2-88

THE GREAT INTERNATIONAL
Cheese Board

THE GREAT INTERNATIONAL
Cheese Board

by Nancy Eekhof-Stork
edited by Adrian Bailey

PADDINGTON PRESS LTD

NEW YORK & LONDON

Library of Congress Cataloging in Publication Data

Eekhof-Stork, Nancy.
  The great international cheese board.

  Consists of selected chapters from the author's The
world atlas of cheese.
  Includes index.
  1. Cheese.   2. Cheese—Varieties.   3. Cookery
(Cheese) I. Bailey, Adrian, 1928–   II. Title.
SF271.E32 1978   64.3'7'3   78–2916
ISBN 0 7092 0048 X
ISBN 0 448 22069 5(U.S. and Canada only)

© 1979 Paddington Press Ltd.

This edition is based on selections from THE WORLD ATLAS OF CHEESE
by Nancy Eekhof-Stork, English-language edition edited by Adrian Bailey
© 1976 Spectrum Amsterdam, for text and illustrations
© 1976 Paddington Press Ltd., for English-language edition

Produced by Spectrum Amsterdam International Publishing,
Amsterdam, The Netherlands.

Phototypeset by Tradespools Ltd., Frome, Somerset.
Printed by Smeets Offset, Weert, The Netherlands.

Jacket photograph by Rex Bamber.
Cheeses provided by the kind courtesy of Paxton and Whitfield, London, England.
Jacket design by Patricia Pillay.

IN THE UNITED STATES
PADDINGTON PRESS
Distributed by
GROSSET & DUNLAP

IN THE UNITED KINGDOM
PADDINGTON PRESS

IN CANADA
Distributed by
RANDOM HOUSE OF CANADA LTD.

Contents

Introduction

Cheese means different things to different people. In Provence, in the south of France, it is probably a small white goat's milk cheese wrapped in chestnut leaves, called a Banon. In Somerset, England, it is likely to be a Cheddar, eaten with bread and a glass of beer. In the Valle d'Aosta, north of Turin in Italy's Piedmont province, the natural choice is Fontina, accompanied by crusty bread and a flask of local wine.

Whatever your preference, cheese is undeniably one of our most basic, nourishing and flavorful foods. It is found in nearly every part of the world, not only in quantity but in enormous variety: from the reindeer cheese of Lapland to a long list of international favorites such as Cheddar and Brie, Gouda and Gorgonzola, Emmental and Parmesan. And now, with gourmet cheese shops well-established in almost every conceivable area, it is possible to sample both staple and gourmet varieties from all over the world.

Cheese lovers are not hard to recognize in these shops. We all have a certain gleam in our eyes as we peer along the shelves and into the refrigerated displays, taking note of a particularly inviting specimen of an old favorite, raising our eyebrows at an unexpected new find . . . getting it home, savoring the aroma, anticipating the first bite, washing it down with a favorite wine. But how many of us have ever really stopped to think what is behind that gloriously melting Brie or that beautifully veined, golden Stilton, or even, for that matter, that penetrating piece of Limburger that we *didn't* bring home? How did these cheeses originate? What is the history behind them? How have climate, geography and technical innovation affected them? How are they made? What accounts for their texture, aroma and taste?

It is with the inquisitive, daring cheese lover in mind that *The Great International Cheese Board* was conceived. Country by country, it explores in colorful detail the cheeses, both famous and obscure, of the eleven greatest cheesemaking nations of the world: the Netherlands, Belgium, Luxembourg, Norway, Sweden, Denmark, Great Britain, France, Germany, Switzerland and Italy. Through an abundance of historical and contemporary detail, folklore and culinary information, as well as photographs and drawings, "cheese" maps and "cheese production" diagrams, the long and intriguing cheesemaking heritage of these nations comes alive. In addition, a data panel for each country provides vital information on specific cheeses: their weight, shape, consistency, rind formation, fat content, and so on. We have also included special sections at the end of the book which deal with the more practical aspects of the world of cheese, where cheese lovers can find tips on serving and storing, preparing cheese boards, selecting complementary cheeses and wines, cooking with cheese and much, much more.

The principles of cheesemaking
Cheese is very much the product of a given land and its people. Indeed, the entire range of the world's cheese is due not only to man's inventiveness, but to a host of other factors that make up the environment he lives in: climate, soil, vegetation, altitude, what milk-producing animals are available, the area's state of economic development, even national taste and customs.

The making of cheese is a domestic skill that became an art, an art that became an industry. The successful combination of art and industry has resulted in the manufacture of durable, high-quality cheese capable of being produced on a large scale and transported over long distances without much loss of original character. Most of the prominent national cheese types have evolved from traditional farmhouse methods. Yet there remain hundreds, perhaps thousands, of small rural types that have never reached the big markets, cheeses that have been made for centuries in secluded valleys or remote alpine meadows.

People have been making cheese for countless thousands of years, ever since they first domesticated and began to milk cows and other mammals. The first cheeses were probably sour-milk cheeses. Set aside in baskets or caskets (often unclean, and thus easy breeding grounds for bacteria), the milk would sour spontaneously and then curdle, separating into curds and watery whey. It was but a small step to discover that by pouring the thickened mass of curd into plaited baskets or perforated pots pots and drawing off the remaining whey, a sort of fresh acid-curd cheese (not unlike German Handkäse or Sauermilchquark) could be achieved.

It was not long before it was found that to make a good-quality cheese which could be kept for long periods of time a considerably more complex procedure was called for, requiring a curdling agent such as rennet. Methods are considerably more sophisticated today, but the basics of cheesemaking have not really changed.

Rennet is usually obtained from the stomach bag of young calves. Provided that the milk has been previously soured (which today is done with a special starter culture), rennet is stimulated by the calcium in milk to convert casein, the major protein in milk, into an insoluble compound. To put it more simply, rennet causes soured milk to separate into curd, which is the main element of cheese, and whey. Curd is a junket-like mass of insoluble dry matter (coagulated particles of protein, milk fat, milk sugar, vitamins and minerals), which before it is drained still contains a large proportion of whey, the watery component of milk which also contains some sugar, fat, proteins and minerals.

The cheesemaker's main task is to separate the whey from the curd particles by stirring and cutting, perhaps the most delicate part of cheesemaking. For fresh and soft-type cheeses, the curd is hardly cut at all. For the hard varieties, it is first cut into large pieces and gradually into smaller ones, expelling as much whey as possible. Finally, a fairly solid mass of curd is obtained, which may be dried even further before being collected into molds and then pressed. For most cheeses this is only half the process: proper texture and flavor are acquired only after curing and ripening.

The mysteries of ripening
After the whey has been drained off, a white mass of curd remains which has little or no flavor. It is hard to believe that it

will ever develop into a tasty delicacy! As the cheese is left to ripen, however, some of its moisture evaporates, increasing the proportion and solidity of the dry matter, which gives it a more decided cheese taste. At the same time, a number of complex biochemical processes are occurring. The starter used to sour the milk is a pure culture of lactic acid bacteria, which convert milk sugar into lactic acid. Eventually the acid level rises to a point where the bacteria perish, leaving behind a protein-consuming enzyme which acts upon casein. As the casein decomposes, the amino acids and other elements it contains are released in the cheese, influencing its taste and aroma. Ammonia may be formed, and its pungent odor is easily detectable in some types.

Milk fat is also subjected to biochemical change. A small part of it is broken down by another enzyme, creating fatty acids which further add to the flavor. Some bacteria, living on the milk sugar, produce gas which sometimes cannot escape from the paste and so forms holes, like those in Emmental.

Apart from natural ripening, specific cultures can be added, perhaps to encourage formation of a white flora on the surface of the cheese (Camembert). Under moist conditions, an orange-red smear of coryne bacteria may grow on the surface (Limburger). Surface ripening is usually faster than normal internal ripening and, in contrast, works from the outside toward the center. In general, the darker the culture's color, the greater the intensity of aroma and flavor. Mold may also be introduced into the interior of a cheese, where it spreads, causing blue-veining and an often sharp, piquant taste (Roquefort).

The optimum ripening period depends on the cheese type. As a rule, the harder the cheese, the longer it should ripen; and the longer a cheese ripens, the harder it gets.

Methods of production
The production of nearly all cheeses today is based on one of the following methods of production:

1. *Fresh cheeses* (Fromage frais, Quark, Cream Cheese): These require more starter and less rennet than other types, a lower curdling temperature and longer curdling time. After curdling, the curd is cut into small cubes and the whey drained off. A very soft curd results, which is homogenized, packed in plastic cups, cooled and sold fresh. There is little, if any, ripening period.

2. *Soft cheeses* (Limburger, Camembert, Brie): These have a soft, usually spreadable paste which tends to stick to the knife. They are lightly pressed, and ripening time is usually short. Soft cheeses often have a surface mold growth. (See Camembert production, pp.50–51.)

3. *Semihard cheeses* (Gouda, Edam, Stilton, Fontina): These cheeses are pressed and have a firm, but smooth, easy-to-cut consistency. The ripening period varies, depending on the cheese. Most blue-veined cheeses are semihard. (See Gouda production, pp.10–11.)

4. *Hard Cheeses* (Cheddar, Emmental, Parmesan): As much whey as possible is drained off. This is achieved in one of two ways: "after heating" or "cooking" (see Emmental production, p.71); or "cheddaring" (see Cheddar production, pp.34–35). Hard cheeses are heavily pressed and have long ripening periods. A surface flora is possible (Gruyère).

5. *Kneaded or plastic curd cheeses* (Provolone, Caciocavallo): The curd is immersed in a mixture of hot water and whey, which renders the curd elastic; it is then kneaded and modeled into fancy shapes. Kneaded cheeses are usually well matured and are often smoked.

6. *Whey cheeses* (Mysost, Gjetost): The whey is heated until it has evaporated and a brown carmelized paste is formed.

Key to symbols in national maps

In the maps of Great Britain, the Netherlands, France, Switzerland and Italy, the important original cheeses of each country have been marked by means of a symbol representing their shapes, and located in the region where each respective cheese originally came from.

The many different shapes in which cheese is made have been grouped in the following categories.

Ball: either a perfect sphere or (mostly) flattened or otherwise distorted.

Cartwheel: a large, relatively flat wheel of heavy weight.

Flat disc: much smaller than the cartwheel and usually weighing under 1 kg (2.2 lbs).

Cylinder: of varying height and diameter, but always taller in relation to its diameter than the cartwheel. In some cases, the two following subtypes have been distinguished.

Low cylinder.

Tall cylinder.

Oval or any similar fancy shape.

Loaf: a large rectangular shape which tends to be higher than its width. The brick shape, the width of which is greater than its height, is also included in this category.

Cube or a similar shape.

Truncated cone, pyramid or similar shape.

Bar.

Rectangular or square. The bigger block form is also included in this category.

Cheese sold in a basket.

Cheese sold in a container, whether this be a bag, sack, pot, jar or plastic cup.

Triangular: this is a rare shape, the triangular portions of cheese usually being cuts of a bigger, cylindrical cheese.

Key to symbols in data panels

Milk

Cow's milk

Goat's milk

Sheep's milk

Refers to a note at the foot of the data panel

A combination of symbols means that more than one kind of milk is used, either alternatively or mixed together. The sequence of the symbols does not indicate any order of importance.

Type

Fresh cheese

Soft cheese

Semihard cheese

Hard cheese

Rind

No rind or hardly any rind

Dry rind

White rind flora

Orange-red rind smear ("washed cheese")

Blue-veined cheese

Form
This is described in the terms explained above, with a few additions for some otherwise unclassifiable cheeses. When a cheese is habitually made in many different shapes, rather than one typical form. the term "varying" is employed.

Weight
The average weights of the usual forms in which the cheese is made are indicated. Where weights vary widely, the term "varying" is employed.

% Fat content
The required minimum percentage of fat in the dry matter is given; where no official regulations exist, the average percentage. Where two figures are given, the cheese may be made in a certain number of percentages between and including the percentage mentioned. Where no reliable information is available,

the symbol "?" is used.

Note
Please note that cheeses are discussed primarily under the country where they originally came from. even if they are produced on a large scale in other countries. Cheeses selected for inclusion have been chosen for their interest rather than their production figures. The list of cheese types of each country is not exhaustive.

Text and data panels describe the usual and typical form in which each cheese type is made. Individual differences can, and will, occur, since cheese is a living thing, made by many different artisans and factories, each with his own methods and recipes.

Netherlands

The sea would claim much of Holland if it could: the northern and western provinces of the Netherlands are below sea level, and their very existence is the outcome of an age-old struggle between the Dutch and the invading ocean. Because the country is flat – save for the tiny, hilly area south of the province of Limburg – the landscape gives the impression of a vast spaciousness, where land, sea and sky become fused together.

Even before the dykes were built to protect the inhabitants from the sea, there were more than enough fertile, green acres to make the Netherlands a prominent dairy country: round, brick containers with perforated bottoms, apparently cheese molds, have been discovered in ancient Frankish dwellings of the fourth century A.D. We learn from ninth-century records, that the Frisians made butter and cheese for the court of Charlemagne. During the Middle Ages, the collective efforts of farmers from all over Holland led to a prosperous period, with the rise of dairy markets and the *kaaswaag* (cheese weigh-house) where cow's, goat's and sheep's milk cheeses were inspected for quality and weight. Haarlem already had a dairy trade center in 1266, Leiden in 1303, and Leeuwarden in Friesland got its town weigh-house in 1386. At the same time, the export of cheese developed, first overland and via the Rhine to Germany (still the biggest importer of Dutch cheese) and later, when the Dutch became the "freight carriers of Europe," by sea to the farthest corners of the Baltic and Mediterranean.

Looking at the bills of lading of the Dutch trading vessels during that time, it seems incredible that such enormous quantities of cheese could be produced since the milk yield was considerably lower than that of today, the farmer-cheesemakers were ill-equipped, and transport was slow.

Cattle now graze on reclaimed land that was once the sea's dominion – the elegant, piebald Frisians and the robust Groningens with their black-and-white faces. Further inland, along the winding rivers and waterways, Maas, Rhine and IJssel cattle are herded to the spotless dairies. More than a third of the land here is used for cattle breeding and milk production so that the Netherlands is now the biggest cheese exporter in the world.

ABOVE: A special postmark of 1918. It states: "Gouda cheese and pig market; market day on Thursday." The cheese market is still held on Thursday, throughout the year, in the triangular marketplace.

Edam 3
Friese Nagelkaas 1
Gouda 5
Kernhem 2
Leiden 4

LEFT: Milking time in a Dutch polder near Volendam. In the summer the farmer goes to the meadow twice a day, but during the winter the cattle are stabled and are milked under cover.

TOP LEFT: The old cheese weigh-house in Gouda, the Kaaswaag, designed and built in 1668 by P. Post. Above the entrance is a fine relief which shows how cheeses were weighed.

TOP RIGHT: A between-the-wars photograph of the famous cheese market in Gouda. This was before the automobile took over, and farmers came to market by horse and cart, bringing their consignment of cheeses. Although most of Holland's Gouda is now made in factories, true farmhouse Gouda is still obtainable everywhere.

ABOVE: A stack of *Boerenkaas* Goudas (*Boeren* means "farmer"). Only factory cheese carries the name "Gouda" stamped on the rind.

BELOW: A typical Dutch farmhouse near Haastrecht. The cheesemaking room lies in the extension of the rear of the house, visible on the far left.

The urban areas that include Amsterdam, The Hague, Rotterdam and Utrecht are grouped to form the modern, industrial heart of the Netherlands – the *Randstad* Holland – and between them, nestling in the green countryside, is Gouda, the birthplace of *Gouda* cheese. Even today there are about a thousand Gouda cheese farms in the provinces of South Holland and Utrecht. Legend claims that the first Gouda cheese was made in the nearby village of Stolwijk; the name Stolwijk is still a guarantee of an extremely tasty type of Gouda.

Traditionally, the area was not only known for the production of excellent milk and cheese, but also for trade and freight: Gouda stands at the junction of two rivers, the Gouwe and the Hollandse IJssel, where shipbuilders once put the resources of the wooded countryside to profitable use. In early times, Gouda was one of the five principal Dutch trading centers, with a flourishing industry in textiles, brewing, leather, pottery and dairy produce. In the thirteenth century there was a thriving cattle market, and also a city market held every six months, where English and Scottish merchants came to buy and sell cheese. According to accounts in old publications, Gouda cheese was compared to England's Derby cheese in freshness and density, and experiments were carried out on the farms with Derby mold cultures.

A good deal in Goudas

Between the famous Gouda Town Hall and the Kaaswaag, which dates from 1668 and sports a marble relief depicting the old weighing trade over the entrance, farmers continue to sell their cheeses according to ancient custom. Each Thursday morning, buyers inspect wagons of cheeses covered with tarpaulins and make their offers – or rather, the buyer suggests a price and the farmer automatically declines. The buyer later returns with a second offer – it's all part of the game – and the farmer suggests a higher figure. Again the buyer walks away, but the third time they will, no doubt, agree. The deal is completed with a slap of hands, and the farmer drives his wagon to the weigh-house.

The number of cheese farms has decreased over the years, so that the

LEFT: Making cheese on the farm. After the curd has been curdled, cut and ripened, it is transferred to a wooden container.

contradictory increase in production can be put down to the improved market value of Gouda farm cheese, and also to the modern methods of manufacture. Since the installation of a cooling system, there is no need to process the fresh milk yield twice daily, as had long been the case. Now "day cheese" is made from fresh morning milk and warmed evening milk from the previous day.

Modern farmhouse ways

The showpiece of modern, hygienic farmhouse cheesemaking is the teak cheese vat, with its stainless steel liner behind which either hot or cold water can circulate. The vat is equipped with an electric mechanism for cutting and stirring the curd, and has a capacity of 1,500 liters (1,650 quarts). An average herd of thirty cows may produce, at the height of the season, about 600 liters (660 quarts) of milk per milking, and for every kilo (2.2 lbs) of cheese about 10 liters (11 quarts) of milk is required.

The making of Gouda cheese is mainly done by women, usually the farmer's wife, assisted by a daughter, and they start at six o'clock in the morning. Long experience has taught them exactly how much rennet and starter to add to a given quantity of milk in the vat, and at what temperature this must be done. Cheese molds are prepared according to the yield of milk: for example, where 400 liters (440 quarts) of milk are used, four 10 kg (22 lbs) molds or five 8 kg (17.6 lbs) molds are needed. The curdled milk is stirred, left for a while, brought to a higher temperature, and then stirred again. When the women have determined with their expert skill that the curd pieces are of the right size and consistency, they fill the molds.

The filling is done in one of two ways: either by dividing the curd into large blocks, and putting a block into each mold, or by crumbling the curd into the mold. This "crumbling" cheese later reveals many small, irregular holes, because of the air incorporated during the process; the so-called "one-piece" shows only a few large and regular holes.

A cheese of great character

After the molds have been filled, the cheese is pressed, stamped with the government mark for farmhouse

LEFT: The curd is then gathered in a cheese cloth.

LEFT: The cloth containing the curd is suspended to allow whey to drain off after which the curd is put into a cheese mold lined with a cloth, well-distributed and firmly pressed.

BELOW: The mold is sealed with a lid, which fits inside its inner rim. The cheeses are then pressed before being given a brine bath.

cheese, wrapped in a clean cloth and pressed again. A period in a tiled, brine bath, with a salt solution of the correct strength, completes the main preparation. During ripening, the Gouda cheese develops its characteristic smell and taste: a farmhouse cheese made from whole, raw milk has a delicious aroma, immediately evident as soon as the cheese is cut. Evident also is the promise of the slightly sweet, full and often somewhat pronounced flavor that surprises the tongue again and again. The cheese remains smooth, even as it gets older. Expert cheese tasters are able to recognize the region – and even the farm – that a particular Gouda cheese comes from. Even those with an untrained palate will at once recognize the subtle transformation that has occurred between an adolescent Gouda and a really mature example, one that has reached, say, the ripe old age of twelve to fourteen months. The rind can become so hard that it needs cutting with a saw before you can proceed with a cheesewire or knife. The paste becomes very firm, rather like Gruyère, and the flavor is slightly salty but full. It has taken on, as wine tasters would say, "a character of great breeding."

Kaasdoop, the Dutch fondu

A small quantity of farmhouse Gouda is retained by the farmer for use in the kitchen. Generous slices are cut for sandwiches, and the rind may be fried with potatoes or added to mashed potatoes or stews. A traditional, simple, utilitarian dish, particularly convenient in the past when the busy farm schedule left little time for elaborate preparation, is the Gouda Kaasdoop, in which cheese is cooked with milk and eaten in the manner of a Swiss fondu, but with brown bread or boiled potatoes. A rather rustic, country dish, it was later taken up by city dwellers who served it in a more elegant fashion with French bread and fondu forks, dipping the bread into the Kaasdoop contained in a fireproof dish over a small flame. The farmers, contemptuous of the Kaasdoop's newly acquired sophistication, eaten in a communal fashion that they considered unhygienic, dropped it from their menu.

LEFT: The official label for Gouda factory-made cheese. The codes refer to the production date and producer.

BELOW: Arrival of milk in a modern cheese factory. An operator controls the fully mechanized process.

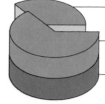

total production Dutch cheese 335,000 tons p.a. (100 %)

production Gouda 202,300 tons p.a. (60 %)

of which exported 103,500 tons p.a. (51 %)

The unique and typical qualities of farmhouse Goudas are notably absent from the factory product. This isn't to say that factory Gouda is robbed of a marked degree of excellence. On the contrary, it is widely exported and enjoyed throughout the world. The factory cheese, however, lacks the subtle, distinct character of the farmhouse variety; for the connoisseur the surprise element is gone.

A safe and sure product

Since factory Gouda is made over a wide area and not restricted to a certain region; since the preparation of the curd often demands production on a massive scale, utilizing 10,000 liters (11,000 quarts) of milk, this loss of individuality is hardly surprising. Furthermore, the milk may come from a considerable distance and may be the product of a number of different farms. For these reasons the milk is pasteurized, so that possible bacteria which might cause defects in the cheese are destroyed, as are, inevitably, the microorganisms that create the farmhouse character. In one respect the factory cheese has the advantage of being standardized: the shopper knows in advance what the cheese will taste like. There are three different kinds from which to choose, according to preference: very mild, young Gouda; a more matured and aromatic variety; and the fully matured, old and piquant type. The *Lunchkaas*, or *Baby Gouda*, is a small, model Gouda, always eaten while young and fresh. *Amsterdam* cheese is a Gouda variety with an increased moisture content and a very smooth, full flavor. There is also a spiced Gouda, flavored with cumin seeds, which is eaten when young. It has a spicy, creamy taste that is best appreciated on a slice of brown bread or on toast.

Gouda in the kitchen

Because its firm consistency varies with age, Gouda has many applications in the kitchen. Irrespective of whether the cheese comes from farm

A. In the cheese-making tank, starter and rennet are mixed into the pasteurized cheese milk (yellow), which coagulates within approximately 20-30 minutes. The curd is cut and stirred automatically according to a preselected program. Part of the whey is run off. The temperature during this 1½-2 hours' treatment is increased from 30°C (86°F) to 35°C (95°F).

B. When the curd is ready, it is transferred to a buffer tank. More whey may be run off from the curd-whey mixture.

C. The wet curd is pumped into a filling apparatus. The precise weight of curd is poured into the molds (nowadays made of steel or plastic rather than teakwood), which arrive on a conveyor belt. Immediately after filling, a circular press descends into the mold where it expels more whey from the curd.

D. The filled cheese molds travel to the press.

E. They are pressed for 1-8 hours under a large hydraulic press. There is now a tendency to use higher pressures for a shorter period of time, since this makes possible a continuous flow of production.

F. After pressing, the cheeses – still in their molds – move slowly up and finally down a high stack of cheeses. This "waiting period" between being pressed and salted improves the quality of the cheese.

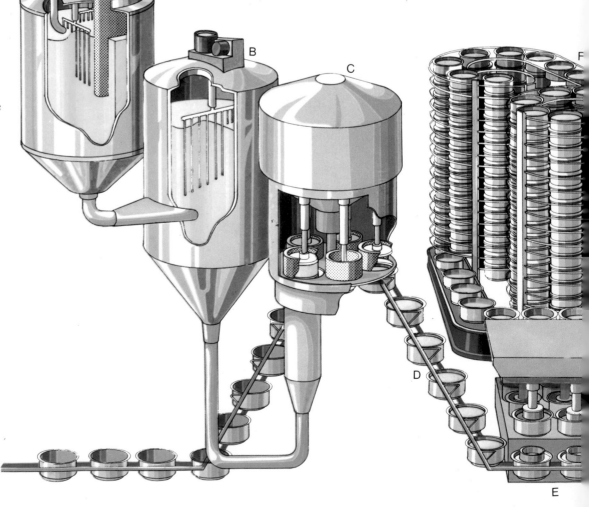

BELOW: Racks of cheeses are lowered into the brine bath and lifted out again by machine.

BELOW: Each finished cheese is given a wax or plastic coating. This minimizes the need to wipe and clean the cheeses during storage and gives additional protection during transport.

or factory, the versatile Gouda is excellent with many types of bread. For cooking, choose a young Gouda when you require a melting cheese; a mature Gouda when the cheese is to be served whole, or remain visible in the dish, as with cheese ragout, cooked dishes with diced cheese, or baked cheese schnitzels; and an old cheese when you need to grate it.

Gouda can be used for a number of recipes calling for a firm cheese or a grating cheese, a quality it shares with Gruyère and Cheddar. It may be used as a basis for such sauces as Mornay Sauce; in certain soups such as onion soup or Dutch cheese soup (see recipe section); in soufflés; in fish dishes where a slice of cheese is melted on the fish. It may also be served in savory omelettes and in the form of a fondu, like the previously mentioned Kaasdoop.

Besides the traditional cartwheel shape, Gouda is made in square or loaf-shaped forms, as is the case with Edam cheese, although the latter is normally globe-shaped. You can spot the difference by looking at the official label: 48% indicates the full-fat Gouda, while 40% refers to Edam, with its lower fat content.

G. They are taken out of their molds – and are quite firm. The cheeses have developed a rind and have lost most of the excess moisture. They are now ready for a brine bath.

H. Big containers loaded with cheeses are lowered into the brine bath and taken out again after 1-2 days.

J. This salt bath serves many functions: it improves the flavor and the structure of the cheese; it acts as a preservative; and it promotes the formation of a hard, dry rind.

K. Finally, the cheeses are transferred to the ripening rooms. Often the newly made cheeses are bought by wholesalers. Gouda is marketed in various degrees of maturity: "young" Gouda cheese has been ripened for at least 3 weeks, "semimature" Gouda for 2-7 months, while the very piquant, crumbly "old" Gouda has matured for no less than 10-12 months.

L. Close-up of a modern polyethylene cheese mold. From top to bottom: follower, inner lid, perforated lining (replacing cheese cloth) which contains the curd, bottom. Plastic molds have proved much better than stainless steel ones, which allow the curd to cool too quickly. Traditional wooden molds are still the best: taste and flavor develop better during the ripening period, but the difference is only marginal. In an automated factory, wooden molds are too heavy and clumsy to handle, and are being replaced.

Edam cheese is named after the old harbor on the Ysselmeer, north of Amsterdam, in the center of the province of North Holland, where Frisian Edam cheese was first marketed and exported abroad. Edam, with its fat content of 40%, is a little less smooth and less creamy than Gouda, and has a slightly sourish taste when young. In fact this is one of the marketing problems associated with Edam – it is often sold before the magnificent, mature flavor has had time to develop. The lower fat content of Edam is due to its being partly made with skimmed milk; Gouda, with more fat, is made from whole cow's milk.

All the world recognizes the familiar, bright red, or yellow, ball of cheese with its waxy coating, yet Edam is seldom waxed for the home market. The process is reserved for export cheeses, which are colored before leaving the warehouse; the treatment gives the cheeses added protection.

The focal point of the cheese industry is not the town of Edam, however, but that of Alkmaar. Here, on a Friday morning, the cheese market becomes an international tourist attraction. Members of the cheese bearers' guild – the last of the medieval guilds – dress in white suits and hats of different colors to identify the various warehouses they represent. The golden balls of Edam cheese, or the flat wheels of Gouda, are piled high upon wooden sleds of a decidedly Japanese-looking design; the sleds are pulled by cheese porters over the gray brick surface of the marketplace.

Edam cheese has always been a profitable product – there has been a weigh-house in the market since the thirteenth century – and Amsterdam merchants acknowledged this by helping to finance the reclaiming of land from the Ysselmeer, to provide more pastures. The original, whole-milk Edam cheese was prepared in more or less the same way as farm-house Gouda. Its globe-shaped, easy-

to-transport form, not unlike a large grapefruit, came from the Edam cheese mold known as the *kaaskop*. This *kaaskop*, meaning "cheese head," was often used as a helmet during riots, which is said to be why the Dutch are known in many countries by this nickname. Edam's spherical shape is almost unique among cheeses, and is achieved by the tendency of the curd to become firm very readily at an early stage in preparation.

The explorer's cheese
Since the nineteenth century, both on farms and in small factories, Edam cheese has been made from a mixture of whole morning milk and the skimmed evening milk of the previous day. In modern factories the old, wooden cheese molds, the *kaaskop* forms, have been replaced by plastic molds; cheese cloth is no longer used.

Unlike Gouda, farmhouse Edam is no longer made. The smallest variety today is the *Baby Edam* cheese weighing about 1 kg (2.2 lbs), a cheese that is eaten young and is less tasty than the larger type, which weighs 1.7 kg (3.7 lbs). *Commissekaas* (in France called *Mimolette* and for marketing reasons is colored orange with anatto dye) is even heavier, while *Middelbare* is the largest Edam of all. In a different form there is the handsome *Broodkaas*, less salty than the regular Edam, and mainly for use in hotels. Some Edam cheeses are spiced with cumin.

The keeping properties of Edam have been known to be remarkable: in 1956 an expedition to the South Pole found a tin of raw-milk Edam cheese, left behind by the Scott Expedition in 1912. The natural protein and fat disintegration had been at work for forty-four years: the cheese was sharp, but not spoiled.

LEFT: Leiden farm-
house cheeses are
stacked one above the
other in this typical
press.

Leiden cheese is made on a number of large farms along the Old Rhine in the dune region near Leiden. It is a spicy, piquant cheese of partly skimmed milk and buttermilk. In the past, the fresh milk was poured into oval vats that stood in cold, running water, and left for the cream to rise. Today the milk is left for skimming after cooling in the same tub in which the cheese is made. In 12 to 24 hours, the cream is skimmed off, left for a day to sour, then churned into a fairly assertive farm butter. The cheesemaker, in the meantime, warms up a portion of the skimmed, pre-ripened milk, using it to bring the remainder of the milk to curdling temperature. Then butter-milk and rennet are added, the curd is stirred and cut, and the whey is drawn off. A quantity of the curd is now separated from the rest, into which cumin seed is kneaded, a treatment which to a large extent dries the curd.

The traditional way of kneading, where the farmer would clean his feet in whey and afterwards tread the curd, is now considered unhygienic; this is rather a pity, since the very special structure that was characteristic of Leiden cheese no longer develops. The

BELOW: The old method of kneading Leiden cheese. It has never been established which suffered most – the farmer's feet or the cheese! The modern method still demands an intensive working of the curd.

spiced, kneaded curd is sandwiched between two layers of the remaining, unspiced curd, bound in a cheese cloth and placed in a mold. The cheese is pressed for 20 to 24 hours before receiving a second pressing with mold and cloth removed. The sides of the cheese develop their spherical shape, and a special cheese mark is applied, consisting of the two crossed keys of the city of Leiden, the name *Boerenleidse* and a fat content figure of 30 + (more than 30%).

Punishment by the beestings
Leiden farmhouse cheese requires a long period of ripening. In the final stages of ripening, the rind is colored by an application of anatto dye, which is well rubbed in. This treatment has largely replaced the old-fashioned method of rubbing the cheese rind with a mixture of coloring matter and beestings. Beestings is the first milk given by a cow after calving; it is much thicker and richer than ordinary milk and contains an unusual amount of protein. This was mixed with anatto to be applied to the rind, which acquired a fine, glossy, mahogany-colored protective layer. This is not dissimilar to the technique used by the makers of the old English Gloucester cheese, which used to be rubbed with a substance obtained from decomposing vegetable matter. Beestings used to be stored in a pot, since it was not always available, and after several weeks it began to smell rather repulsive, to say the least. Some farmers used to punish their children by forcing them to sit by the beestings pot – a corrective measure that doubtless did very little to increase the consumption and appeal of Leiden cheeses on the farms.

Irrespective of the beestings treat-ment, a well-ripened Leiden cheese is very piquant and almost sharp of taste, with a dry but elastic structure. The fat content varies from 32 to 36%. The indication of 20 + on the govern-ment cheese mark is, in fact, too low, although legally prescribed. The farmers ignore this and put their own additional mark of 30 + on their cheeses. Factory-made Leiden cheese is allowed a 20% and a 40% type: the first is eaten young, the second when more mature. This factory cheese has a piquant taste, but is less sharp than the farmhouse variety.

LEFT: The milk is poured into the metal containers seen in the foreground. The machine at the rear pumps cold water to thoroughly chill the milk. In this way a natural creaming process takes place: the cream floats to the surface and can then be skimmed off; it is usually made into butter. The remaining skimmed milk is made into farmhouse Leiden cheese, which can have a varying fat content.

ABOVE: The drained curd is well mixed with cumin seed, a particu-lar feature of Leiden cheese. Other cheeses also contain cumin, but lack the unique taste of Leiden, which is fairly sharp and dry.

The beautiful, black-and-white Frisian cattle are one of the finest dairy breeds in the world. In spite of this indigenous stock, Friesland is not noted for its cheeses, because the manufacture of butter has always had top priority. The lean, skimmed milk *Friese Kanterkaas* and *Friese Nagelkaas* had a hard time competing with farmhouse Leiden and *Delft* cheese, and even the Delft fell out of favor and is now extinct. The Frisians, however, survived. The quantity of starter is all-important to the making of Frisian cheese. So is the addition of fresh buttermilk, the milling of the curd and the hot water bath. The cheeses also are subject to long pressing and covered ripening; the process is not unlike the one used for English Cheddar.

Cumin and caraway seeds are wonderful additions to rye bread, which was made in northern Europe during Roman times. They are also used to flavor several Scandinavian and Dutch cheeses. Perhaps the ancient breadmakers, who also made cheese, decided to try to spice their cheeses as they did their bread – and thus a taste for spiced cheeses developed.

Nagelkaas is a spiced cheese, flavored with cumin and cloves, hence the name – *nagel* means "nail" and refers to the shape of the clove; the cheese is said to go well with a glass of Gewürztraminer. The unspiced *Kanterkaas* is a product of the processed cheese industry. The cumin-spiced Kanter is so like Leiden factory cheese that it shares the same classification. After about six months' ripening, the aroma and flavor are fully developed. Both cheeses have a 40% and 20% variety, the latter possessing a higher moisture content, which makes it smooth in spite of the low percentage of fat.

The accident that led to Kernhem

During wet winters before the days of improved storage conditions, Edam cheeses in the warehouses of the tenant farmers sometimes collapsed into strong-smelling, flat discs with an orange-colored rind flora of coryne bacteria, and when cut the cheese stuck to the knife. The farmers found, however, that this "knife sticker" was a delicacy. The Netherlands Institute for Dairy Research experimented with this accidental cheese, and from it developed *Kernhem* cheese, a totally new type with a creamy flavor.

Since 1906, strict controls regulate the high standard of Dutch cheeses, and those that pass the inspection receive the government mark which indicates the country of origin (Holland), the producer and production date in code and, in most cases, the name of the cheese and the fat content. Export cheese is even more thoroughly inspected and, as we have mentioned, the Dutch are the biggest cheese exporters in the world. Even so, it is odd that cheese fails to play a more important role in the Dutch kitchen. Cheese is used for sandwiches and snacks, but is rarely used in dishes apart from a few homely applications of Gouda, the fondu-style Kaasdoop, and Houtsnip (white bread with a slice of cheese topped with a piece of rye bread, and cut into small pieces). Over the last few years, however, foreign influence has brought about certain changes, and Dutch cheese features in many imported, international recipes.

BELOW: A nineteenth-century print showing an old cheesemaking room. The cheese press stands on the left; to the right is the curd mill. In the center, wet curd is pre-pressed under a stone.

Name	Milk	Type	Rind	Form	Weight	% Fat content
Edam	◪	◼	◻	ball	1-6.5 kg	40
Friese Nagelkaas	◪	◼	◻	cartwheel	7-8 kg	20-40
Gouda	◪	◼	◻	cartwheel	2.5-20 kg	48
Kernhem	◪	●	❖	flat disc	1.8 kg	60
Leiden	◪	◼	◻	cartwheel	7-8 kg	20-40

Key to symbols on page 6. 1 kg = 2.2 lbs.

ABOVE: Leiden cheese is colored by rubbing the rind with anatto dye, and sometimes with beestings, the first milk obtained after a cow has calved.

Belgium and Luxembourg

In the Middle Ages, the southern Netherlands occupied most of the area which is now Belgium, and was a major center of trade and commerce. Most international routes over land or sea met in Bruges, but towards the close of the fourteenth century, Antwerp began to overtake Bruges. The city became a great trading port for Spanish and English wool, French wine, Portuguese spices, Dutch butter and cheese, Scandinavian wood and fish, and flax from the surrounding districts.

No dairy produce of any consequence was produced in the southern provinces of the lowlands bordering the North Sea, even though the ground was fertile enough. There was more money to be made from arable farming, for those traders who supported and propped up the country's living standards. Neither was the cow highly thought of as a producer of milk, unlike the sheep or the goat, the farmer used his cattle for pulling the plow, and as a source of manure, rather than milk or cheese – as with everything in farming, it's a matter of carefully judged economics.

Cheese from a crisis

Serious problems affected agriculture at the end of the nineteenth century, forcing drastic changes on Belgian farming, especially in the wheatlands, following the fall in grain prices. Farmers turned to cattle breeding, and the economic value of meat, milk and other dairy produce soon rose; the cows quickly left the sheep and goats well behind. Although Belgian farmers maintained their agrarian traditions, they began to pay careful attention to cattle breeding; this combined with good feeding soon increased the milk yield. Before 1900, the first dairy factories had been established, mainly for the processing of butter; after the Second World War, more factories were built and cheese began to be produced. New cheese factories were constructed to meet the growing demand, and existing plants were modernized.

Until the mid-1960s, Belgium's main production was centered on the semihard cheeses of the Gouda and Saint-Paulin variety, but a change in the national preference led to the rehabilitation of original Belgian soft cheeses.

ABOVE: Cows grazing in a meadow in the Belgian Ardennes. Frisian cattle, together with this white or blue-spotted breed, are found all over central and southern Belgium; the white breed represents about half the cattle stock of the country.

ABOVE: A philatelic rarity: a Belgian postage stamp dating before the Second World War, joined to a Dutch official cheese control stamp.

The return of the farmhouse cheese

The most famous of all Belgian cheeses is, or rather was, the *Limburger* – famous if only for its persistent, omnipotent aroma. It was made in the Liege region, and sold in Limburg, but it has now been almost totally superseded by the *Herve* cheeses, Limburger itself having been adopted by the Germans, who make it in considerable quantity.

Although Limburger failed to make a comeback, the renaissance of farmhouse cheeses is well established. Among them are such types as *Remoudou, Brusselsekaas, Fromage en panier* and *Plattekaas* (curd cheese). Herve comes from the grazing area of that name, in the north of the province of Liège, a rolling stretch of country between the Vesdre and the Meuse. Herve is the generic name of a number of different types, of which Remoudou is the most valued. The name comes from the Walloon word *remoud* or, roughly, "after-milk." It is made from the milk that a cow gives at the end of the lactation period, when the milk is very rich in fat. With the introduction of artificial insemination, the cows are continuously productive, and are never dry all at the same time.

The stinking cheese

The preparation of Herve begins with the pouring of warm, raw milk into a metal cheese vat, called a *tine* (a word found both in Dutch and Norwegian) where, with the aid of a little rennet, it thickens within $1\frac{1}{2}$ hours. After a rest period, a perforated pot or colander is placed on the curd; the pot fills with whey, and 40 to 50% is ladled off. The next stage introduces the traditional *spantafel*, a large draining board with a rim about 6 inches high, divided lengthwise by planks to form gutters, down which the whey runs to be drained through apertures. The entire contraption – made by local craftsmen – is built on a stand so that it slopes to allow drainage.

The cheesemaker pours the wet curd from a pan quickly and evenly along the gutters, until they are completely filled. The whey is drained off, the longitudinal strips of curd are then turned through 90°, with a practiced, deft movement of the cheesemaker's arms, and the curds rest while further whey is strained off. This process is repeated three times. The strips are

then cut into cubes, placed back onto the *spantafel*, between planks now arranged to form rectangular divisions, and each cheese is turned regularly by hand for the next 48 hours. Air currents in the room must be avoided, as they would spoil the newly made cheeses.

In the old days, the cheesemaker would then place the cheeses next to one another on a cheese board, where they were treated by dusting with salt, but today a special salting table is used. The unripe cheeses are collected by so-called *affineurs*, who take them from the farm to their establishments, where the cheeses are washed and again treated with salt and lukewarm brine. Due to this process, and also the damp air in the processing room, the initially hard, chalk-white cheese becomes soft and smooth, while the ripening bacteria present on the reddish-brown rind imparts an outstanding aroma and penetrating flavor, especially with Remoudou, which has earned the dubious nickname of "the stinking cheese."

The final packing shape is a cube, measuring 6 × 6 cm (about 2.5 × 2.5 in). Factory-made Remoudou,

ABOVE: This drawing shows the traditional method of making farmhouse Remoudou cheese. The girl on the left is cutting the curd by hand, with the aid of a curd knife. In the center is a metal container called a *tine*, and filled with curd on top of which a small, perforated colander rests. The colander fills with whey, which is then scooped out. When most of the whey has been strained off, the curd

is poured onto the long table (behind the girl on the left) called a *spantafel*, a draining board fitted with longitudinal planks. The man turns the long strips of curd which form between the planks. When the strips have drained and are firm, they are cut into cubes and placed on another, similar table (right). Here the cheesemaker turns them regularly for a period of 48 hours. The cheeses are

then salted by hand on the salting table (far right), then left to dry. During the maturation time of about six weeks, the cheeses are regularly turned and washed with lukewarm brine, as the woman on the right is doing. The washing technique encourages the growth of a reddish, bacterial flora, which gives the cheese its unusual, piquant taste and sharp aroma.

RIGHT: Remoudou is the name given to a special type of Herve cheese, and is similar to the Limburger, now made mainly in Germany and elsewhere.

like so many mass-produced cheeses, uses pasteurized instead of raw milk, and the refining process takes place either in the factory, or on the premises of the *affineurs*.

The methods of manufacture, as used by traditional craftsmen, can be seen in the Musée du Remoudou, a museum devoted to cheese and established by the Seigneurerie Folklorique du Remoudou. The premises are the ripening cellars of an old cheese factory in Battice, close by the town of Herve to the east of Liège. The Seigneurerie keeps the rightful fame of real, old Remoudou alive in more than one sense, for the odor of the famous "stinking cheese" is impregnated in the stones of the museum.

Cheeses of Flanders and the south
A variety of the washed cheeses is the *Plateau* cheese, with a consistency that is somewhere between soft and semihard; during ripening the rind is kept moist by regularly dampening it with fresh water. In Flanders, *Plattekaas* (fresh curd cheese) is a type that includes many fresh, unripened varieties, cheeses with different fat

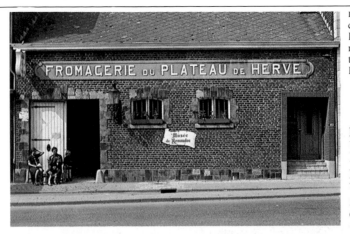

LEFT: Once a cheese dairy in the village of Battice, now a small museum devoted to the history of Remoudou.

contents according to the amount of cream added. Skimmed-milk cheese has less than 20% fat; the semifat variety has 20% to 35%; the full-fat cheese, from 35% to 45%; cream cheese has more than 45% fat in dry matter.

The French-speaking part of the country has its own fresh cheeses: *Fromage en panier* and *Fromage en cassette*. These are still made in limited amounts in southern Belgium, from either buttermilk, skimmed milk or whole milk, and sold in small baskets covered with walnut leaves. Often, the curd is flavored with pepper. The Belgians enjoy eating this cheese on toast, with a layer of butter on the cheese – a local delicacy.

In fact, the Belgians are great eaters who have invented some classic – and filling – soups and stews, and dishes that include cheese. Excuses for festivals and communal feasts are not exactly numerous, but when they do arise the quantities of food that appear are prodigious: plates are overfilled with cold cuts of assorted meats, sausages, selections of cheeses, bread, wine and beer – especially beer.

A scene straight out of a Brueghel

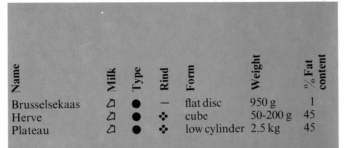

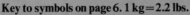

Name	Milk	Type	Rind	Form	Weight	% Fat content
Brusselsekaas	⌂	●	—	flat disc	950 g	1
Herve	⌂	●	❖	cube	50-200 g	45
Plateau	⌂	●	❖	low cylinder	2.5 kg	45

Key to symbols on page 6. 1 kg=2.2 lbs.

painting is enacted every three years in the town of Wynghene south of Bruges. The local residents honor the painter by dressing in the costume of the period, and members of several guilds – bakers, butchers, brewers and cheesemakers – present their products to the general enjoyment of all.

Other cheeses from Belgium and Luxembourg

The most typically Belgian cheese is the *Brusselsekaas* (Brussels cheese), or *Hettekaas*, and it is made in two phases from pasteurized, skimmed milk. The coagulated mass is cut into small blocks, and in the 12-hour rest period that follows, they contract, acidify and release whey. Afterwards this fresh curd is put into sacks and placed on a grid to drain. The curd is then ground, salted and molded to shape with metal hoops. The cheeses must first be laid out on planks to drain further, and then on rush matting to dry. The second phase in the complicated process allows the cheeses to ripen for two months in a humid ripening room. Every eight days they are dipped and turned in lukewarm water and then finally in a brine bath. The cheese is then cut into pieces and packed in cellophane and, after yet another bathing and draining treatment, is packed in boxes or plastic containers. The end product is very moist and salty, and very much to the national taste.

Finally, Belgium produces many imitations of foreign cheeses, including *Gouda, Edam, Emmental,* and, for the export market, large quantities of *Cheddar, Camembert, Brie* and *Saint-Paulin*.

In Luxembourg, the cheese industry concentrates mainly on the fresh types, like the skimmed-milk *Fromage blanc, Cottage cheese,* and *Kachke's Fromage cuit,* a cheese that can be favorably compared to the Cancaillotte from Franche Comté.

The quality of the Belgian, hard-cheese types is guaranteed by regular official inspection. Two favorable judgments out of three inspections allows the cheese to carry a mark denoting quality, stamped in purple ink on the rind, plus the Belgian emblem of origin – a Breughelian picture of two porters bearing a pile of various cheeses on a plank.

LEFT: In the monastery of Lesse, cheese is sold by the monks. It is a Saint-Paulin type which has been prepared in the cloisters since ancient times.

ABOVE: The wrapping for the cheese produced by the monastery of Lesse, near Dinant.

LEFT: A dairy-worker monk, using the cheese press at Lesse.

17

Norway

If Scandinavia were likened to a piece of cheese, then Norway might resemble the rind – a hard, irregular and crumbled crust. The elongated stretch of land consists for the most part of an imposing but inhospitable plateau of barren rock, some 70% of which is above the tree line. For over a million years the Atlantic ocean has frayed the Norwegian coast. The sea borders the country in all directions save that of the east, driving deep into the fjords and fissures that were first cut by the retreating glaciers during the Ice Age.

From early times the Norwegians have made a virtue out of necessity, turning to the oceans for their livelihood. The sea was full of fish, and the rugged coast formed many a natural harbor for the ships built by a nation of master shipbuilders. Although the fishing industry has played an important part in Norway's economy, only a small proportion of Norway is under cultivation. The country has thus had to rely on foreign trade since the days of the Vikings. Oslo, Bergen, Stavanger and Trondheim were trading centers that were thriving even during the Middle Ages. The Norwegians exported timber and fish, and the holds of the returning ships often contained cheeses brought from other lands. An early cheese type that dates from this period, and is still being made, is the semihard, spiced cheese called *Nøkkelost*, which bears some resemblance to Dutch Leiden cheese. It used to carry the mark of St. Peter's crossed keys, the arms of the city of Leiden; hence its name: *nokkel* is the Norwegian word for "key."

Early farmhouse cheese

Only some 3% of Norway can be successfully cultivated, although the warm Gulf Stream influences the climate. Even as far north as the Lofoten region, the weather can be mild and the grass is of excellent quality. Until the beginning of the twentieth century and the introduction of hydroelectric power, Norway was almost entirely agricultural. A source of cheap power, electricity brought about the growth of manufacturing industries, and especially the pulp paper, wood and canning industries.

Norway's pasture land, albeit of limited acreage, provides good grazing for cattle. Consequently, cattle breeding and dairying have made a substantial contribution to the na-

ABOVE: Norway is a sparsely populated country with the majority of people living in the south. This isolated church is situated on the northern coast.

BELOW: Farmhouses on the plateau of Geiranger, between Bergen and Trondheim. Here you might still find farmhouse goat cheese.

tional economy for centuries. The early farmers quickly learned how to make the very best of their dairy product. They found that the skimmed milk, left behind after the butter had been made, could be used to produce a delicious cheese. Cheesemakers used beautifully carved and decorated cheese molds, and for transporting their cheese and butter there was the traditional *tine*, a strikingly shaped, elegant wooden container. The symbol of this container, rendered in the national colors red, white and blue, is today the emblem of the entire Norwegian dairy industry.

Although Norway has many farms, they are among the smallest in Europe, and in past times the cheese production per farming family was not very high. Much of the cheese was made for immediate consumption and eaten fresh. *Pultost*, the nonfat cheese made from sour, skimmed milk, is an early cheese type, produced long before the arrival of manufactured cheeses. This soft cheese is made throughout Norway, and there are seemingly endless varieties with only very slight differences in preparation. Some might contain caraway seeds, others have had cream added to them to make the cheese richer. Pultost is also known as *Ramost* and *Knaost*, according to the locality.

When you consider Norway's mountainous character, it is not surprising that goat's milk was once as popular, if not more so, than cow's milk. The two were frequently mixed to give variety to the taste. This taste for sharp, pungent cheeses remains, and goat cheeses are still made here and there on the farms, as is the whey cheese *Gjetost*.

Farmer to factory

Even now there are several farmers who still make cheese for their own consumption, but the production of cheese for the market has long since moved from the small farms to the factories. The development of the factory industry started as long ago as 1856. The farmers in some of the valleys decided to build a communal farm in the mountains, where the cattle grazed during the summer months. The aim was to process the rich quality summer milk, and the move heralded the first cooperative dairy plant in northern Europe. The initiative was so well received that

dairy factories began to appear everywhere throughout the country. Today there are an impressive two hundred or so cooperative establishments. In keeping with the progressive approach to farming and cheesemaking, an improved road system was planned. Roads were laid to the farms, even those outlying properties in the mountains, so that the transportation of milk from farm to factory is fast and efficient. While the traditional origin of the cheeses formed the basis of their quality, the cooperative effort enabled mass production to get under way. Factories are now not only making Norway's standard cheese types, but new brands as well, including *Norbo*, *Ridder* (a cheese similar to St.-Paulin) and the easy-melting, rindless *Norvegia*, so popular in the kitchen. Also being produced are blue *Normanna*, Norwegian *Gouda*, *Edam*, *Tilsit*,

Port-Salut, *Camembert*, *Brie*, *Emmental* and the glorious cream cheeses *Crème Château* and *Château Bleu*, to mention but a few. The entire cheese production, its inspection and marketing both at home and abroad, is controlled by the Norske Meierier, which works together with the Ministry of Agriculture.

Cheese for the long winter

In addition to fresh cheeses, the dairy farmers used to make cheeses that could be kept for eating during the long winter months, when milk was not so plentiful. As a rule, the cheeses were prepared during the summer from the milk surplus to be stored for the coming winter. It has been suggested that the unique, brown cheese called *Gammelost* owes its name to its long-keeping properties. *Gammel* is the Norwegian word for "old"; while *ost* simply means "cheese." Another explanation is that Gammelost is a cheese made from a very old recipe. A more likely explanation, however, is that it got its name because of the cheese's appearance – not only did it turn a greenish-brown color, but it developed a mold growth as well. Whatever its origin, the present factory-made Gammelost is ready for consumption within four to five weeks, and is one of Norway's freshest cheese types.

The mold spores that settle on Gammelost endow it with a delicious flavor. In the dark days before the sterilization of cheesemaking equipment, the farm cheeses grew a spontaneous mold culture. When the cheese was made in wooden vessels and molds, there were always traces remaining from the previous batch and mold spores were extremely productive. This is considered unacceptable in the hygienic modern factory, and the result is that spontaneous growth is now completely suppressed. However, the soft and smooth Gammelost would not be Gammelost without its unique, distinctive flavor: sharp and aromatic. For this reason, to maintain its character, the dairies inoculate the cheese with laboratory-grown molds. Once these have settled on the cheese they develop a kind of long, furry texture, the fur is pressed into the paste by hand to spread through the cheese, which slowly turns a brownish color. Gammelost contains less than 3% fat.

ABOVE: A row of Gammelost cheeses in the ripening room. The mold is regularly pressed into the cheeses by hand. With its unique, pungent aroma and taste, Gammelost is a real contribution to the range of world cheeses.

LEFT: A wedge cut from a Jarlsberg cheese. Jarlsberg is a large, full-cream, firm cheese with many regular holes.

Ancient revival

Another true veteran among Norway's cheeses is *Jarlsberg*. Its name derives from an old estate on the west bank of Oslo Fjord in the south, where the Vikings first settled. The farmers of this region made a large, firm, full-cream cheese with holes. The cheese more or less died out when attention shifted to the products of the dairy plants, but it was not totally forgotten. In the laboratories of the University of Agriculture in Ås, experiments were continued until the correct method of preparing the original product was established. As Norwegian taste had not changed over the ages, Jarlsberg once again became a popular cheese, both in Norway as well as abroad. The taste is somewhere between a Gouda and an Emmental: mild and nutty, with a slight hint of sweetness.

Morning begins with Mysost

The most popular Norwegian cheese on the home market is undoubtedly *Mysost*, a cheese made from whey – *Myse* is the Norwegian word for "whey." Without a piece of Mysost on the table, the Norwegian breakfast is incomplete. More than 30 % of the total cheese production consists of this brown whey cheese, which is marketed in various forms.

Whey cheeses, like skimmed-milk cheeses, were originally products of expedience, but in Norway and other Scandinavian countries, their status has been considerably elevated. The whey cheese types originated from goat's milk, because cow's milk was made into butter and the whey was consequently deprived of butter fat. Goat's milk, on the other hand, was used only for drinking, or for cheesemaking. The whey cheeses were

LEFT: *Landgang* (meaning "gangway"), the Norwegian version of a hero sandwich – a meal in itself.

ABOVE: Warehouses in the old harbor in Trondheim. Situated as it is on a fjord, Trondheim is one of Norway's many natural harbors.

Name	Milk	Type	Rind	Form	Weight	% Fat content
Crème Château	⌂	●	—	flat disc	1.5 kg	60
Gammelost	⌂	◖	☐	cylinder	2-3 kg	0.5-3
Jarlsberg	⌂	◖	☐	cylinder	10 kg	45
Mysost	⌂	●	—	loaf	1.5 kg	10-33
Nøkkelost	⌂	◖	☐	cartwheel	12-15 kg	45
Norbo	⌂	●	☐	cylinder	4 kg	45
Norvegia	⌂	●	☐	loaf	4.5 kg	45
Pultost	⌂	○	—	container	varies	varies
Ridder	⌂	●	❖	low cylinder	1,5-2 kg	60

Key to symbols on page 6. 1 kg = 2.2 lbs.

known as *Gjetost*, *gjei* being the Norwegian word for "goat."

The manufacture of Mysost starts with either goat's milk or cow's milk, or a mixture of both. When made with pure goat's milk whey, the product is called *Ekte* (genuine) *Gjetost*. The cream is skimmed for butter and the milk goes to make cheese. The remaining whey is heated very slowly until the water has evaporated, and the milk sugar forms a kind of brown, caramelized paste known as *prim*. At this stage milk or cream is often added, which changes the fat content of the

RIGHT: Old label from a Gammelost cheese. The making of this ancient cheese type is a tradition on Norwegian farms. The cheese is said to date back to Viking times.

ultimate product. However, the brown color, sweetish flavor and firm, tough consistency remain the general characteristics of all Mysost varieties.

Mysost is not, strictly speaking, a cheese, since cheese is, by definition, a product made from pressed curds. Dairy-made Mysost, the commercial variety, is still similar in quality to that originally produced by the mountain farms in former times, and in the distant past it must have been a real champion among the Norwegian cheeses. It is even said that this was the cheese the Vikings carried with them as food when they went on their predatory raids, and from it they got their courage and endurance. Whatever the truth, their present descendants still consider Mysost an essential beginning to a busy day.

Food for hearty appetites

For centuries the Norwegian way of life demanded that the people be independent, especially with regard to the food supply. Foodstuffs had to be preserved during the long winter months, especially in the isolated mountain farm dwellings. For this reason many of Norway's traditional foods are smoke or salt-cured – salted mutton, salted ham and salt fish. Norway's cuisine can engender some fabulous thirsts, hence the popularity of beer and the powerful aquavit. Today the Norwegian larder is supplemented by a variety of imported foods, but the Norwegian diet continues to remain simple, robust, filling and fresh. With fish as a staple food, the national menu consists of such delights as fish soups, herring, salt fish and pickled fish (salmon is a particular delicacy); there is also an abundance of roast lamb, veal, fine vegetables, crusty flatbreads, potato cakes, fruit, cream, buttermilk and – of course – cheese. Cheese, especially Gjetost or Mysost, is used in sauces and on their famous open sandwiches. An impressive example is a French loaf cut lengthwise, well buttered and decorated with a selection of fish, meat, salad and cheese, according to taste. This arm's-length sandwich is called *landgang*, meaning "gangway," and is best indulged in when preceded by a glass or two of aquavit and accompanied by Norway's favorite drink – beer.

BELOW: The range of Norway's cheeses: on the extreme left is a speckled, half-circle of spicy Nøkkelost. On top of it, next to a Norwegian Edam is a white Gjetost, a goat's whey cheese. In the foreground is a dark-brown, round Gammelost; to the right of this, a half Jarlsberg with its characteristic, large holes. In front is Cheddar, blue Normanna and Port-Salut. At the extreme right an orange Ridderost sandwiched between Gouda and Tilsit. In front are two triangular portions of Crême Château. The cheese with the paprika on top is Norvegia; to the left a Swiss type. A number of foreign cheeses are also included.

Sweden

Sweden's geographical position, with Norway to the west and the Baltic to the east, has by no means isolated her from contact with other nations. In common with her adventurous, sea-faring neighbors, the Swedes were also traders who, according to an ancient runic inscription carved on a stone at the Rännarebanan, "courageously sailed to the gold in the West, and in the East they fed the eagles."

Visby, the oldest Hanseatic League settlement on the Baltic island of Götland, was the junction of overseas trade routes between Russia and the West during the Middle Ages. Even in the country's early history, dairy farmers were making and exporting large quantities of butter, but no cheese, or at least very little, as cheese was imported from other countries – Sweden was one of the principal importers of Dutch cheese until well into the nineteenth century. Yet it is an established fact that cheese was made on both sides of the Vättern Lake over a thousand years ago: *Götaost* (Göt-land cheese) in Västergötland and goat's milk cheese in Östergötland. The social, cultural and economic life of the Scandinavian peoples has

TOP: Although only 9% of Sweden's land area is suitable for any form of agriculture, the country has over 2.5 million head of cattle. Much of the milk is made into cheese, which has an important place on the national menu.

ABOVE: A wooden church spire at Trono, Ålsingland, a fine example of traditional country architecture.

always been finely interwoven, and since curds and buttermilk were staple foods of the Vikings, there is little doubt that cheese varieties and methods of preparation were exchanged during that period of Scandinavia's history.

The parson's cheese
Cheese was valued as an item of currency in sixteenth-century Protestant Sweden. In areas where pastures were owned by the church, the local vicar exacted rent from the parishioners who farmed the land in the form of quantities of milk and sometimes of fresh cheese. The vicar or his wife would make cheese from the milk, which could then be bartered in exchange for other necessities – meat, perhaps, or butter, eggs and fish. The name *Prästost*, literally "parsonage cheese," is a reminder of this old custom. Such cheeses were often highly valued. *Småland-Prästost*, named after the district of fertile meadows in the south of Sweden, was widely known, far beyond the boundaries of the region where the cheeses were made. It has remained a popular country cheese, but it is now factory-

made from a mixture of fresh and pasteurized milk, the fresh milk giving the cheese an extra aroma and flavor. The cheesecloth in which it is pressed remains around the cheese.

Cheese in a cold climate

Lappernas Renost, made from reindeer milk by the seminomadic Laplanders, can hardly be considered one of Sweden's most popular national cheeses – but it is probably the most northerly cheese in the world. The Laplanders make the cheese in small quantities for their own consumption, sometimes as an accompaniment to coffee, into which the cheese is dipped. Reindeer milk is characterized by its extremely high fat content, but it is a scarce commodity, as one animal can only produce about 25 liters (27.5 quarts) of milk a year. The production of reindeer cheese is thus minimal, its enjoyment limited to the Lapps.

Sweden's sharp and spicy cheeses

Very much in vogue, and one of Sweden's biggest-selling cheeses, is the tall, round *Hushållsost*, or "household cheese." Hushållsost is a traditional farmhouse cheese, which for centuries had been made from whole milk by the farmers of southern Sweden. Now a modern factory product, it can be found in a variety of shapes and with a varying fat content. The name also varies: *Boxholms Gräddost*, *Lilliput* or *Smålands Gräddost*, the last type being characterized by many small holes. The taste is mild, and the cheese only requires one or two months to ripen.

A much longer ripening period is needed for the extremely popular *Svecia* cheese to reach its ultimate perfection. Svecia is a true Swedish speciality; it has an abundance of irregular eyelets and a smooth consistency. Like the Hushållsost, it is marketed in various types. There are mild Svecias and deliciously piquant ones, with a range of nuances in between. A well-matured Svecia, one that has been ripening for more than twelve months, is a splendid cheese with a pure, fresh and yet definite flavor. One type of Svecia is spiced with cumin seeds and cloves, and is ready to eat after only two months' ripening. Another clove- and cumin-flavored cheese, the *Kryddost*, takes much longer to mature, and after one year it possesses an extremely sharp, spicy taste. It is often recommended as

LEFT: These symbols and runic inscriptions were carved on rock surfaces by the Vikings. Runes played an important part in divination and were thought to have influenced weather, crops and cattle.

an ingredient for lobster dishes, as it is one of the few cheese varieties able to hold its own beside the pronounced flavor of lobster. Kryddost is available in fat contents of 30 and 45 %.

Even larger and heavier than Svecia, to which it is comparable, is *Västerbotten* cheese. Originally called Burträsk cheese, it was first made during the middle of the last century, in a cheese dairy in the old village of Burträsk. It became widely copied, however, and changed its name to Västerbotten, and was registered as such. Today only a cheese from the Västerbotten region can carry that name; each is stamped with the letter W following careful inspection to see that regulations have been met. One Västerbotten cheese weighs approximately 20 kg (44 lbs), and usually has a fat content of 50 %. After ten to twelve months of ripening, it has a dry and somewhat crumbly texture, and a very pronounced flavor.

Cheeses for the smörgåsbord

During the past twenty years or so, the Swedish cheese industry has not only concentrated on the manufacture of traditional varieties, but has also added to the range of national cheeses. Today local cheeses are being made and foreign cheeses imitated. There are a number of ways by which a cheese manufacturer can increase the selection and the simplest is to produce a specific type of cheese, but with varying fat content. A factory can also

RIGHT: Kryddost cheese, spiced with cumin and cloves. When well matured it is a very tasty, semi-hard cheese with many small eyes.

LEFT: The Swedish Santa Claus features on this old cheese label. At Christmas, the Swedes enjoy the special, festive cheese God Julost.

introduce new shapes and sizes, or it can experiment with various mold cultures and with shorter or longer periods of ripening, which can influence the appearance and taste of a cheese. The atmosphere in the ripening room can significantly affect a cheese's character. If, for example, a cheese is stored in a moist atmosphere, the rind growth will develop much more vigorously. Finally, technical and marketing influences may lead to entirely new innovations, such as the production of prepacked cheese, which ripens inside its foil.

Sweden's weeping cheese
One of the main types of foil-ripened cheese is *Riddarost*, which is sold with a fat content of either 30 % or 45 %, both spiced and plain, and has no visible rind. Some examples of the cheese have a faintly theatrical quality: for special occasions you can order from the factory in Götene, a cheese weighing 500 kg (1,100 lbs), measuring a cubic meter (3⅓ cubic feet). Two representatives from the factory accompany the giant cheese, so that they may cut it in the presence of the customer – always a spectacular event. The large pieces are then divided into loaves of approximately 1 kg (2.2 lbs), from which manageable portions are cut.

Another principal cheese type, also available with fat contents of 30 % and 45 %, is the currently popular

TOP: Supervisors at work in a modern cheese storeroom. They use a special knife to take samples from cheeses selected at random in order to assess their progress and development.

ABOVE: A display of some fine Swedish cheeses. The big wedge with the large eyes is Grevé. A piece of Tilsiter-style cheese sits on top of some Kryddost. The drum-shaped cheese with the slicer is Swedish Cheddar, behind it a portion of Västgötaost. Far right is a sample of red-waxed Fontina, and far left some Swedish Camembert.

Herrgårdsost. As it matures it acquires a mild, nutty flavor, and if stored for a year or more its eyes, as they say, "start to cry," the holes becoming shiny and moist. It melts easily when heated, and is therefore an ideal cooking cheese. A version of Herrgårdsost is the foil-ripened *Drabant*, very popular at the breakfast table due to its surprising mildness. There is a still mellower version known as *Billinge*.

One of the finest of all Swedish cheeses is *Grevé*, a cheese of the Emmental type, but ripened with a different mold culture which gives it a slightly less dry texture. After some ten months' ripening, the Grevé has the same moist-looking eyes as the Swiss Emmental, with its aroma and flavor similar as well.

Many of the lesser-known Swedish cheese varieties have developed from such regional types as *Västgötaost* from Västergötland, *Hälsingeost* from Hälsingland, and *Buost* and *Vålåloffen* from Jämtland. Decidedly non-fat is the Buost, a long, flat, rectangular cheese, which after its salt bath is kept moist. Hälsingeost is soft and smooth, but somewhat sharp and even slightly bitter to taste; it is made of a mixture of cow's milk and 10 % goat's milk. These last two cheese varieties are not paraffined, but develop a rind growth, as does Vålåloffen, with its pale orange rind like Port-Salut.

Passed by the runes
The farmhouse heritage of certain other varieties is more difficult to establish. *Fontina* and *Scandia* both have a fat content of 45 % and are made in the shape of a wagonwheel with sharp edges; the Fontina is red-paraffined.

Swedish Fontina should not be confused with the famous Italian cheese of the same name, the Fontina d'Aosta, although the shape is vaguely similar.

Any country that has a progressive dairy industry like that of Sweden, and that has a large public demand for foreign cheeses, strives to produce good, competitive imitations. It is thus not surprising that a whole series of Swedish cheeses has been copied or derived from foreign cheese types: *Tilci, Havarti, Ambrosia* (of the Tilsit type), Swedish *Cheddar, Gouda, Edam, Port-Salut, Brie, Camembert, Party* (somewhere between Brie and Camembert), *Stilton, Stockkumla dessertost* (like Stilton, but without the

Name	Milk	Type	Rind	Form	Weight	% Fat content
Getost		■	—	cube	200-500 g	30
Grevé		■	□	cartwheel	12-14 kg	30-45
Herrgårdsost		■	□	cartwheel	12-20 kg	30-45
Hushållsost		■	□	cylinder	2 kg	45-60
Mesost		■	—	loaf	1.5 kg	10-30
Prästost		■	□	cylinder	12-15 kg	50
Riddarost		■	—	loaf	1 kg	30-45
Svecia		■	□	cartwheel	12-24 kg	30-55
Västerbotten		■	□	cartwheel	20 kg	30-50

Key to symbols on page 6. 1 kg = 2.2 lbs.

characteristic rind), *Ädelost* (Roquefort type, but made from cow's milk instead of sheep's milk), full-cream cheeses such as *Crème Chantilly, Crème Château, Crème Noisette,* and various types of *Färskost* (cottage cheese and curds).

By far the greater part of Swedish cheese production finds its way to the consumer in small packs under the new trademark "Ostmästeren." All cheeses are given an official inspection, and those that are accepted are stamped with a *runmärkt* ("rune brand"). As a rule, the Swedes are expert cheesemakers, and the quality is high. Those cheeses that are pressed and bound in cheesecloth are additionally protected by a paraffin covering; the Swedish cheesemakers prefer this to plastic wrapping because of effects on the ripening process. With paraffining, the curds must be finished dry, and not too much salting can take place. Thus the salt content of most Swedish cheeses is quite low.

Swedish farmhouse cheese

Traditional farmhouse cheesemaking still survives in spite of the newly developed methods and the internationally inspired factory cheeses. In the north of the country, on the summer farms, a quantity of *Getost* is made from raw goat's milk. Production of this cheese has been commenced on a fairly limited scale by small dairies and is based on pasteurized milk. After about one month,

Getost is ready to eat. The Swedes like to serve it on tunnbröd (very thinly sliced bread, not unlike a matzo in appearance), often with a slice of brown whey cheese called *Mesost*. Mesost – to the Norwegians, "Mysost" – is a caramel-like substance derived from thickening the whey, which has been separated from the prepared curd. Noteworthy, too, is *Getmesost*, a whey cheese made from goat's milk and formerly prepared in iron pots, from which it obtained a relatively high iron content.

The Swedish table

At its most sophisticated, the famous smörgåsbord is an awe-inspiring selection of dishes, a very extensive buffet with a tempting display of hot and cold meat and fish dishes, salads, sauces, cheeses and breads. The rustic and traditional affair from which it derived is a meal of salt fish, cheese, bread and butter – smörgåsbord means "bread and butter table" – washed down with aquavit. Many Swedes begin their smörgåsbord meal with knäckebröd and paper-thin slices of hard rye bread with *Potkäs*, or Pot cheese – a mixture of grated cheese, butter, brandy and various herbs. Camembert is eaten in Sweden in a manner all on its own. The cheese is cut into sections, then breadcrumbed and fried. A compote is served with it made from *hjortron*, yellow, marble-sized berries from the mountain swamps of north Sweden, with a very delicate, somewhat raspberry-like flavor.

Cheesemaker's cake

One of Sweden's special, sweet delicacies is the traditional and festive *ostkaka*, a cake which is practically made in the manner of a cheese. It differs from other cheesecakes in that cheese is not one of the added ingredients. The cake calls for a large quantity of milk mixed with cream. This is curdled with rennet before the remaining ingredients are added: eggs, sugar, flour and flavorings. The mixture is then poured into a copper mold, and baked. As is happening in many countries today, people are forgetting how to prepare these dishes, now that they are commercially available.

BELOW: A characteristic raised house in Dalarna, central Sweden.

RIGHT: A nomadic Laplander in his tent of reindeer hide. The rare reindeer cheese is stony-hard, flat, and round in form. The Lapps often dunk it in coffee.

Denmark

To produce cheese in quantity, quality and variety you need large herds of dairy cattle; these in turn demand wide acres of lush pastures encouraged by a temperate climate. This is why Denmark, of all the Scandinavian countries, is by far the most important as a producer of cheese. Unlike Norway and Sweden, it has no rough, mountainous countryside. The highest point is only 1,770 meters (1.3 miles) above sea level, and nearly everywhere there are green fields and fertile soil. The bitter winter can suddenly turn into a mild spring with sunshine and gentle rain – a more favorable climate for farming and cattle raising is hard to imagine.

Denmark's agricultural policies came about as a result of two main factors. To begin with, an intensive reclaiming of sandy heathlands and marshes eventually provided large areas of fertile grazing, and this compensated for unpromising mineral wealth and lack of industrial raw materials. The second factor is that Denmark occupies a very advantageous position between the North Sea and the Baltic and lies on the path of several important trade routes. Today, about 95% of the land area is cultivated, and there is a well-organized system of cooperative farming. Denmark has become one of the world's great producers of bacon, butter, cereals and meat – and, of course, cheese.

The cheeses of prehistory
Some of the earliest settlers on the Danish mainland were primitive tribes from Finland and Lapland, who arrived more than four thousand years ago. Archeological finds show that they kept goats, sheep and cows, and doubtless cheese formed a part of the daily menu. The Danes became skilled in the art of cheesemaking, learning from other countries special techniques of preparation, skills which they generously shared and spread abroad through the agency of the Vikings. Denmark was the real homeland of these fierce sea warriors, and it is likely that the inhabitants of the regions in which Vikings permanently settled became familiar with Danish cheeses, perhaps also with cheeses from elsewhere in Europe which the Vikings, like modern tourists, brought home in their ships.

The next important influence on

LEFT: The wealth of Denmark. A rich land of pastures, well-fed cows and dairy farms, some of the important aspects of the national economy. Perhaps this is why the windmill in the background is featured on the Danish 10-kronen banknote.

BELOW: A beautiful old farmhouse with decorative copperwork windows. The windows are curved to give the occupants a wider angle of vision than would plain, flat ones.

Danish cheese came from the Cistercian monks of the Middle Ages, who developed new methods of manufacture, which they passed on to the farmers and landowners in districts adjacent to their monasteries. It is not strange that the first simple cheese dairies were found particularly in these monasteries. The Cistercians were forbidden to eat meat, and experimented to find a nutritious replacement.

Avoiding the use of rennet as a starter, they found that the leaves of certain insectivorous plants, probably of the genus *Drosera* (e.g., the Venus' flytrap and the Sundew), could be used instead. The juice released by these plants to dissolve trapped insects contains the same enzymes as rennet. The monks probably taught the farmers the art of maturing cheeses in addition to making fresh ones. Gradually the goat's milk and sheep's milk were replaced by cow's milk.

Smoked cheese, status cheese
The Scandinavians developed a taste for certain smoked foods, following the need to preserve, and thus smoke, their fish. It was but a short step to the

smoking of cheese. In Finland fresh cheeses were smoked over a straw or hay fire in the open air. Such a cheese is *Fynskt Rygeost*. Traditionally a farm cheese, it is now mainly produced in factories, where the curds are conveyed in aluminum containers through a smoke chamber. Afterwards, cumin seed can be added, either sprinkled on the curds or mixed with them. The cheese does not mature and can only be kept for a few days.

Originally farmers made cheese for their own consumption, and for use as currency, to pay the taxes levied by the church.

As towns began to grow, the demand for cheese increased and production kept pace. Among those considered to be very experienced cheese makers were the inhabitants of the island of Samsø (which would one day make Danish cheese world-renowned). The annual production of Danish butter and cheese during the first half of the thirteenth century reached nearly 60,000 kg (132,000 lbs). In the province of Thy in North Jylland, from which *Tybo* cheese takes its name, cheese became a status symbol: the larger the cheeses, the

BOTTOM: Havarti is a semihard cheese of the Tilsit type. The cheese is named after the farm of one of Denmark's greatest cheese pioneers, Hanne Nielsen. In the nineteenth century she experimented with foreign and local cheeses, and produced much cheese of excellent quality.

BELOW: The harbor of Århus, Denmark's second largest city and home of the Danish Cheese Export Board.

greater the professional skill of the makers, and on this skill the prosperity of the region depended. Some cheeses reached such colossal dimensions that several men could hardly lift them.

Royalties from cheese
During the reign of King Christian II at the beginning of the sixteenth century, religious observance held that it was forbidden to eat cheese during Lent. Christian's position was somewhat ambivalent: he was the upholder of the faith, but also a champion of Danish cheese, and those Danes who took the trouble could obtain from the king a special letter of dispensation (for a suitable fee, of course) by which cheese and religious observance became reconciled.

Christian was responsible for considerable improvements in the quality of Danish cheese and other dairy products. Deciding that the industry needed foreign expertise, he sent for some Dutch farmers, cheesemakers from near Edam, who settled on the island of Amager near Copenhagen.

The first export market
The Dutch cheesemakers' example had an inspiring effect on the Danish cheese industry. Many landowners, who were previously only interested in horses, became involved in dairy farming. On the estates and the large farms, cellars were turned into cheese dairies, where an even temperature was maintained throughout the year. Production demanded a greater work force, and the ripened cheeses piled up in the cellars in such quantities that the supply outstripped the demand, however great the latter was. New markets had to be found. *Tybo* cheese was an early export, finding its way to Britain before the nineteenth century, where its highly flavored aroma was much appreciated. *Ejdersted* and *Tyrstrup* were exported from Schleswig-Holstein (then a part of Denmark), albeit in small quantities only. The Danish cheeses of this period differed from region to region: there were both firm and soft cheeses, spicy and simple.

As often happens in the course of progress, many have disappeared forever.

The cheese pioneers

In keeping with the practice of many European cheesemakers, experiments were started in an attempt to produce foreign types of cheese for the home market. Around 1800 Constantin Bruun, owner of the Antvorskov estate, invited Swiss cheesemakers to make Emmental from the entire milk yield of his dairy cows. Although production was successful, Danish Emmental gradually developed into a smaller cheese with a character all its own – the present *Samsø*.

On his Bekkeskov estate, Baron Selby adopted British methods of cheese preparation. He did not press his cheese underneath stones, as was the normal practice, but used a screw press. The young engineer Jørgenson of Knabstrup also became famous as a cheesemaker, with his fine examples of Dutch, Parmesan, Swiss and Cheddar cheeses. He startled the Danish cheese world by publishing his manufacturing secrets with a frankness unknown since the days of the medieval monks.

Of all the great cheese pioneers, the most important was Hanne Nielsen. Born in 1829, Nielsen was a country-woman who was interested in farm produce – so interested that she purchased a farm, named Havarthi, from her husband and decided to make cheese. Undaunted by her lack of foreign languages, she traveled abroad to study cheesemaking. Returning to Havarthi, she started to experiment with Norwegian goat's milk cheese, English Cheddar, Dutch Edam and Gouda, French Camembert and Roquefort, East Prussian Tilsit and Swiss Emmental. Her farm, which gave its name to the modern *Havarti* cheese, was soon producing enormous quantities of cheese, some of which was sold to the Royal Court. In Denmark her influence was far reaching, and she found time to give lessons in cheesemaking to farmers' wives, who in turn taught others, so that the constantly increasing home industry became a chapter in the country's agrarian history.

The foundation of cooperatives

Around the year 1880, Denmark had three types of dairy establishment in existence: the small farms; the estates where local milk was made into butter

LEFT: The production of factory-made Cheddar cheese for export.

LEFT: Newly cut portions of curd receiving a liberal dose of salt.

ABOVE: Factory workers packing the famous blue-veined cheeses. The triangular wedges of cheese are packed into round containers, and each portion receives a label. The label below is of a similar type of Danish Blue to those being assembled above.

and cheese; and the small cheese factories which processed the milk of associated farms. Originally the best cheese came from the estates. Most farmers felt more secure concentrating on crops rather than dairy farming, and many grew wheat for export. But towards the end of the nineteenth century, grain prices fell by 40 %, due to the enormous export activity of the now superproductive wheatlands of the world – North America, Australia and Argentina. The Danish farms could only survive this crisis by shifting to dairy and meat production; but to achieve a competitive price for their dairy products they would have to work through close cooperation.

In 1882 the first cooperative dairy factory was opened in Hjedding, in southwest Jutland. Six years later 215 of them had been established throughout the country. While some operated as private concerns, most maintained the cooperative system. A further stimulant to trade was the invention of the centrifugal cream separator, which enabled butter to be made on a much larger scale. These kind of improvements also helped the cheesemakers to improve their product.

Denmark's world exports

Even before the nineteenth century, Denmark was a dairy country of world repute, but it was her butter rather than her cheese that attracted foreign buyers. Relatively little attention was paid to cheese production, which could only just satisfy the home market; cheese was available in variety, but not in quantity. This state of affairs persisted until after the Second World War. Then, owing to land consolidation, progress in combating cattle disease, and the establishment of cooperative stables which could hold over four hundred cows, milk production greatly increased, despite the decreasing number of farmers. Today cheese factories have completely taken over production from the farmers, the milk from the farms being collected by modern refrigerated tankers. Denmark has grown in importance and become the third largest cheese exporter in the world, after Holland and New Zealand.

Pride of place

Foreign influences can still be found in the Danish cheese varieties. The establishment of the national range was originally based on cheeses from foreign countries, mainly from Europe, yet these eventually took on a genuine Danish character, due to the properties of Danish milk.

As a further step towards establishing the origin of Danish cheeses, the authorities decided to change the names of many types, especially those with foreign origins and those that might be confused with other Scandinavian cheeses. Thus Danish Emmental was renamed Samsø, after the island in the Kattegat. Port-du-Salut became Esrom, after the town where it is made. All the members of the Samsø family, which were made in different towns or districts, such as Mols, Thy and Fyn, were given the possessive suffix "bo" so that Fynbo means "from the island of Fyn." To these we can add Molbo, Elbo and Tybo; also Maribo, which is named after the town on the island of Lolland.

The Samsø family

Samsø, the Danish cheese with Swiss origins, is round like a cartwheel with sharp edges, and weighs approximately 14 kg (30.8 lbs). It is a full-

LEFT: Cattle breeding in Denmark is far more important than crop farming, which usually serves the cattle industry.

BELOW: Large, round Samsø cheeses in the brine bath. The label on the left was one used for exported cheese.

cream cheese: the paste is firm but not hard, the color is pale yellow. It has shiny holes or "eyes" the size of cherries, and a fine nutty flavor that varies from sweet to strong, depending on the duration of ripening. Some prefer to eat it soon after it has been made, when sweet and very mild, while others maintain that age improves the flavor.

Samsø became established as the grandfather of all Danish cheese types. It is typically Scandinavian in spite of its Swiss origins. While it may not be counted among the really great cheeses, it is extremely versatile, lending its characteristics to a number of descendants. *Danbo* differs from Samsø in shape, being square instead of round, and sometimes contains caraway seeds. Well-ripened (up to two years) spiced Danbo is called *Gammelost* and considered a speciality. *Fynbo* is round like Samsø, but smaller and without the sharp edges. It has eyes which are somewhat smaller than the original Samsø. The mild, aromatic *Elbo*, with its very firm paste, is made in a loaf shape and has fewer holes. *Tybo*, the most solid-looking member of the family, is half the size of Elbo. *Molbo* is the last member of the clan, a round cheese with a red rind. The distinct, nutty aroma is immediately apparent on cutting. Highly flavored, and widely exported, Molbo has a firmer consistency than the other Samsøs. Most of these cheeses are made in varying fat contents, usually between 20 and 45 %. All the varieties of Samsø lend themselves well to cooking.

Esrom and other semihard types

The Samsøs are not the only semihard cheeses found in Denmark. The Gouda-like *Maribo* is either flat and round, or square in shape, and full of very small holes due to the curd's being crumbled, kneaded and then salted. Maribo has a red-paraffined rind and is made with fat contents of 20, 30 and 45 %. Its paste is yellow to reddish-yellow in color, and it possesses a distinctive flavor, with a characteristic, quite pronounced aftertaste. *Havarti*, one of the most heavily exported of all Danish cheeses, is loaf or cylindrical in shape, and rather like Tilsit. The rind of Havarti can be left dry or washed. As the cheese ages, the washed rind makes the taste of this cheese, originally fresh and slightly sour, somewhat sharp.

In the monastery town of Esrom, the monks used to make an excellent cheese, which was later forgotten. The monastery is now in ruins, but the Danish Dairy Research Institute has rediscovered Esrom. This full-cream cheese, probably finer and richer than the original, has a deliciously sweet taste, its paste is golden yellow and with small holes. The washed rind gives the cheese so much flavor that lovers of Esrom will advise you not to cut it away, but to eat it with the cheese.

Blue-veined specialities

Denmark makes a selection of blue-veined cheeses, whose origins were greatly influenced by the examples of Roquefort and Gorgonzola. The most famous is the Danish Blue or *Danablu*.

Danablu was first produced before World War I, when Danish cheese-makers were experimenting with various types of mold cultures. Realizing that the mold in cheese is similar to that which grows on stale bread, a cheesemaker by the name of Marius Boel introduced a bread mold culture onto a high-fat cheese made with homogenized milk.

Danablu comes in several types: cylindrical, rectangular or square, with fat contents of 50 to 60 %. The paste ripens swiftly and looks milk-white, with a delicate network of blue-green veins. Danablu cuts easier than one would normally expect from such a soft cheese, even though it is some-times rather crumbly. Its flavor is very pronounced, often distinctly sharp. If you find it too salty, it can be im-proved by crumbling and mixing with butter or cream. In this form it spreads easily on sandwiches; it is also a favorite Danish accompaniment to meat.

Mycella is a larger cheese, milder in taste, more yellow in color, with a veining nearer green than blue. This is a different mold than that of Danablu. It is called *mycelium*, which gives the cheese its name, and has characteris-tics in common with Gorgonzola. Apart from the production of national cheese types, Denmark continues to make imitations of foreign varieties, such as *Camembert, Brie, Emmental, Saint-Paulin, Mozzarella*, various whey cheeses, *Hytteost* (cottage cheese) and *Flödeost* (cream cheese).

ABOVE: A picturesque old dairy farm on the island of Fyn. The house is half-timbered, and the ridge of the thatched roof is strengthened with wood.

Name	Milk	Type	Rind	Form	Weight	% Fat content
Danablu	△	■	✂	cylinder	2.7-3.2 kg	50-60
Danbo	△	■	▢	rectangular	6 kg	10-45
Elbo	△	■	▢	loaf	5-6 kg	20-45
Esrom	△	■	❖	loaf	0.5-1.5 kg	45-60
Fynbo	△	■	▢	cartwheel	7-8 kg	30-45
Fynsk Rygeost	△	○	—	container	100-600 g	5-45
Havarti	△	■	▢❖	loaf, cylinder	4-5 kg	30-60
Maribo	△	■	▢	cartwheel, rectangular	13-15 kg	20-45
Molbo	△	■	▢	ball	1-3 kg	40-45
Mycella	△	■	✂	cylinder	5-9 kg	50
Samsø	△	■	▢	cartwheel	14 kg	30-45
Tybo	△	■	▢	loaf	2 kg	20-45

Key to symbols on page 6. 453 g = 1 lb; 1 kg = 2.2 lbs.

Smørrebród and the *lur* mark

The Danes are champion cheese eaters. On average, they consume some 10 kg (22 lbs) per person a year, mainly on open sandwiches – the famous smørrebród.

Cheese, of course, is a very popular ingredient on these open sandwiches, and may be combined with other foodstuffs, such as chopped egg, mushrooms, bacon slivers, shrimp and smoked fish. These are tastefully arranged with practiced skill on thickly buttered bread, usually rye bread and white bread.

The consumption of cheese has increased to such an extent that a large proportion is marketed pre-packed. For this purpose the cheese is made slightly drier than normal, and then is allowed to ripen in the packag-ing, which prevents a rind from form-ing; the remaining moisture is retained, but the gases are able to escape.

All cheeses for export must be pro-vided with the *lur* mark, denoting that it has been passed by state quality control. The mark shows four inter-woven horns, or *lurs*, which, in the Bronze Age, formed a wind instrument used only on ceremonial occasions. It is applied on a casein disc, which in addition records the fat content and the coded production date; the label grows to form a part of the rind.

Great Britain

For the succession of British poets, there have never been enough words to describe the English landscape, which can change not only from county to county, but from mile to mile. In the east, where the land is flat as a table, the soil is black, and the roads of the fen country run straight and true, there commences a gradual confusion of hills and forests, meadowland, villages and towns. Ignore the big cities and follow the rolling, twisting roads. They will take you to the mountains and valleys of Wales, or they will skirt the Pennine chain of hills – the spine of England – to take you north into the rocky, wild Scottish Highlands. Here, the coastline is indented by deep and narrow estuaries, called firths, in contrast to the wide, placid rivers of England. From the sea ports along the coast, seafarers and explorers swarmed over the globe, and wherever they went they left a small corner of Britain in every foreign field – and possibly a cheese recipe or two.

Britain is steeped in traditions, and its institutions, from parliamentary democracy to fish and chips, have become known all over the world. But the British have often been among the first to start important new developments. Chief among these was the Industrial Revolution, begun here in the eighteenth century when farm workers, hoping to escape rural poverty, sought work in the cities – and found urban poverty instead. They left the farms by the thousands, and the cities began to expand. Yet in spite of the ensuing urbanization and industrialization, a great deal of Britain remains rural and agricultural. The country is rich in cattle and sheep, and has a true maritime climate: mild winters and cool summers, the perfect conditions for dairy farming. It is not surprising, then, that Great Britain has several unique cheese varieties of superb quality. Yet because the British drink a large quantity of milk, they are obliged to supplement their equally heavy cheese consumption by importing cheese from abroad. Over 130,000 tons of cheese are brought in each year, in addition to the 199,000 tons produced at home, of which only 3% is exported. Everybody in England, regardless of class, eats cheese, for along with bread, bacon and beer, it has been a staple for well over a thousand years.

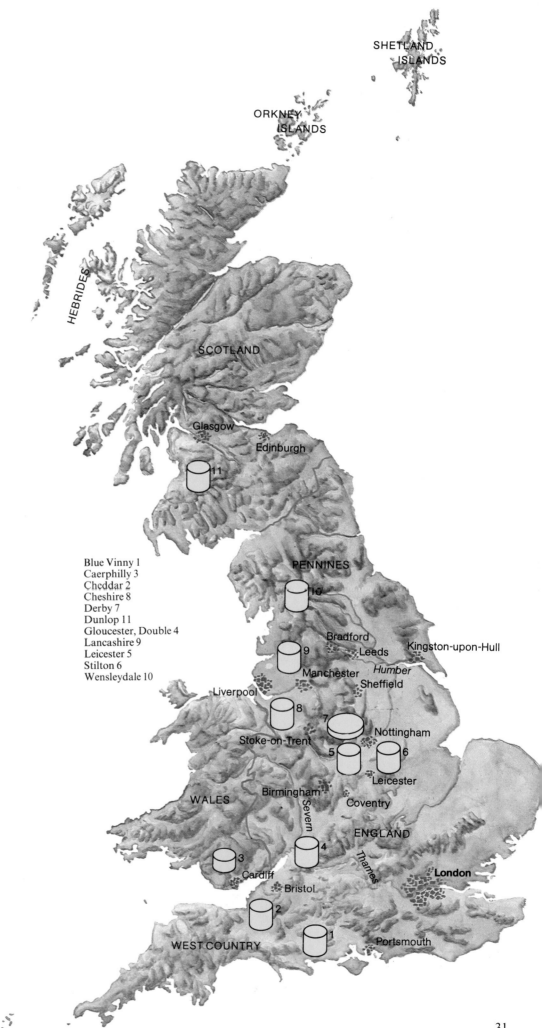

Blue Vinny 1
Caerphilly 3
Cheddar 2
Cheshire 8
Derby 7
Dunlop 11
Gloucester, Double 4
Lancashire 9
Leicester 5
Stilton 6
Wensleydale 10

Of the English cheeses that have survived the passing of time to take their places among the great cheeses of the world, there are less than a dozen. The most popular and widely-consumed British cheese is unquestionably the great *Cheddar*, from the county of Somerset in the West Country. Here is a region where for centuries cows have grazed and cheese has been made. Somerset, together with its southern neighbor Dorset, supply well over a quarter of all the cheeses produced in England and Wales. The lovely landscape of Somerset rises abruptly in the northeast to scale the Mendip Hills, where the stalactite caves and the winding, narrow cleft known as Cheddar Gorge leads to the small village of Cheddar. The village with its souvenir shops for tourists is not particularly memorable, yet this is the cradle of a world-famous cheese, once made locally on numerous farms, as well as in some adjoining parishes.

The history of English cheese

In the Middle Ages, a farmer and his family were almost entirely self-supporting, living mainly on the produce of the farm, which included buttermilk, butter, whey and cheese. Whether they made Cheddar as we know it today is an open question, but Cheddar cheese was already in demand in the Elizabethan period, when it was described as an excellent cheese of delicate taste. Cheese was then made from both sheep's milk and cow's milk, but by the seventeenth century the preference for cow's milk was thoroughly established. Traditionally, the farmer or laborer made ''common cheese'' for his own consumption, a low-fat, skimmed-milk cheese which turned very hard and crumbly. But there were others who

ABOVE: Although England has densely populated industrial centers, there remain large areas of beautiful, remote countryside. Some rural villages, and habits too, have hardly altered since the eighteenth century. From this past, several great cheeses have survived.

ABOVE: Traditional milk cans. Most British cheese is now made in factories. The milk is transported daily from the surrounding area, usually in large tankers.

RIGHT: In the carefree, rustic days of cheese-making, when a hefty dairymaid would use her ample weight to squeeze the whey from the curd, cheese was pressed with a heavy stone. Later versions of the cheese press employed a screw device or a pulley, so that greater pressure was exerted. Iron cheese presses, which also employ the screw system, date back to the early nineteenth century and are still in use on a few farms.

made whole-milk cheeses, called "rich cheese," a luxurious, golden-yellow variety sold to the local gentry in the manor house, or in the nearby market town. It was made from full, fresh, morning milk, mixed with skimmed cream from the previous evening. No wonder that this "new milk," or "morning cheese," was described as long ago as 1655 as the best in England.

Not unnaturally, attempts were made to copy it on a cheaper scale. Farmers and merchants began coloring their simple skimmed-milk cheeses to give them the appearance of a richer variety. In some parts of the West Country, cheeses were dyed with saffron, long cultivated there as a food flavoring and as a dye for home-spun yarn. In the eighteenth century it was found that an extract from the fruit of a West Indian tree, *Bixa orellana*, was cheaper to use than saffron and more permanent than carrot juice. This dye, called anatta or anatto, is still the most satisfactory way of coloring cheese; the most notable examples are the bright orange *Leicester* and certain makes of *Scottish Cheddar*.

"The bigger the maid, the better the cheese"

In the good old, hit-or-miss days of cheesemaking, when Britain was entirely agricultural, most cheeses were made by a traditionally buxom, rosy-cheeked dairymaid. There were milkmaids too, and equally endowed, who feature often in English folk songs. In fact, their lives were hard and their work tedious. When no milkmaid was available, the dairy-maid had to milk the cows herself, every morning and evening. She was responsible for the upkeep of the dairy

TOP: In the heart of the Cheddar cheese country is the cathedral city of Wells, where cheeses are graded.

LEFT: Milkmaid with a yoke. The old rhyme, "Where are you going to, my pretty maid? / I'm going a-milking, sir, she said," ignores the fact that prettiness in itself was no virtue – brawn and stamina were what was required. A story tells of one village where girls were asked to lift – with one hand – the exceptionally heavy lid of an old chest. Those that failed forfeited their chance of marrying a farmer, for farmers demanded a partner who could pull her weight in the business.

ABOVE: The birthplace of Cheddar cheese. According to legend, the caves that are a feature of Cheddar Gorge, Somerset, were once used to mature the cheeses.

and its equipment – such as there was – and she was required to have perfect knowledge of the cheesemaker's art: how to treat the milk, prepare the curd and press the cheese. Before pressing could begin it was of the greatest importance to have the vessels firmly filled. This the dairymaid achieved by climbing onto the lid of the cheese vessel, then pressing down on the curds with her hands, using her full weight, until most of the whey had oozed out. This pre-pressing was essential, because the primitive cheese presses of the day were unable to cope with moist curd. As the old saying goes: "The bigger the dairymaid, the better the cheese."

In the little spare time remaining, the dairymaid had to prepare rennet from the stomachs of calves, churn the butter and attend to the ripening of the cheese. Owing to this intense work program, mishaps did occur with the ripening process. The rule then was, "Save what can be saved." Because cheesemakers were ignorant of critical temperatures, acid percentages and moisture content, cheese had to be saved as often as made.

As far back as the seventeenth century, when the production on farms increased, the neighboring farmers of the Cheddar district began to work on a more or less cooperative basis. Their collective milk output was taken to a cooperative dairy, and from it cheeses of 20 to 120 pounds were made. According to their size they could be kept between two and five years. Towards the end of the seventeenth century a lively cheese trade had developed across the country and abroad, to the considerable profit of the cheese districts.

Cheese as a family secret

Apart from the cooperative cheeses, the majority of Cheddars were farmhouse cheeses. The quality varied greatly, as did the recipes for making them – recipes that were closely-guarded family secrets passed down from mother to daughter. In the second half of the nineteenth century, a widespread reform was heralded by Joseph Harding who showed the cheesemakers a more enlightened system of production. His slogan was: "Cheese is not made in the field, nor in the byre, nor even in the cow – it is made in the dairy."

What Harding taught became known as the "cheddaring" process. The curd is cut into pieces in the normal manner. When most of the whey has been expelled, the curds are stacked in the vessel to form thick blocks, or parcels. These are turned about and folded, releasing as much moisture as possible. The temperature required during this process is approximately 37°C (98.5°F). The thick pieces, in the meantime, become very firm but "tender like the breast of a chicken." Now the moment of milling has arrived. Formerly, the dairymaid tore the curd by hand into small pieces. At the end of the eighteenth century a curd mill was invented, making the task somewhat lighter. The milled curd is placed back in the vessel, stirred and salted, and finally pressed into a mold. After maturing, the cheese should have a close, but not hard, texture without eyes. Nowadays, the farms that make their own Cheddar are few and far between; the ones that sell it are even fewer. Important customers, such as the Court, restaurants, special establishments and London clubs have a regular order for Cheddars.

Cheddar, the great traveler

The traditional farmhouse Cheddar used to be made between April 1 and November 1, but is now made throughout the year. It is usually produced from the milk of a specific breed of British cow, the Shorthorn. The cheese should have a firm, elastic consistency and a slightly nutty flavor; it must be neither too sweet nor too sour. It should ripen for at least six, but preferably twelve months or longer. The real connoisseur eats mature Cheddar with fresh bread, brown or white, or crackers; butter; sweet pickle

BELOW: A sample of milk is examined in the laboratory. For all cheese products pure milk, hygienically processed and transported, is the first requirement.

BELOW: The blades of this mechanical cutter stir and cut the curd in large troughs.

BELOW: Milling the firm, drained mass of curd. This series of photographs shows the so-called horizontal system in which the curd is processed in long, usually open, cheese tubs or troughs. The most up-to-date system is shown in the drawing below, where a vertical tower is employed.

A. The cheese-making tank. The pasteurized cheese milk (yellow) is pumped into this vat, which has a mechanical stirring and cutting device to handle the curd. The temperature of the curd-whey mixture in the tank is controlled by steam circulating between the double walls of the tank. The milk enters at a temperature of about 30°C (86°F).

B. From the starter tank a calculated amount of starter culture (gray) is added to the cheese milk.

C. Rennet (red) is also added, which causes the cheese milk to coagulate and to separate into curd and whey.

D. The curd is successively cut, stirred and heated to 35–40°C (95–104°F); some of the whey is then drawn off by suction. When these processes have been completed – which may take some 2½ hours – the mixture of curd and whey is pumped to the cheddar tower.

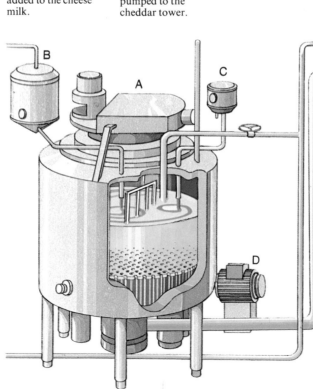

G. At the foot of the cheddar tower, the curd mass is cut into long strips and milled into finger-size pieces.

BELOW: Salt is added to the milled curd, either by hand as here, or automatically as part of a continuous production line.

BELOW: Filling the molds. In times gone by, the dairymaid had to "dress" the cheese with a "skirt" and "cap" of fine muslin cloth. Cheeses are now bound by machine and emerge from the molds in finished form.

BELOW: Cheddars are made both in the characteristic drum shape and in blocks to simplify cutting and prepacking.

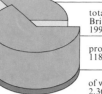

total production British cheese 199,000 tons p.a. (100%)

production Cheddar 118,000 tons p.a. (60%)

of which exported 2,360 tons p.a. (2%)

E. The cheddar tower. Cheddaring is a decisive step in the making of Cheddar cheese. The manual method consists of piling and repiling blocks of warm curd, so that the curd particles fuse together and form a fibrous mass. At the same time, moisture is expelled and the acidity of the curd increases. In the cheddar tower, this process has been successfully mechanized;

the curd is cheddared, so to speak, by its own weight.

F. In the tower, the curd moves slowly downward, reaching the correct fibrous texture by the end of its path. Whey (blue) separates from the curd through the perforated lining and is partially drawn off. Temperature in the tower is maintained at 32–38°C (90–100°F).

M. In a modern production line like this, cheesemaking can proceed virtually automatically, with a very high output, and in a continuous flow. The end product is uniform, usually of good quality, but lacks individuality. It has been estimated that the cheddar tower alone replaces the equivalent of five skilled cheesemakers, and that labor costs can be cut by more than half; on the other hand, the investments are considerable. This is another factor that forces cheese factories to become larger and larger.

or gherkins; crisp lettuce or celery; and a glass or two of hard cider. Cheddar is also an excellent companion to English draught beer, or a good Burgundy. But then, what isn't!

Since the middle of the last century, Cheddar has been made in cheese factories, also known as "creameries." Today there are more than thirty, spread right across Britain. Factory Cheddar is usually eaten at a somewhat less mature stage than the farmhouse variety, from six to eight months old. It has a very pleasant, mild flavor – milder and less sharp than the tasty farm-made cheese. It melts easily, and is therefore popular as one of the varieties used in Welsh rarebit, where cheese is cooked with beer to make a thickish sauce which is then poured onto buttered toast and browned under the grill. Of all British cheeses, Cheddar has the biggest production, sales and consumption figures. Its fame has reached far beyond the British Isles, traveling with emigrants to parts of the world where the cheddaring process could be established. Thus we have New Zealand and Australian Cheddar, New York State Cheddar and even, it is whispered, *French* Cheddar: *quel triomphe!* The cheese further owes its foreign success to the fact that it travels well and keeps its excellent quality for a long time.

Britain's Gruyère
Yet another reason for Cheddar's popularity is its application to processing. Many varieties of processed cheese use Cheddar as a base, owing to its great stability and wide appeal, qualities which it shares with Gruyère, another favorite of the processers.

Cheddar has always been a cheese demanding much time and investment, if only because of its long ripening period. It is evident that, like so many other "difficult" regional cheeses, Cheddar might have vanished forever, a victim of technical progress and economic efficiency, had it not been for a providential occurrence: the doomed Cheddar found a benefactor, a fresh cheese from Wales – Caerphilly.

H. A conveyor belt feeds the milled curd into a rotating drum, where it is thoroughly mixed with the correct dosage of dry salt.

J. The curd is poured into hoops or molds. Automatic weighing apparatus ensures the correct filling of each mold.

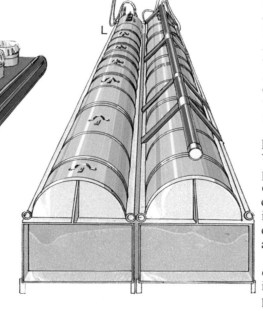

K. The molds move on conveyor belts to the filling machine and from there to the presses. Each mold has a piece of cheesecloth folded into it.

L. A cheese press of the horizontal type, in which the cheeses in their molds are heavily pressed for 12 to 24 hours. After pressing,

they go to air-conditioned ripening rooms, while the molds are cleaned and returned to the production line.

A hundred years ago, fresh and snow-white *Caerphilly* cheese was made twice daily on nearly every farm. Contrary to the usual practice, the morning and evening milk were never mixed in making the cheese, most of it was eaten on the farm; the rest was sold in and around Cardiff. Caerphilly was very popular with the miners, because it was easily digested in the confined, cramped conditions, and being very fresh did not dry out at all.

How Caerphilly rescued Cheddar

Compared to most other British cheeses, Caerphilly is quite modern, perhaps no more than 160 years old. It was named after the village of Caerphilly where it was first made. The cheese rapidly became so popular that Welsh farmers, finding it impossible to cope with the demand, turned for help in the late nineteenth century to their neighbors across the Bristol Channel – the Cheddar makers. So it came to be that two very different types of cheese were produced on many farms in Somerset: the traditional Cheddar, a cheese that demanded considerable labor and long periods of ripening; and also Caerphilly, requiring less milk (a Cheddar requires 10 times its weight in milk; a Caerphilly only 1.1 times its weight), and offering a fairly rapid turnover – a Caerphilly could be sold after five to ten days. The Cheddar makers could thus wait patiently for their Cheddars to ripen.

Caerphilly is a soft, fresh cheese, with a mild, slightly sour flavor reminiscent of buttermilk. It is easy to cut into slices and goes well with summer salads, with bread, butter and celery.

The Single and Double Gloucester

Along the Vale of Gloucester and the Vale of Berkeley is the land of the Gloucester cheese. It is likely that cheese has been made here for over a thousand years. The cheeses were known as either Gloucester or Berkeley cheeses, probably according to the district in which they were made. They came in two sizes, the generous, well-matured *Double Gloucester* and the thinner, milder *Single Gloucester*. Of the two, only the Double has remained, perhaps because the cheesemakers, keeping an eye on export markets, appreciated its large proportions and good keeping qualities. Also, a Double Gloucester never becomes sharp, in spite of its long

ABOVE: Caerphilly Castle, in the county of Glamorgan, Wales, lies in the middle of the region where fresh. white Caerphilly cheese is made.

ABOVE: Double Gloucester cheeses. The factory-made cheese on the left is smaller than the traditional size, and is called a "truckle" cheese. On the right is a mature farmhouse cheese.

ripening period of six to twelve months.

Although Gloucesters are ancient cheeses, they were only established as a popular type at the beginning of the eighteenth century, owing to the treatment of the rind. The floor of the curing room was regularly rubbed with bean and potato stalks, leaving a wet, black deposit. The Gloucesters were placed on this and turned twice weekly, which made the rind tough as leather and improved the keeping properties of the cheese. Then came the widespread practice of coloring cheeses with carrot juice, by which it was hoped to convince buyers that the rosier the cheese, the richer was the content of milk. Still later the cheesemakers decided to enhance their product further by painting the rinds with red ochre, instead of the traditional black treatment, sometimes mixing the pigment with beer. Today the cheeses are usually found with a natural, uncolored rind.

The handsome, red cheeses featured in festivals to mark the beginning of spring. They were decorated with flowers and carried through the streets of the small village of Randwick which in old Anglo-Saxon means "the dairy farm on the hill," an additional testimony to the lineage of Gloucester cheese. A similar folklore event is still celebrated on Coopers Hill near Gloucester City on Whit Monday, when cheese wheels are rolled down the hill among great festivities.

RIGHT: Customary cheese rolling on Coopers Hill, near Gloucester city. The figure wearing the white coat and tall hat is the master of ceremonies. The decorated cheese bounces downhill, pursued by a crowd of children. This ancient custom used to be held on Midsummer Day, but has now been changed to Whit Monday.

Cheshire cheese is Cheddar's great rival. Many declare it to be the oldest of all England's cheeses. That it was also a famous cheese is evident by the fact that Cheshire was mentioned in the Domesday Book, by which time it was well established. The Roman soldiers of the 20th Legion, garrisoned in the town of Chester, possibly enjoyed the taste of this salty, crumbly cheese, made from the milk of cows that were gradually superseding the shaggy goats that had grazed here for centuries.

Cheshire cheese is named after the county, although the French, who have appreciated Cheshire for a long time, call it *Chester* after the capital, perhaps because the city was a large cheese market where cheeses were sold for export. The particular appeal and flavor of Cheshire cheese is due not only to the preparation and ripening techniques, but to the quality of the region's soil. Local farmers declare that the Cheshire meadows are the finest in England, and perhaps the most unique, due to salt deposits found in the lands below Nantwich and Middlewich, dating from a period when prehistoric seas covered the area.

Cattle that graze in Cheshire pastures are noted for the high salt content of their milk, which then endows the cheese with such a characteristic flavor that it is impossible to imitate outside Cheshire. The cheese ripens slowly and possesses a fat content of 48%.

LEFT: A fine farmhouse Cheshire cheese. Until well into the nineteenth century, farmers paid their rent in Cheshire cheeses.

ABOVE: Excellent, rare and expensive – a blue Cheshire cheese. Note the holes where the cheese has been skewered, the mold may then develop in the channels thus formed, a matter of luck and judgment.

LEFT: Making cheese in Wensleydale, Yorkshire. It is important that the curd and whey are well separated, and that the curd is thoroughly drained.

Until the Second World War, the cheese was mainly farm produced. There are still some twenty farms making their own cheese, and fortunately it looks as if their number may be increasing. Cheshire is made in three varieties – red, white and blue – and is thus said to endear itself to Union Jack patriots. White Cheshire is a quick-ripening product which uses a larger quantity of rennet as a starter; it is pale cream in color and mild in flavor. Its keeping properties, however, are poor, and it turns acid and bitter in flavor. The red, semimature cheese is made from May to October, has a mild, nutty flavor and is ready for sale after about six weeks. Anatto dye is used to create the orange color of the cheese.

Blue Cheshire is an almost totally different cheese, and one of the greatest "blues" in the world. The invasion of the blue mold is always accidental, although slightly encouraged. The cheesemaker never adds special doses of mold culture, but with an expert eye selects those cheeses which seem to have the propensity for turning blue. He then places these cheeses in a very humid cellar, skewering them occasionally with the hope that the blue may develop in the air channels. His satisfaction when the mold takes is considerable, because this splendid cheese, quite the equal of Stilton, has become rather rare and fetches high prices.

A blue Cheshire cheese is distinctive in appearance, being orange with blue veining. It has turned from the crumbly texture of the ordinary cheese to a soft, buttery one with a unique taste. There are no better accompaniments than crusty, fresh bread, farmhouse butter and ale, or fruity Burgundy, or – it's up to you.

The good cheese of Mrs. Paulet

Fortunately for the devotees of blue cheese, there is plenty of *Stilton* to supplement the lack of blue Cheshire. This almost sounds as if blue Cheshire would naturally be the first choice, but to the majority of Englishmen, Stilton is *the* blue cheese, and has been aristocracy's companion to Port wine for over three hundred years. Stilton is made in tall, cylindrical shapes weighing either seven or fourteen pounds. Together with Cheddar and Cheshire, it is among the most famous of English cheeses, dating back to the seventeenth

century. Some have suggested that Stilton may have derived from goat's or sheep's milk cheeses which "blued" like Roquefort and were made in the Vale of Belvoir in the Middle Ages.

Popular legend has it that Stilton was first made at Quenby Hall, Leicestershire, the country seat of Lady Beaumont. Her housekeeper, a Mrs. Paulet, had a brother-in-law who was landlord of the Bell Inn in the small village of Stilton. She supplied him with the home-made cheese which was surplus to the household requirements. The Bell was a coaching stop on the Great North road, and the cheese soon became famous as "Mrs. Paulet's cheese." The writer Daniel Defoe, however, reports having enjoyed Stilton cheese at the Bell in the year 1720, some ten years before the arrival of Mrs. Paulet's cheese. Furthermore, there were others who claim to have invented Stilton, notably a Mrs. Orton of Little Dalby near Melton Mowbray. The origin of Stilton remains a mystery, but Mrs. Paulet's complicated recipe was still being used even in this century, until Stilton became a factory cheese.

It is made of the richest whole milk. After curdling, cutting and stirring, the whey is separated from the curds, which are then salted and placed in deep, wooden hoops. The curd is regularly turned so that adequate drainage can take place. Stilton is not pressed. After about one week the curd is removed from the hoop, bound in calico, and left in a cool, moist atmosphere for another week. During this period the characteristic brown rind begins to form, and the cheese gradually becomes firm enough to keep its shape without the cheese cloth.

A fresh, white Stilton is also made. It is very crumbly, with a strong smell and a flavor that is mild and gentle, yet sourish. Only in the cool, humid ripening cellars does the blue mold develop. Fine, steel skewers or needles are driven into the cheese, and the blue mold develops in the resulting channels to spread throughout. Stilton needs four to six months to mature properly; unfortunately, it is often sold when too fresh, when it is hard, white, chalky and acidic in flavor.

Just as the firm of Hutchinson in Whitchurch, Shropshire, store and age their own blue Cheshires, so the world-famous cheese department of Fortnum & Mason in London stores its Stilton.

RIGHT: A small Double Gloucester cheese next to a pot of Fortnum & Mason's best blue Stilton. In the background is a white Stilton.

In the cellars beneath the premises, assistants turn the cheeses daily and regularly brush the rind clean to avoid fungi and mites.

In the seventeenth and eighteenth centuries no such care was taken. Cheeses tended to be stored in damp and dirty cellars, and, interestingly enough, many connoisseurs did not consider a cheese fully matured unless it was swarming with mites. When you consider the prevailing lack of attention to hygiene – even in the dairy – it was not surprising that many cheeses turned blue, and it was the blue cheeses in particular that received the attentions of mites. Today Stilton and other English blue cheeses are made with fine-quality milk and ripened in a carefully controlled environment.

Ripe Stilton should have a well-crinkled, brown rind and a pale, slightly flaky texture. The flavor is smooth and mellow, much milder than other blue cheeses. The blue-green mold should be evenly distributed, although it is often inclined to concentrate towards the center. When the edges are brown the cheese is fully ripe, and although Stilton is available all the year round, it is at its best from November to April, and is especially enjoyed at the Christmas table.

The best way to cut a Stilton is in horizontal slices across the top. The alternate method – that of scooping out the center with a spoon – causes the cheese to go dry and crumbly. This is sometimes remedied by pouring

LEFT: A perfect example of a well-matured, royal Stilton cheese. Fruit and nuts are by no means essential accompaniments. All that is required is a biscuit or a slice of crusty bread, plus a glass or two of Port or Burgundy. Stilton may be purchased almost everywhere throughout the year, but is held to be at its best during the Christmas season.

LEFT: A motorway now by-passes the historic Bell Inn at Stilton, Leicestershire. The inn, which is now closed, was where Stilton cheese was sold in the seventeenth century.

LEFT: Blue Wensleydale, the Yorkshire cheese which can compete with the more famous Stilton. Some people claim (Yorkshire folk, no doubt) that Stilton is but a variation of the original, blue Wensleydale. White Wensleydale is said to be *the* cheese to eat with apple pie.

Port wine into the cavity, but this does little to improve matters. Better to cut a modest piece and enjoy it with a few dry biscuits and a stick of celery, and perhaps a glass or two of Port or Burgundy.

Apple pie and cheese
There is another fine British blue, made like Stilton in both white and blue varieties. This is *Wensleydale*, a Yorkshire cheese of more ancient lineage. It is said that Wensleydale was made by the Cistercian monks of the now-ruined Jervaulx and Fountains abbeys, from an original Norman recipe. This would imply that blue Wensleydale is perhaps an ancestor of the Norman Bleu de Bresse, but in many ways it is a closer relative of Roquefort – or rather, it used to be, as the cheese was originally made from sheep's milk (as is the great French cheese), or occasionally from goat's milk, whichever happened to be available.

For centuries the monks had upheld their traditions of agriculture, cattle breeding and dairying, and after the dissolution of the monasteries by Henry VIII in the sixteenth century, they taught their cheesemaking methods to the local farmers' wives.

It was sometime during the seventeenth century that most farms turned to whole cow's milk. In those days, blue Wensleydale would have been eaten on the dale farms, along with the famous York ham and pieces of the oatbread called havercake, alas now extinct. A local rival to the Wensleydale cheese was called Cotherstone, and was made in the village of that name in Teesdale. It was also known as "Yorkshire Stilton," and if it is still being made it's a well-kept secret.

The term "blue" Wensleydale

BELOW: Hebden Bridge in the Pennines, close by the industrial heart of Yorkshire. Britain's largest county has wild moorland, alternating with good pastures and industrial areas.

implies that there is a white one. This is indeed the case, and it is a much bigger seller. White Wensleydale is often sold when very young. It has a slightly sour, buttermilk flavor not unlike Caerphilly.

Making Wensleydale cheese requires careful attention. The great secret is that the curd must not turn sour, and this depends on the freshness and sweetness of the milk, the quantity of rennet and the slow drainage of the curd. Slices of curd, wrapped in calico, are placed on drainage receptacles and turned every twenty minutes. When the whey has been expelled, the curd is salted and put into vessels, where it remains overnight without pressing. The next morning it is bound with calico and pressed for just a few hours; the impression of this calico band can clearly be seen on the cheese afterwards.

During ripening, the cheese, which is still very soft, is turned every day for the first few weeks, and later every other day. It is ripe after some months, and velvety in texture. The majority of Wensleydale cheeses on the market are the white, unripened sort. Blue-veined Wensleydale is fairly rare: it can be spread like butter and has a mild, creamy flavor. A daunting rival of Stilton, it has practically the same shape and weight, but differs in having a gray-white rind.

In the north of England, apple pie and white Wensleydale cheese are a favorite combination. The saying goes in Yorkshire: "Apple pie without cheese is like a kiss without a squeeze." Another well-known verse concurs: "But I, when I undress me / Each night, upon my knees / Will ask the Lord to bless me / With apple pie and cheese."

BELOW: The rugged landscape of Skye in the Hebrides. Although the islands are noted for their whiskey, some still produce their own cheeses.

Centuries ago, when most farms made their own cheese, English cheeses were found in great variety. They say that the railways put an end to the variety, for milk could be transported in bulk to dairies, and cheeses became regional. While it remains true that the odd farm still makes its own cheese, such local specialities as Bath cheese, Oxford, Suffolk (said to be the world's hardest), Essex, the blue Cottenham from Cambridge, the Daventry and the Lincoln have disappeared forever; only the great ones have survived.

The quality of *Leicester* has always been protected, as witness the town crier of Leicester who used to call out a list of fines and punishments for spoiling or adulterating the cheese. In its crumbly structure it resembles Cheshire cheese, but it receives a much greater dose of anatto coloring to give it the familiar, deep orange hue. On the cheese board it contrasts pleasantly with others. Leicester is one of the finest and mildest of English cheeses, and it reaches the peak of perfection after about six to nine months. As it melts easily, it is useful in cooking, especially for Welsh rarebit.

In the kitchens of the scattered farmhouses on the lonely hills of Lancashire, white *Lancashire* cheese is still made, as of old, from a mixture of two days' curd. The curd is kept for a fortnight, during which time the acid develops that is responsible for the whiteness of the cheese. After passing through the curd mill, Lancashire is salted and pressed. At present, a total of about 150 cheeses are made every week on the farms, the rest coming from the creameries. Lancashire is ripe after two to three months and should then be eaten at once, which means that practically the entire production is consumed in the immediate vicinity. A soft cheese, after three months it can still be spread like butter, but it is by no means as mild, having developed a strong aroma and a more pronounced flavor than either Cheddar or Cheshire. Like Leicester, the cheese melts easily, and for this reason used to be called "the Leigh toaster," after the town of Leigh, near Manchester.

The popularity of *Derby* cheese suffers from the fact that it closely resembles Cheddar and, quite simply, most people prefer Cheddar. Production is on a fairly limited scale, and the cheese is not subject to the rigorous grading scrutiny of Cheddars. Derby

ABOVE: Dunlop cheese under the press in an old cheese factory still operating today. Dunlop is often compared with Double Gloucester, which it somewhat resembles, and with Cheddar is the biggest selling cheese in Scotland.

LEFT: There's a lot to be said for a piece of Lancashire cheese and a good glass of ale.

is a mild, pleasant cheese, a solid, hard-pressed type with a fairly high moisture content. It is sold from six weeks old, when it is rather unripe, but the ripening defects from which it once suffered have been eliminated, and a mature Derby – like any good cheese – is worth waiting for.

There is a flavored variety known as *Sage Derby*, which has undergone several changes in its history. Originally, it was flavored with finely chopped, fresh sage leaves, which were mixed with the curd. The next development was to grind the leaves and add spinach juice, which gave the cheese a bright, green streak through its center, like a sandwich. Then the makers created a marbling effect, which is the current fashion. The original type is once more available in limited quantities, however, especially at Christmas time.

The three counties where farmhouse cheese is still made have united to form the "Golden Cheese Hoard of Farmhouse Cheddar, Cheshire and Lancashire." The Milk Marketing Board organizes its production and, with the English Country Cheese Council, promotes both farmhouse and factory cheese produced in England and Wales.

A few other varieties are made, which are of importance in their own region, and are sometimes to be found in the shops of big cities, where they are appreciated as special cheeses.

Regional specialities

More of a curiosity than a speciality is the *Dorset Blue*, otherwise known as *Blue Vinney*. The word *Vinney* is thought to derive from the Old English *fyniz*, meaning "mold." It is a hard, blue-veined cheese that was once produced on nearly every farm in

RIGHT: A fine display of British cheeses, photographed at Wells Stores, Streatley. Next to the Stilton, on the left of the top shelf, is a blue Wensleydale and three Leicesters. Below is a small Double Gloucester perched on two Cheddars; between these and the half of a full-size Gloucester are some baby Cheshires. On the lower shelf is a white Lancashire (far left) next to a white Wensleydale, and various Scottish cheeses (the small round ones at the back are from Islay and the Orkneys). In the front is a large Derby cheese, two Gloucesters and a piece of Sage Derby.

LEFT: The label from a Caithness cheese, made in the far north of Scotland.

Dorset from milk that had been skimmed by hand. Consequently it was fat-deprived, and its chalky, loose consistency caused air pockets favorable for mold development. There were other factors too. In former times, the milk was often contaminated and dairy conditions unhygienic; cheeses would be stored in a shed together with leather horse harnesses and wet boots – conditions ideal for mold development. Blue veining will occur much more readily in a full-fat cheese, with more enjoyable results, and so the spontaneous growth in a Dorset cheese was a rare event – even then, the cheese required eighteen months to mature. It was said to be so hard that the people of Dorset used it to make locomotive wheels.

Blue Vinney is now almost extinct, and attempts to revive it have been unsuccessful. It is possible to find a shop that sells a cheese purporting to be "Blue Vinney," but it is more likely to be a second- or third-grade Stilton.

In recent times a number of new cheeses – some good, some bad – have appeared on the market. There is the upstart *Red Windsor* (a Cheddar impregnated with wine) and a Stilton encrusted with walnuts, not really to be taken seriously. A very pleasant newcomer is *Caboc*, a full-cream, cylindrical cheese covered in oatmeal, and made in Scotland; its taste is sometimes slightly sourish, and nutty due to the oatmeal. There are also several small, soft cheeses from the north of Scotland: *Caithness* cheese, *Orkney* cheese, and *Islay* from the Hebridean island of that name. The most famous of the Scottish clan is certainly the *Dunlop* from Ayrshire. During the lactation period, Ayrshire cows provide an amazing 11,600 kg of milk – nearly 40 liters (48.4 quarts)

per day. Dunlop is said to owe its existence to an Irish refugee of the late seventeenth century, one Barbara Gilmour, who arrived in Ayr and made her cheeses according to an Irish recipe. It is not unlike Cheddar, but light of color and rather bland and moister, even when well-matured. Dunlop is usually eaten quite young, when only a few months old; it goes well with buttered oatcakes and Scotch ale.

The modern, younger generation of Scot seems to prefer the anatto-dyed *Scottish Cheddar*, while the older generation still enjoys such rough-hewn country cheeses as the nameless "farm cheese" flavored with caraway seeds, found in Aberdeenshire. Then there's *Crowdie*, a full-cream, fresh cheese made in country farms by adding rennet to tepid milk straight from the cow. As soon as the curd is formed, it is put into a colander with a cheese cloth and left to drain. After some hours the curd is placed in a basin and mixed with cream and a pinch of salt.

It would be a mistake to suppose that British farmers' wives throughout the country make *cottage cheese* and *pot cheese* to any extent or variety. A few do, here and there, especially in summer when milk tends to sour, but the majority go to the local supermarket and buy processed Cheddar – it's one of the sad facts of our advanced civilization.

The British tend to be resistant to changes in their daily diet. Although they have embraced hamburgers and spaghetti (they even manufacture their own spaghetti and, it is rumored, export it to Italy), only the indigenous cheeses are made in the United Kingdom; one does not find in the range of cheeses any of a clearly foreign origin. In this sense all cheeses made in Great Britain are British originals, stemming mostly from an ancient tradition which has inspired a degree of pride and prejudice: the British seem to prefer their own cheeses to anyone else's.

Name	Milk	Type	Rind	Form	Weight	% Fat content
Blue Vinny	△	■	⋈	cylinder	6-7 kg	15-45
Caerphilly	△	●	□	low cylinder	3.6 kg	48
Cheddar	△	■	□	cylinder, cube	18-27 kg	48
Cheshire	△	■	□⋈	cylinder	22 kg	48
Derby	△	■	□	cartwheel	13-14 kg	48
Dunlop	△	■	□	cylinder	27 kg	48
Gloucester, Double	△	■	□	cylinder	28 kg	48
Lancashire	△	●	□	cylinder, loaf	22.5 kg, 4.5-5.5 kg	48
Leicester	△	■	□	cylinder	13-18 kg	48
Stilton	△	■	⋈	cylinder	6.4-8.2 kg	48
Wensleydale	△	■	□⋈	cylinder	4.5-5.5 kg	48

Key to symbols on page 6. 1 kg = 2.2 lbs.

France

The cheeses of France are renowned for their excellence and astonishing variety – no other country has so many different types, and many of them are copied all over the world. Second only to the Greeks in their consumption of cheese, the French eat a yearly average of 14.8 kg (32.6 lbs) per person. Like the wines they so perfectly accompany, French cheeses – unique and delicious – are the pride of both their region of origin and France herself. They vary considerably in flavor and appearance: some are wrapped in straw, others in paper, or in leaves. Some are coated with grape seeds, coarsely crushed peppercorns, herbs or halved walnuts. They may be round, square, lozenge or heart-shaped, in a roll or a pyramid; soft and tender, hard as a rock, blue-veined, snow-white, red, black or speckled. Dozens of once rare local cheeses now enjoy a wide reputation, though many others are still found only in remote places where family cheesemakers have been producing them for hundreds of years.

As General de Gaulle once said, comparing the pastoral and political character of France, "How can one possibly govern a country that produces over 370 different cheeses?" We cannot, in this book attempt to list them all. Let us instead make a tour of France, to sample not only the humble village cheeses, but those aristocrats of the French table, the Gruyères, Camemberts, Bries and Roqueforts, which many people maintain are the finest cheeses in the world.

The flavor and fragrance of Provence
The Mediterranean climate has made Provence one of the most attractive areas of France. Stretching from the Italian border to beyond the wild Camargue, the landscape can be both arid and harsh, soft and abundant. The mountains, gorges and valleys produce a glorious profusion of sub-tropical fruits and flowers. The cuisine matches the varied character of the land and its people; it is rich, spicy, oily and pungent. How odd, then, that Provence boasts no great regional cheese, but only small, unpretentious ones made for local consumption. You have to search for them: *Cachat*, for example, a sheep's milk cheese, eaten either fresh or in a marinade of brandy, vinegar, local herbs and spices. Then there's *Banon* with a

ABOVE: A fine display of French regional cheeses. Nowhere in the world can such variety be found as in France.

BELOW: Château-renard near Avignon, a typical southern French town in lovely surroundings.

striking aroma and a powerful, nutty flavor, covered with savory and wrapped in chestnut leaves. Banon is fortified with brandy or white wine, and subjected to five weeks of mysterious fermentation in a sealed earthenware pot. *Poivre d'Ane* is a simple *chèvre* (goat's milk cheese) sprinkled with savory and rosemary, giving it the fragrance of the Provençal countryside.

To the north of the area, local specialties are easier to find – *Picardon* in the Drôme region and *Pelardon* across the Rhône are tiny, goat's milk cheeses, white and fresh, with a lovely full flavor. *Saint-Marcellin* from the Isère is a dairy milk cheese to be eaten fresh (usually mixed with herbs) or ripened in chestnut leaves. Further into the mountains, at the foot of Mont Blanc, is the original home of *Bossons Macérés*, a special *chèvre*, ripened with alcohol, olive oil and fragrant herbs, to give the cheese a very strong, tangy flavor. It is here, in the French Alps, that we meet the first of our great French cheeses – the Gruyères.

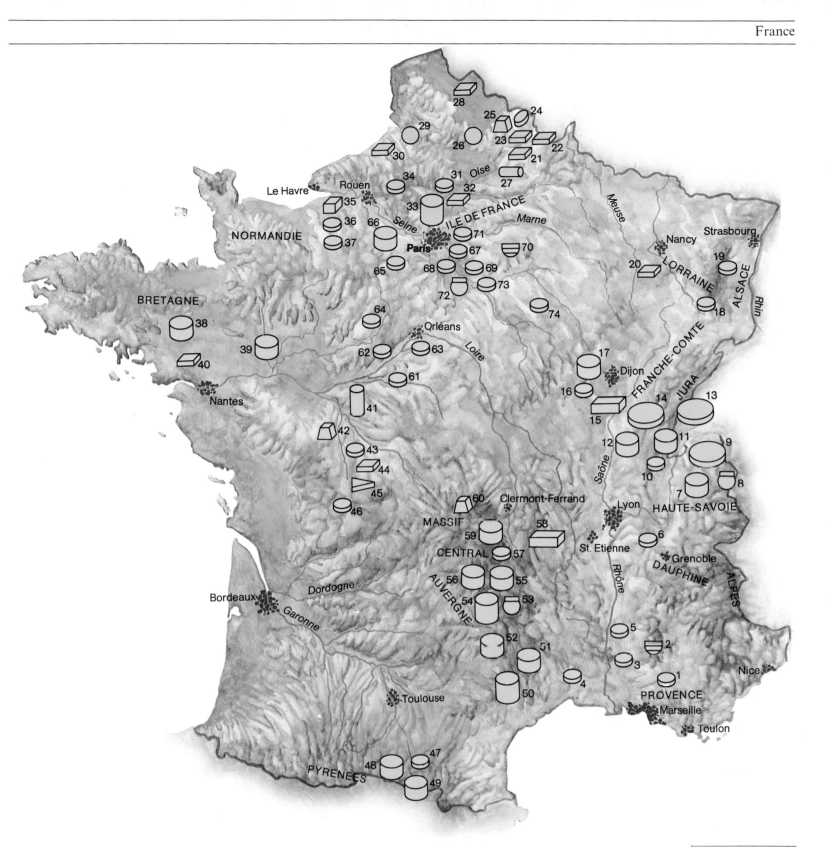

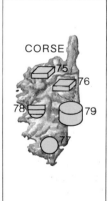

CORSE

BELOW: Saint-Claude in the French Jura, where alpine pastures produce many excellent cheeses.

The birthplace of *Gruyère* cheese stretches across the French-Swiss border. On the French side it encompasses the Haute Savoie and the region of Franche-Comté; on the Swiss side the cantons of Fribourg, Vaud and Neuchatel. Here, language and landscape are shared alike, but the exclusive right to use the name "Gruyère" was long a bone of contention between France and Switzerland – it was granted to both countries by the Convention of Stresa in 1951.

The French border country has high mountains and deep valleys with many springs and rivers. The climate is often harsh, with marked seasonal changes. The rural character of the land and people is such that, even today, many farmers live far from the market centers and transport is difficult. For this reason, the medieval farmers decided to make a cheese which could be kept for the longest possible time, and so Gruyère was born. The trouble with Gruyère, however, is that one cheese demands from 500 to 1,000 liters (550 to 1,100 quarts) of milk – too much for one farm to produce. Thus the farmers began to form cooperatives. Cheese was made from the communal milk in small huts called *fruitières*, as these produced the fruits of communal effort. The first *fruitières* were already in existence in the Middle Ages. In 1267, the farmers of a small Jura village were making a cheese called *Vachelin*, an ancestor of the Gruyère. Also recorded in early historical documents were small goat's milk cheeses called *Chevrets*.

Fine art of cheese

Today, the main types of French Gruyère cheese are *Comté*, *Beaufort* and *Emmental*. Nowadays many experts regard Emmental as a cheese apart from Gruyère; the two others are still considered subvarieties of Gruyère.

Both Gruyère and Emmental have achieved great stature in the world of cheese, because they fulfill so many requirements with such success. From very simple beginnings they have evolved to become fine works of art: Emmental with its wide-eyed honeycomb texture and bold, wagon-wheel proportions; Gruyère, the smaller of the two – in size, but not in character. Yet they have much in common, although confusion may arise over the appearance of the paste. Emmental

LEFT: Saint-Véran in the French Alps, the highest inhabited village in Europe.

has big holes while many varieties of Gruyère have a closed body with a few cracks here and there. On the other hand, there are Gruyères with holes. Gruyère de Comté, for example, has large, elliptical holes in the paste, as can be seen in the picture on the opposite page; the princely Beaufort may have a few small holes or none at all.

These cheeses are splendid additions to the range of table cheeses. In the kitchen their uses are legion: few cheese types are more adaptable to the repertoire of French cooking, a fact that is recognized by great chefs and ordinary housewives alike.

Comté – the choice of the French

Like champagne, France is its own biggest customer for *Gruyère de Comté*. The cheese has a slightly moist and crumbly rind: the consistency is firm, with a bit of give, and the holes – or "eyes" – are as big as nuts. Owing to the molds that form on the rind, the taste and smell of the cheese have a more pronounced character than that of Emmental. Comté is made from evening milk, set aside in wooden or metal dishes for ripening and creaming up. When the cream has been skimmed off, it is mixed with morning milk, processed raw, and not subjected to the heat treatment of the Swiss Gruyère. This influences the slow ripening process: it requires at least six months at a temperature of 18° to 20°C (64° to 68°F), and needs continuous attention to encourage the development of the rind mold. This is why the cheese is not brushed, as Beaufort is, but wiped with a brine-soaked cloth. The cellars of the cheese huts are too small to store the cheeses for the required six months while production continues, so the nonripened *Comté Blanc* cheeses are sold to *affineurs*, who let the cheeses ripen in their spacious storage cellars before sending them to market. Farmers, cheesemakers and *affineurs* have together formed the *Syndicat du Véritable Gruyère de Comté*, which has set up strict regulations governing production to protect the quality of the cheese.

Beaufort, the prince of Gruyères

Compared to Comté, the *Beaufort (de Montagne)* is almost "blind," as the experts say: it is not allowed to form eyes, or holes. It has a smooth and

LEFT: Here in the Haute Savoie is the original home of the great French Gruyères: Comté, Beaufort and Emmental.

creamy consistency, with an excellent fruity aroma and taste. The shape of a Beaufort is somewhere between the straight-sided Comté, and the convex-sided Emmental and the cheese usually weighs from 30 to 60 kg (66 to 132 lbs). The French author Brillat-Savarin, one of the most famous gourmets of the early nineteenth century, called Beaufort "the prince of Gruyères."

Its fame is due mainly to the use of extremely rich milk, collected in the valleys of Tatentaise and Maurienne, 1,500 to 2,500 meters (about 20,000 to 32,000 feet) above sea level, luscious alpine meadows affording excellent summer grazing. The milk is made into cheese according to methods passed down by generations of farmers over the centuries. The cheeses ripen in the cooperative Cave de Gruyère de Beaufort at a temperature of 10° to 12°C (50° to 54°F). For the first two months they are salted in the morning, brushed in the afternoon and turned the next day; later, this treatment is carried out every third day. The production of Beaufort de Montagne is relatively small, however, though in the valleys some *Beaufort d'Hiver*, or *Laitier*, is additionally made in the winter.

Emmental, a labor-saving giant

Emmental is descended from the famous Swiss cheese of the region around Berne, but in France it is considered one of the original types of French Gruyère. Today Emmental is equal to them both, and is the pride of the Haute Savoie, Haute Marn Haute Saône and Côte d'Or. Nowhere in the world is so much Emmental cheese made as in France: the nation produces more than its greatest competitors: the United States, Germany, Austria, Finland and even Switzerland itself. In spite of this, the French decline to make the cheese for export. Almost all French Emmental is eaten by the French, who have created such a demand that they themselves are believed to import it from Switzerland, the country of origin. In any event, Swiss Emmental doesn't have far to travel, since the area around Lake Geneva is really one great cheese-producing region.

Normally a meter (39.37 inches) in diameter, French Emmental is a huge cartwheel of a cheese, which might weigh anywhere from 60 to 130 kg (132 to 286 lbs); it can be recognized by the red mark signifying its origin. The mild, somewhat sweet taste is reminiscent of fresh nuts; the consistency is softer than that of Gruyère, and it has many large holes. During ripening, the hard rind turns a dark yellow or light brown. One of the most remarkable things about this giant among cheeses is that it is entirely produced by mechanical means, in large dairy factories. Even the brushing, polishing and turning are done by machine. So well developed is the process of automation, that a modern Emmental factory requires a very small labor force.

LEFT: The characteristic large-holed texture of a fine Gruyère. Nearly all the Gruyère produced is consumed in France itself.

BELOW: A Gruyère cheese factory at the end of the nineteenth century. Although the process may now seem primitive, it was the start of mass production. In the center stands the great cheese kettle. The curd hangs above in a cloth. The man on the right tends to the fire, which is necessary, among other things, for rewarming the cheese. A double press is seen in the foreground.

Choisissez votre coupe de GRUYÈRE le kilo 9.95

BELOW: Alsace is famous for cheeses as well as wines – the two are splendid partners. Here is the famous wine town of Riquewihr, with its picturesque houses and steep main street

In addition to the hard Gruyères and Emmental, the mountain slopes along the Swiss border yield several kinds of soft cheese. In Savoie these are generally called *Tommes*, the *Tomme de Savoie* being one of the more familiar varieties. When made according to the ancient farmhouse methods, they are ripened in natural caves; they may be treated with brandy and brushed, or sometimes, in the variety known as *Tomme au raisin*, they are coated with grape pulp. After each turning, the cheesemaker presses the mold into the rind by hand; the crust which forms gradually develops gray, white, yellow and red spots, and becomes very dry. Modern production procedures demand that they be prepared in a more simplified manner, to develop a natural rind. The ivory to yellow-colored cheese, which has a fat content varying between 10 and 30%, has a fresh and particular taste, which is occasionally slightly bitter or sourish. *Reblochon* is another mountain cheese, ripened like the Tommes in caves. It is a semihard cheese, with a dark, yellow-washed rind. The rich, unskimmed milk that makes the cheese is processed immediately after milking, when it is still warm. This, it seems, gives Reblochon its characteristic flavor – mild, creamy and fragrant.

In the Haute Jura, in Gex and Septmoncel, we find two fine blue cheeses, both of which are entitled to use the name *Bleu du Haute Jura*; individually they are identified as *Bleu de Gex* and *Bleu de Septmoncel*. Like the Tommes, they are an ancient variety, once made in huts high on the mountain slopes, but today production takes place in small, central cheese dairies. Twice a week, even during the cold weather, milk is brought down the winding, narrow roads to the two dairies, which handle more than 2,000 liters (2,100 quarts) a day. From the curds comes a firm, white cheese, evenly blue-veined after maturing, with a fresh though modest flavor. Like certain wines, these cheeses do not seem to travel well, which is why most are consumed in the region where they are made; small quantities can be found, however, in Lyon, St. Etienne and Grenoble.

Cheese with a fortified flavor

A far more stable and hardy blue

LEFT: Grape skins and pips from the wine press cover the rind of a Fondu au Raisin.

BELOW: Cheeses in the cellar of a well-stocked cheese shop. Top left is Langres, below is Carré de l'Est. At the bottom are heart-shaped Rollots, right are cream cheeses.

cheese is the popular *Bleu de Bresse*, which comes from the rich meadow country between the Saône and the Jura. Although small in size, the cheeses share certain characteristics with Gorgonzola, except that they are much milder. *Cancoillotte* (or *Cancaillotte*) is an unripened curd cheese, mostly a home-made product from the vicinity of Besançon. The curds are placed in a warm part of the kitchen to ferment, and to develop a strong, unique flavor. They are then heated with milk, or butter and white wine, according to the family recipe. The melted cheese, a *fromage fondu*, is then poured into a dish, and left to form a thick paste, to be used in combination with various dishes: in a savory pastry, with potatoes and fried eggs, and so on. As a snack, hot Cancoillotte is eaten with fresh bread or toast.

Quite a number of these regional, farmhouse cheeses are specially prepared, in order to enhance or increase their flavor. Herbs may be added, or the cheeses may be soaked in wine, brandy or even coffee, as is a cheese called *Laumes*.

In the Burgundy country of the Côte d'Or, a little further to the west past Dijon, is the small village of Epoisses, where *Fromage d'Epoisses* is made from well-chilled evening milk mixed with fresh morning milk. As soon as the mold forms, the cheeses are soaked in water and an *eau de vie* made from grape pulp, called *Marc de Bourgogne*. Just before they are sold, they are again soaked in the *Marc*, which has been fortified by a good, white Burgundy. Cheeses thus treated are called *Epoisses confits au vin blanc,* or *confits au Marc*. A variety of the *Tomme au Raisin* is the *Tomme au Marc de Raisin,* which is coated with grape pulp and left to form a hard crust of pips; *Fondu au Marc de Raisin* is similar, but is made from pasteurized milk. A challenge to strong teeth and robust digestions, the pips in both varieties are best left on the plate, even if the manufacturers do suggest otherwise!

An inheritance from Ireland

Where France meets the German border to the northeast, the rolling fertile meadows merge into the wooded Vosges, a land of mineral springs and spas, of light and delicate wines, of dialects blending French and

Also from Vosges and other provinces of the northeast comes the square-shaped *Carré de l'Est*, with its spotlessly white mold. *Carré* ripens on screens, and its paste is homogeneous, with a fat content of 40 to 60%. The cheese is slightly salted, and its flavor resembles that of Camembert, the famous Normandy cheese to which Carré de l'Est has become a forceful competitor.

A royal favorite

The extreme northwest of France, along the Belgian border, is rich pasture land. The cheeses produced there are strong and full-flavored, the most famous of which is named after the town of Maroilles. *Maroilles* is the great speciality of the region, which has been making similar cheeses for over a thousand years; by the sixteenth century the fame of the cheeses was so widespread that they found their way to the court of Spain. Sometimes the cheese was made by order: in the twelfth century on the feast of St. Jean-Baptiste (June 24) certain villages were required to make their milk into cheese for the abbey of Maroilles, where St. John was the patron saint. The cheeses are allowed to mature for several months, during which time they are carefully washed with water and then turned. Maroilles is a square cheese with a reddish rind, the paste being pale, soft and slightly salted; its flavor is delicious, strong and full, without being sharp. Each weighs approximately 800 g (1.8 lbs). A smaller version, *Sorbais*, weighs only 600 g (1.3 lbs); the even smaller *Mignon* 400 g (.9 lb), and the very smallest – the *Quart* – only 200 g (.4 lb). Other Maroilles-type varieties include *Manicamp* and *Monceau*; the French loaf-shaped *Baguette* and the twice-salted *Maroilles Gris* or *Vieux Lille*, with its grayish rind. The latter matures for five or six months in very moist cellars, by which time the *Vieux Lille* has become liquid and might be considered over-ripe. It has a very pronounced flavor, and the aroma is distinguished by a definite smell of ammonia. A large proportion of various Maroilles types continues to be made on farms.

According to legend, Louis XIV and the Crown Prince, the Dauphin, when visiting the north of France, were served nonripened Maroilles that had been flavored with garden

ABOVE AND RIGHT: Munster cheese labels. There are only a few farms remaining where traditional farmhouse Munster is still made. You can find them along the *Route de Fromage*, along the top of the Vosges, west of the small town of Munster.

German, of sausages and beer and farmhouse cheeses. The cheeses are eaten with finely chopped onions, caraway seeds and crisp bread, together with beer or, better still, the spicy, white Gewürztraminer wine. This is the area of France known as Alsace-Lorraine, and its greatest cheese is *Munster*.

It is said that the cheese was first made by Irish monks who settled in Vosges in the seventh century. Munster is a round cheese with an orange-red rind, a yellow and very soft consistency, and a quite distinct, tangy flavor. Real farmhouse Munster is becoming very rare, and consequently more and more expensive; the few farms still making it can be recognized by the new small Munsters left outside to dry; the cheeses remain outdoors for a week before being stored in the cellars. Here they ripen for two months on beds of rye straw alongside the now mature cheeses, from which they acquire the rind flora. Factories in Vosges, as well as elsewhere in France and abroad, have adopted this method; they also manufacture a large Munster called *Géromé*, nicknamed the "red head," which was originally made in the mountain huts of Gerardmer, on the east slopes.

LEFT: "Good cheese from Maroilles, who wants my good Maroilles," cried the street vendor. From a print by Carle Vernet, 1815.

LEFT: A label from a small Maroilles cheese weighing 300 g (10.5 oz). This cheese is made in Thiérache in northern France, primarily from the milk of Pie Noir cattle.

herbs, specially chosen for the occasion. The cheese was so greatly appreciated that it was allowed to be called *Dauphin* from that day onwards, or so the story goes. The name is still given to a herb-and-cloves white Maroilles, which is ripened in molds for three to four months. The taste resembles that of *Boulette d'Avesnes*, a small farmhouse cheese from Avesnes and surroundings, which is made of buttermilk curds to which finely chopped herbs have been added. After three months' ripening the flattened cones have a reddish-yellow surface and a crumbly consistency, and one must be prepared for the first, sharp taste. Neither should the taste of *Rollot* be taken lightly; this is a treacherously innocent-looking, full-cream cheese from Picardy, small and flat, with a round or sometimes heart-shaped form. Another local Boulette comes from Cambrai, the *Boulette de Cambrai*; it is flavored with herbs and spices and eaten fresh.

By no means are all of these northern cheeses sharp and strong flavored. *Mimolette* is a pleasant, mild cheese weighing about 3 kg (6.6 lbs), and is orange-colored with a gray rind. It bears such a close resemblance to the Dutch cheese Commissie, a large type of Edam, that the Dutch call their export version Mimolette, while the French cheese has been nicknamed "Vieux Hollande." The Mimolette is also made in other parts of France, particularly in Brittany.

BELOW: The heavily-salted Maroilles Gris, or Vieux Lille. It is matured for a particularly long period and acquires a gray crust.

The Swiss secret of a French cheese

In the 1850s a farmer named Héroult had a farm in the *département* of the Oise, to the north of Paris. Nearly every day his wife sent her fresh cheeses to the Halles market in Paris. A Swiss cowherd, living on the farm, suggested that she should add some fresh cream to the curds, as was sometimes done in his home country. The result was so successful that Madame Héroult soon had trouble meeting the increased demand, and so it was that *Petit-Suisse* was born. Together with a partner, Charles Gervais, she started the Gervais cheese factory, which is now one of the largest in France. Because of its creamy, very soft consistency, Petit-Suisse is packed in small plastic or paper containers. It has a 60% fat content, and the taste is very fresh, slightly sourish and nutty. Petit-Suisse is popular with both adults and children as a dessert served with fruit, or alone, with a little sugar. So too is the closely related semisalted *Demi-sel*.

An ancient Christmas delicacy

Where the river Epte runs before and beyond the town of Gournay, some of the finest dairy country between Paris and the sea is to be found. This fine butter and cream area is known as the Pays de Bray, and its most famous cheese is *Neufchatel*. As long ago as the fifteenth century, English merchants arrived via Dieppe and, along with other goods purchased in the region, they took back some of these cheeses for the Christmas market at home – the cheeses were probably much the same as now: small, weighing about 100 g (3½ oz) each. When purchased fresh, the white flora can just be seen, but it is sometimes left to ripen further. Neufchatels have a soft paste, which is lightly salted and has a pure and refreshing flavor. They come in various shapes which determine their names: the best known is the cylindrical *Bonde or Bondon*; there is also the square-shaped *Carré*, the rectangular *Briquette* and the heart-shaped *Coeur*.

LEFT: The rich pasturelands of Normandy here reach the sea at Etretat, near Le Havre. The region to the south produces some famous cheeses: Pont-l'Evêque, Livarot, Camembert.

BELOW: An early print showing Camembert made in the traditional way: the curd is removed by hand from the basin while still fairly wet, and then ladled into small molds. The art lies in filling the molds in a number of consecutive layers. The cheese drains further by the pressure of its own weight, the whey draining through the perforations.

Camembert cheese takes its name from the Normandy village of Camembert in the *département* of the Orne. Legend says that the cheese was first made in 1791 by Marie Harel, who eventually passed the recipe on to her daughter, also called Marie. She and her husband, Victor Paynel, sold the cheese at the local markets, and it became so famous that a statue was erected to the elder Marie at nearby Vimoutiers.

Like many legends, Camembert's exists on fancy rather than fact. Marie Harel did not invent Camembert cheese – she didn't even live in Camembert. The cheese had already been described in a seventeenth-century dictionary as a splendid cheese which, like the excellent *Livarot*, was for sale in the market at Vimoutiers. It is likely that cheeses of the Camembert type were enjoyed by William the Conqueror, when they were known as *Augelot*, now a local name for the famous cheese *Pont-l'Evêque*. Augelot cheese came from the Pays d'Auge, where Camembert, Livarot and Pont-l'Evêque have been made for centuries.

In the old days, the ripening of Camembert was left to nature. At one time it had a red rind; later it became blue-crusted because the cheese was very sensitive to the formation of undesired molds. Marie Harel was the first cheesemaker to establish a regular mold flora and, in this respect, was the inventor of *modern* Camembert.

Factory production commenced towards the end of the last century, and has been improved since the introduction of *Penicillium candidum*, a white inoculated mold, in 1910. Unfortunately, the cheese is sometimes oversalted, which interferes with its true characteristics.

A real Camembert has a fine, supple consistency, a taste reminiscent of mushrooms and a strong aroma; a Camembert cheese inspired the Surrealist poet Léon-Paul Fargue to call it "les pieds de Dieu" – "the feet of the Lord." When the first Camembert factories were established outside Normandy, the Syndicat des Fabricants du Véritable Camembert de Normandie was founded, in order to identify and protect the cheese of the region. Special regulations also exist concerning *Gournay*, the smaller Camembert, and other similar types.

LEFT: The familiar, chipwood box for Camembert superseded the straw packaging. Patented in the 1890s, the box helped preserve the cheese and improved exports.

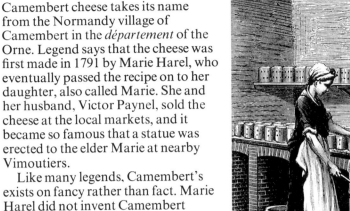

BELOW: Norman farmers have made butter, cream, cheese and cider for well over a thousand years. The products have greatly influenced Normandy's regional cooking.

LEFT: An estate in Normandy. The region has abundant orchards in addition to its pastures. Cider and Calvados, the Norman brandy, are made from the apples.

BELOW: The idyllic river valley of the Risle, one of the small rivers which meanders through Camembert country to the Seine estuary.

BELOW: The cheese-making room of the Coopérative Laitière at Vicq, France. In the foreground are a number of cheese-making vats, considerably smaller than those in the large drawing below. To the right, workers remove the distributor plates and stack the trays of molds.

BELOW: The correct quantity of wet curd is discharged onto the distributor plates. It is important that each mold be evenly filled.

LEFT: The trays of molds are continuously stacked and turned. Note the wet curd in the tall molds; it will eventually settle into the familiar, round cheese we associate with Camembert.

A. This buffer tank contains pasteurized cheese milk. After addition of starter, the milk is pumped into one or more of the cheesemaking vats. Its temperature should be 31-32°C (88-90°F).

B. The cheesemaking vats are large, open vats, similar to the traditional type. Rennet is added, and in very modern production lines (as the one shown here), the Camembert mold culture is also added directly to the cheese milk. It takes about an hour for the milk in the vat to coagulate. From right to left, the successive stages are shown: the first vat is filled with milk; in the second vat milk is curdling; in the third vat milk coagulates to form curd; from the fourth vat the curd is poured into the molds; the last vat is empty and ready to be filled with prepared milk.

E. The molds stand on trays; on top of them sits a distributor plate with openings that channel the right amount of wet curd into the molds.

C. This apparatus, which is anything but traditional, is a stirring device. Lowered into any of the vats, its slow rotation mixes and gently stirs the curd. This phase is preceded by careful cutting of the coagulum, which may be done mechanically or by hand; the curd layer should measure about 1.5-3 cm (½-1¼ in). In the meantime, some whey can be run off.

D. When the curd is ready, this feeder screw is lowered into the vat, into which it fits closely. It rotates, expelling the curd-whey mixture through the opening in the end of the vat and into the molds. One full turn of the screw displaces enough curd to fill one tray of molds.

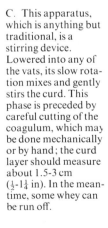

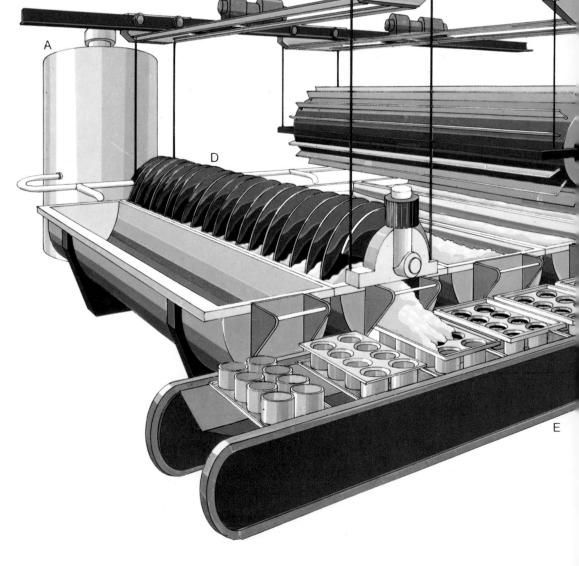

LEFT: Originally, the white mold grew spontaneously, and slowly, on the cheeses. Modern manufacturers encourage the action by spraying the cheeses with *Penicillium candidum*, while in the drying and ripening rooms.

LEFT: Fresh Camemberts in the ripening room. On some of them the white mold is beginning to appear.

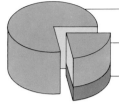

total production French cheese 898,800 tons p.a. (100 %)

production Camembert 186,000 tons p.a. (20.7 %)

export soft cheeses 57,100 tons p.a.

F. At the end of the conveyor belt, the trays of molds are stacked. A considerable amount of whey is drained off, the cheeses being pressed so to speak, by their own weight. Workers turn the trays a few times during the draining process. As the excess moisture is expelled, the volume of the curd diminishes.

G. After about twenty-four hours the cheeses are taken from their molds and salted, usually by means of a brine bath. Large containers, filled with the young cheeses, are immersed in a salty solution.

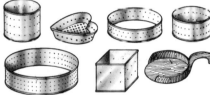

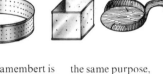

ABOVE: Camembert is made in the traditional tall, narrow molds (top left); other soft cheeses are made in a wide variety of mold shapes. Note the perforations that allows the whey to drain. For the same purpose, some molds have no bottom at all.

H. The cheeses are dried and transferred to the high-humidity ripening room. At a temperature of 13-15°C (55-59°F), the characteristic white mold begins to appear on the surface. After 7-12 days the cheeses are packed and distributed. The cheese has an even, pure white growth of mold, but the ripening of the interior has only just begun, and will require further maturing before it is "à point," as the French say. During transport, and in the shop, the ripening process slowly continues.

Many soft cheeses, with or without surface molds, are prepared along these lines, among them Brie and Carré de l'Est. Camembert, however, represents no less than two-thirds of all soft cheese produced in France.

RIGHT: A stock of small Camemberts in the storage cellars of a Paris cheese factor.

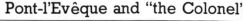

LEFT: No fewer than twenty-two gold medals testify the high standards of craftsmanship that have gone into the making of this brand of Pont-l'Evêque.

LEFT: One of the three great cheeses from the Pays d'Auge – Livarot. The cheese has a supple consistency with small holes, the taste is fresh and mild, the aroma surprisingly strong.

With Camembert, Pont-l'Evêque and Livarot are the three world-famous cheeses of the Pays d'Auge, and guaranteed as original by the mark of the Syndicat de la Marque d'Origine Pays d'Auge. Like most widely marketed cheeses, Pont-l'Evêque is mainly factory produced, made from very fresh milk, and then cured for four to five weeks. The small cheeses are then washed, causing the rind to turn yellow and the flavor and aroma to become stronger. If the cheeses are not washed, the rind becomes gray instead, and slightly cracked. The consistency of the pale-yellow cheese is soft and supple. Other varieties of Pont-l'Evêque are *Trouville* and the much larger *Pavé de Moyaux*.

Livarot – there is also a local variety sold as *Lisieux* – was once a skimmed-milk cheese, but it is now made from the skimmed evening milk of the previous day, mixed with the full-cream morning milk. The cheeses do not ripen on the farm but are sold on the market in Livarot or Vimoutiers as *Livarot Blanc* to *affineurs,* who in Normandy are called *cavistes.*

However, the farmer-cheesemakers, and with them the professional *cavistes*, are being replaced by factories, where the fresh cheeses are placed in a drying room in order to develop the bacteriological flora on the rind. After some weeks they are transferred to caves possessing a strong, ammoniac atmosphere, where they remain for two months. Because a maturing Livarot cheese is inclined to dip in the center, each cheese is bound with five strips of cattail leaf or paper; the stripes left by this corset have earned Livarot the nickname of "the Colonel." The consistency is soft, with small eyes, the flavor is mild and fresh, and the aroma quite strong. If the cheese is found to have a chalk-white center, it indicates that the whey has not been adequately drained during the manufacture.

"The cheeses have arrived"
Toward the south, where the river Mayenne idly threads its way through the Normandy countryside in the direction of the Loire, stands Entrammes with its abbey of Notre Dame de Port-du-Salut, built in 1233. After Napoleon's reign, Trappist monks returned from exile, bringing with them a dozen dairy cows; they settled here and began producing a

LEFT: This Trappist monk is washing the small Port-Salut cheeses, made by him and his fellow monks at the Abbey of Notre Dame de Port-du-Salut in Entrammes.

BELOW: The small, delicate goat's milk cheeses (*chevres*) called Sainte-Maure are recognized by the straw or stick which pierces the length of each cheese. Some maintain that without it the Sainte-Maure would fall apart! It is an unusually fine and tasty cheese from Touraine, "the garden of France." The Sainte-Maure is locally very popular, especially when accompanied with a cool, dry Loire wine, such as Muscadet.

LEFT: A great deal of goat's milk cheese is made on the island of Corsica. The cheeses are notoriously strong and, like the Corsicans themselves, highly individual.

splendid cheese for their own consumption. Increased production followed a decision to use milk supplied by local farmers, and *Port-du-Salut* cheese soon reached the street markets of Paris. A cheese factor named Mouquet, who sold cheese in the capital over a hundred years ago, would put out a notice board proclaiming the arrival of a new supply – "*Arrivage des fromages*" – and within the hour his entire supply would be sold. Production, still done according to the ancient recipe, now amounts to some 200,000 cheeses a year. Port-du-Salut is a flat and cylindrical cheese with a pale yellow rind. It is semihard, has good keeping properties and a mild flavor.

Other Trappist monasteries soon followed with a cheese "*façon de Port-du-Salut*"; in 1878, however, the name of the original abbey cheese was placed under legal protection. In 1909 the monks from Entrammes helped to establish, far from the abbey, a then ultramodern, commercially run factory where cheese was made under the name of *Port-Salut*. The cheese called *Saint Paulin*, made in all parts of France, can be considered a close relative, although it is prepared somewhat differently.

Rare and spicy cheeses of the southeast
Between Tours and Poitiers is a land watered by tributaries of the Loire, a land so abundant that it is called the "garden of France" – Touraine; in Tours, they say, the very best French is spoken. The farmers of Touraine make a flamboyant and popular goat's milk cheese, *Sainte-Maure*, which is influenced by the Camembert in the way it is made and ripened.

East of Touraine, on the Atlantic Ocean, is the *département* of Vendée. Here we can taste *Fromage Nantais*, also called *Fromage de Curé*, a small, square cheese first made in 1890 by a local parish priest. In those days the cheese was known as *Petit Breton*. Production increased sharply after the arrival of a Belgian cheesemaker, who added a professional touch and modified the recipe a little, to suit the taste of his own country. It now slightly resembles Remoudou. Fromage de Curé is also made in Brittany. If we journey south and southeast of Vendée, to Vienne, Deux-Sèvres and Charente, we come to a country where farmers are prolific in the making of

BELOW: In the Pyrenées, a region of spicy, Spanish-style cheeses, much of the milk from sheep is made into fresh cheese and sent to Roquefort. Once there, it ripens in the famous caves where it develops the inimitable, blue-green mold.

dozens of different cheeses, mostly unripened dairy cheeses, and an ever increasing number of *chèvres* – goat's milk cheeses, which ripen only for a short time and are hardly ever seen outside the district of origin. There is *Fromage de la Mothe*, for example, which is left to dry for about fifteen days between vine or plane tree leaves; the *Chabichou*, the *Carré de Saint-Cyr* and the *Fromage de Ruffec*. Finally, an extremely rare collector's item: a small triangular cheese made of sheep's milk, called *l'Aunis*.

Perhaps the individuality and the rarity of these small cheeses is intended to compensate the cheese explorer for the scarcity that exists in Bordeaux, to the south. No indigenous cheese is found in claret country – the vineyards leave precious little room for meadows. Beyond the *département of* Landes, the foothills of the Pyrenées yield good grazing land for dairy cattle. Influenced by Spanish cookery, the mountain herdsmen make their own fresh cheeses, strongly spiced with pepper and pimento, especially in the Basque country. Such are the cheeses *Orrys* and *Castillon*. In wintertime, when the cattle are kept in stables, *Bethmale* cheese (also known as *Aulus* or *Oustet*) is made, a hard spicy cheese, very suitable for grating. Some cheeses from this area of the Pyrenées are made from the milk of ewes, and they are sent uncured to ripen in the unique caves of Roquefort, home of the famous blue cheese.

The rural cheeses of Corsica
The rugged, mountainous Corsican landscape of pine forest, tumbling, icy streams, ravines and precipitous tracks is strictly sheep and goat country. Mountain herdsmen make cheese from both kinds of milk, sometimes mixed together. From the north and center of the island comes the square and creamy *Niolo* and the slightly more salted *Venaco*, which is ripened for three months. In the south, *Sartenais* is made, and then there is *Bruccio*, a fresh cheese which is sometimes salted and preserved for the winter. Most of Corsica's cheeses are powerful, rough and "goaty" as you might expect. The island also produces a blue-veined cheese, *Bleu de Corse*, which resembles Roquefort; most of the sheep's milk, however, is processed to "white" Roquefort and sent "home" to ripen in the Roquefort caves.

Lovers of cheese may become ecstatic when presented with a *Roquefort*. They describe it as a fine, noble cheese, delicately veined and marbled with a bluish-green mold. Some would say that Roquefort is peerless, the greatest cheese in the world.

Roquefort cheese comes from an area south of the Massif Central and east of the beautiful Gorges du Tarn, an area of poor pasture land. The village of Roquefort-sur-Soulzon stands on the remains of a mountain, Combalou. In prehistoric times, rainwater drained through the porous limestone strata to form a gigantic underground water basin, so weakening the foundations of Combalou that one day the entire mountain collapsed.

Due to the collapse and subsequent displacements, cracks formed called *fleurines*, which serve as natural chimneys and air filters. In the underground caves there is a continuous circulation of fresh air, which distributes the moisture evenly over the entire mountain. Combalou breathes. Condensation and evaporation balance each other, air pressure and temperature are in equilibrium, and the micro-climate is of unequalled purity. Here, the *Penicillium roqueforti* developed, mold families that grow on organic substances.

The poor soil of the arid *causses* made all but the most primitive agriculture impossible, and although grass could hardly grow, the sheep thrived. Their milk was made into a cheese that

LEFT: Roquefort cheese. The legend of Roquefort tells of a herdsman who left a loaf of bread and some fresh curd cheese in the caves of Roquefort. He returned to discover that the cheese had turned moldy, but it was so tasty that the local farmers decided to mature all their cheeses by the same method.

RIGHT: The tall, round forms are filled with curd.

ABOVE: Samples of cheese and cultures of mold are continuously tested and examined in the modern laboratories.

RIGHT: The cheeses mature slowly in the cool cellars, where there is always a gentle flow of air to distribute the spores of *Penicillium glaucum* var. *Roqueforti* to all parts of the caves. These conditions give Roquefort cheese its unique character.

brought fame and prosperity to the *causses* in general, and Roquefort in particular. There is nothing special about the milk of these Lacaune sheep; it is only when a cheese is ripened in the center of Combalou that it acquires from the *Penicillium roqueforti* its greenish veins and unique flavor.

A blessing of blue

The inhabitants of the *causses* protect their prosperity by the Confederation Générale des Producteurs de Lait de Brebis et des Industriels de Roquefort. Its members are the sheep breeders, who twice daily bring their sheep from the *causses* to the hygienic stables, where they are mechanically milked. Also members are the hundreds of manufacturers of "white" Roquefort, both here, on Corsica and in the Pyrenées, and the producers in the caves of Combalou.

A Roquefort cheese receives its blessing of blue by being covered in a thin layer of salt, brushed and pricked, and then stored in the caves in such a way that the moist air can easily reach it. After some weeks it is wrapped in foil, where it continues to ripen. A Roquefort cheese weighs approximately 2.7 kg (5.9 lbs) and is cylindrical in shape. It is also marketed in smaller, pre-packed portions. Its paste is white with blue-green veins and is somewhat crumbly. The smell and taste of this great ewe cheese, the only sheep's cheese in the world to gain such renown, is highly flavored, but nobly so. The cheese is provided with a guarantee label for export purposes.

Roquefort has a long export history. Monastery chronicles of the eighth century mention the transport of Roquefort across the Alps, by which time it was well established: the Romans were acquainted with it, Charlemagne enjoyed it, and by the eleventh century we find it recorded on customs' lists. For hundreds of years, Roquefort cheese has been praised by authors, including Casanova, who had it served with ice-cold ham.

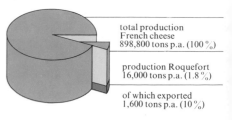

total production French cheese 898,800 tons p.a. (100%)

production Roquefort 16,000 tons p.a. (1.8%)

of which exported 1,600 tons p.a. (10%)

ABOVE: The breed of cattle, as much as the pasture land, determines the quality and the character of French dairy cheeses.

Popular breeds are Normandy, Jersey, Saler and Aubrac, the latter being particularly suited to mountain grazing.

A volcanic, mountainous area of mineral springs, of towns and villages built upon rocky outcrops, of herbal pastures and high passes, the *département* of Cantal gave its name to a mighty cheese that was probably being made during antiquity. Pliny the Elder describes a cheese from near Lozère and Gévaudan, which in many respects resembles the present Cantal. In the second half of the eighteenth century we meet the cheese in the encyclopedia of d'Alembert and Diderot, with an illustration of all the equipment needed for the preparation of a *Fourme du Cantal*. These enormous, drum-shaped cheeses have been sold in the Haute Auvergne and Cantal for centuries, and *Cantal Fermier* is still prepared according to the following, ancient tradition:

Between the middle of May and the beginning of October, the herdsmen tend their cattle in the upland pastures; each herd consists of fifty or sixty cows, usually the mahogany-colored Salers or the smaller Aubracs, a hardy mountain stock. The herdsmen make cheese from the milk, in their old, dilapidated stone huts, using a very laborious process. After being pressed for an hour, the curds are cut into strips and pressed again, a process which is repeated six to ten times. The curds are then left in the cheese press for twenty-four to thirty-six hours, during which time they begin to ripen. They are pressed again and turned at intervals. The turning procedure continues every other day for three months, and at each turning the rind is polished. Twice during the season the herdsmen undertake the journey down the mountain roads to deliver their cheeses, some specimens weighing as much as 45 kg (99 lbs).

ABOVE: Tall, drum-shaped Cantal cheeses – *Fourmes de Cantal* – maturing in a cellar. The Cantal is a beautiful cheese from the Massif Central.

Sometimes called "the French cheddar," it has a smooth texture and a fragrant aroma of the Auvergne meadows.

Modern preparation techniques

Initially, the rind of a Cantal shows golden-colored spots, which vanish as the cheese matures. Gradually, the rind turns darker, nearly black. Later it becomes almost red, and finally grayish white. The full-cream, smooth consistency retains the herbal flavor of the mountain meadows. The climate, the altitude, the type of cattle and especially the condition of the soil make something very special of Cantal Fermier. For this reason, great care has been taken to locate other places where identical natural conditions exist, and where this regional cheese can be produced as original Cantal. The places are: the entire *département* of Cantal itself, eight municipalities of Aveyron, twenty-five of Puy-de-Dôme and one of Haute-Loire. The heaviest cheeses are those from the region of Salers. If a Cantal is made at an altitude of at least 850 meters (33,500 feet), it is entitled to bear the additional label of "Haute-Montagne."

In the cheese dairies of the valleys, away from the pure mountain air but with the help of modern equipment, *Cantal Laitier* is made from pasteurized milk. The method of preparation is the same as that of the Fermier, but the cheese ripens for a maximum of two months, and has a less pronounced taste. These factories also produce smaller Cantals of 8 to 10 kg (17.6 to 22 lbs), called *Cantalets*. Cantal cheese is also permitted in a rectangular shape, provided that it ripens for not less than two months. Finally, there are several partially cured Cantals, such as *Tomme d'Aligot* or *Tomme Fraîche*, which are used a great deal in the preparation of regional dishes.

ABOVE: The process of manufacturing Cantal cheeses. The curd is first prepared in metal tubs.

ABOVE: From the tubs, the curd is cut into blocks to be laid out on a bench or table for pressing.

RIGHT: After a short time the curd is cut into strips and pressed again.

Bleu d'Auvergne

Mountain country seems to go hand in hand with blue cheese. Several prime examples are found in the Massif Central, not the least of which is the *Bleu d'Auvergne*, a dairy cheese that comes from more or less the same area as Cantal. The cheese is flat and cylindrical, and weighs between 2 and 2.5 kg (4.4 to 5.5 lbs); it has a refined taste and a very special bouquet. It is said to stimulate the appetite and be good for the digestion.

As the cheese is rather small, not a great deal of milk is required, which is just as well, considering the scarcity of pasture. In places the landscape is rough, with deep valleys and ravines, and a few winding, narrow roads. From early times, the small farms of the region, which often keep no more than ten to fifteen cows, have made their own cheeses. Since 1870 the farmers have been inoculating their curds with *Penicillium glaucum*, in the manner of the makers of Roquefort. The major part of production has been taken over by cheese dairies, but there are still a few farmers around Thiézac who make their own blue cheese, called *Bleu de Thiézac Fermier*. Twice weekly the farmer must take his cheeses (until recently by donkey or mule) to the *affineur*, who then sets them to ripen in the valleys.

Only carefully collected, high-quality milk is suitable for *Bleu d'Auvergne*, as it is made into cheese when raw. The deep-cooled evening milk of the previous day is warmed shortly before the processing and added to the fresh morning milk. The mold culture, again *Penicillium glaucum*, may be added to the milk, but it is usually sprinkled on the curd after it has been transferred to the molds. After three or four days of washing and turning, the cheeses are taken to the salt rooms, which are kept at a temperature of 10°C (50°F). Here they are rubbed with dry salt and pricked with needles, which enables the air to penetrate and encourages the formation of mold. This process is completed within three to four weeks in a humid room at 8° to 10°C; by then the rind has discolored from yellowish-red to white with reddish spots. As soon as the green veins become visible, the small cheeses are packed in metal foil; they are then stored for another few weeks at a temperature of 2°C (about 36°F).

From moldy bread to monument

Owing to the inherent expertise of the makers, the various blue cheeses of the Massif Central are the best in France. Some are named after their place of origin, such as *Bleu d'Aveyron, Bleu de Thiézac* (which has an entirely different flavor because it is salted when warm) and *Bleu de Laqueuille*. The latter, from the Laqueuille district of Puy-de-Dôme, has a somewhat drier rind and a less distinct flavor than the others mentioned, but it possesses an attractive veining, introduced by Antoine Roussel in 1850. Roussel dipped a piece of moldy bread from his home kitchen into the curds, and subsequently produced a blue cheese that, like Marie Harel, was to earn him a monument.

Finally, we must mention *Bleu de Causses*, which ripens in natural caves in the manner of Roquefort, and is found everywhere in the Auvergne. Its taste greatly depends on grazing conditions, including the composition of the local soil and the hours of sunshine during the summer.

The tender touch

In addition to the illustrious Roquefort and the much-decorated Bleu d'Auvergne, *Saint-Nectaire* cheese deserves to be mentioned. Made in Puy-de-Dôme in the immediate environment of Mont Dore, the cheese was already well known during the reign of Louis XIV. It's a fragile little cheese, prepared from the carefully collected milk of Salers cows and sold by the farmers once every fortnight to private or cooperative *affineurs*. Cylindrical in shape, the cheeses are left to ripen on straw in damp cellars, often the old cellars in Clermont-Ferrand, once used for storing wine. After three months the rind is spotted yellow to ochre-red. After six months the taste of the cheese is at its best: it is then supple and mild, and as they say in France, "*à ta tendre pression il répond.*" The major part of the produce is consumed in the region itself. The farmhouse cheese is recognizable by an oval casein disc

ABOVE: This nine-teenth-century farmer from the Auvergene is manually pressing the cheese curd. The whey runs into a wooden tub on the left.

bearing a green guarantee imprint; the factory-made cheese has a rectangular label.

A traditional Christmas soup is made with St. Nectaire, where slices of the cheese are mixed into a broth made of water, stale bread and salt. A few spoonfuls of whipped cream may be added before serving.

There is hardly a cheese-producing area of France that cannot boast a *chèvre* or two, and the Massif Central is no exception. It sports a number of these small, characteristic goat's cheeses. Perhaps the best known is *Chèvreton d'Ambert*, or *Brique de Forez*, which is sometimes partially made of cow's milk giving the cheese a less pungent taste and aroma. Mostly, though, only goat's milk is used. A maturation period of fifteen days on rye straw makes the *Chèvreton* a creamy, smooth cheese with a firm texture. Another local cheese is *Chevrotin*, nearly always eaten while fresh, often with double cream and sugar, or with salt and garlic. When left to ripen, these cheeses are placed in dovecot-like cages mounted on high poles, so that the wind may circulate about them. They must be protected

ABOVE: Built on a rocky outcrop, La Roque-Sainte-Marguerite in the district of Aveyron, where a variety of Bleu d'Auvergne is produced.

LEFT: A family lunch *en plein air* in the garden of the Château de Montmelas, Beaujeu. On such occasions local cheeses and wines may be enjoyed at the peak of their perfection.

by the shade of trees, for they quickly ferment and rise if the sun reaches them, spoiling the *Chevrotin's* particular flavor.

All roads lead to Paris

In Paris and the surrounding countryside our tour through the cheese areas of France comes to an end. For many centuries Paris has been the political, administrative and cultural center of the country. It is here that the great traditions of *Haute Cuisine* were established. In the old days, the regional produce of the land, including many varieties of cheese, reached Les Halles, the Paris market. Here the cheeses became nationally known and would gradually achieve world fame. Let us turn then to Brie cheese, the "Roi de Fromages," which is so closely associated with the capital city.

BELOW RIGHT: Brie de Meaux Fermier is not only the "Brie of Bries," but has been honored as the "Roi de Fromages."

LEFT: A wedge of a delicious and noble cheese – Brie de Melun. Ripe Brie has a soft, golden-yellow consistency, should not develop a white core in the paste, and should be slightly runny.

Paris lies in a basin in the earth's crust; it is as if nature had pressed down a pile of dishes until the edges remain slightly above the surroundings, gently sloping inwards, steep to the outside. The hollow in the center forms the Île de France – the area immediately east of the capital – and Champagne, fertile districts with lush pastures. Here is the home of the large *Brie* cheese, known as the "jewel of the Île de France."

Brie became world-famous overnight. At the Vienna Congress in 1814 and 1815, when statesmen of Europe were laying the foundations for the post-Napoleonic period, there were great celebrations, banquets and dinners between negotiations. During one such occasion an argument arose as to which country produced the best cheeses – or so the story goes. Always the diplomat, the Frenchman Talleyrand proposed that the different national cheeses be allowed to compete with one another at a large banquet. But Talleyrand was a gourmet and a cook as well as a diplomat: it is probable that he never doubted the outcome of the competition. *Brie de Meaux* emerged as the very best of some sixty cheeses – unanimously it was crowned "*Roi de Fromages.*" Indeed, Brie was both the king of cheeses and the cheese of kings and king's consorts: Louis XII and Henry IV enjoyed the cheese, as did the wife of Louis XV, Maria Leszczynska, who included Brie in her favorite patties, *bouchées à la reine*; then there was the writer Alexander Dumas who provided his Three Musketeers with meals that always ended with Brie sprinkled with Burgundy.

The first mention of this cheese can be found in the records of the Court of Champagne, dating from 1217. Its name comes from the province of La Brie in the *département* of Seine-et-Marne. Until the middle of the last century, Brie was exclusively made on the farms, often with a red rind flora. Since it now has become almost entirely a factory-made cheese, produced under rigidly controlled hygienic conditions, the desirable red flora only occurs along the edges of the cheese. Preripened evening milk of the previous day is used, mixed with fresh morning milk. The art lies in spooning the curds in six successive layers into a formerly wooden, but now stainless

steel, ring, and then removing the whey with the aid of a perforated spoon. The cheese is turned, and on each turning clean reed mats are placed on top and underside. After six or seven days, it is sprinkled with powdered *Penicillium candidum* and then allowed to ripen for four weeks at a temperature of 11-12°C (52-54°F). Should the temperature either rise or fall, immediate changes in shape, color and taste result. A correctly prepared Brie should have an evenly distributed mold layer, a cream-colored soft paste without holes, and a flavor – depend-

ABOVE: The Rue de Mouffetard in Paris, a happy memory for anyone with an appetite who has ever been there. The shop windows display a wonderful variety of foodstuffs and wines: fresh vegetables from all corners of the earth, fresh fish from the Atlantic and Mediterranean, meat, poultry and cheese. Every cheese shop has its own specialities (right).

ing on the variety – which ranges over all nuances, from mild to very strong. After ripening, the cheeses are wrapped in waxed paper, packed in chipwood boxes and provided with a label that guarantees their origin.

Formerly, Brie often carried the name of the place of origin, and varieties still exist with a unique, local character. *Brie de Coulommiers*, for example (also called *Petit Brie*, as it weighs only 450 g [1 lb]) is prepared with fresh or pasteurized milk; it is frequently eaten unripened, at the first appearance of mold, and has a

Name	Milk	Type	Rind	Form	Weight	% Fat content
Aunis		●	□	triangular	250-300 g	45
Baguette		●	❖	bar	500 g	45
Banon		●	—	flat disc	100-150 g	45-50
Beaufort		■	□	cartwheel	14-70 kg	50
Bethmale		■	□	low cylinder	5-7 kg	45
Bleu d'Auvergne,		●	⌇	low cylinder	2-2.5 kg	40
- d'Aveyron		●	⌇	low cylinder	2-2.5 kg	45
- de Laqueuille		●	⌇	low cylinder	2-2.5 kg	45
- des Causses		●	⌇	low cylinder	2-2.5 kg	45
- de Thiézac		●	⌇	low cylinder	2-2.5 kg	45
- de Bresse		■	⌇	low cylinder	0.1-2 kg	50
- de Corse		●	⌇	low cylinder	2 kg	45
- de Gex		●	⌇	low cylinder	5.5-6.5 kg	45
- de Septmoncel		●	⌇	low cylinder	5.5-6.5 kg	45
- du Haut Jura		●	⌇	low cylinder	5.5-6.5 kg	45
Boulette d'Avesnes		●	❖	truncated cone	200-300 g	50
- de Cambrai		○	—	ball	250-300 g	45
Bossons Macérés		●	—	container	varying	45
Boursin		○	—	low cylinder	100 g	70
Brie de Coulommiers		●	❖	flat disc	0.4-3 kg	40-50

BELOW: Market porters enjoy a drink in a café bar. Outside, a stack of cheeses stands on the pavement.

very mild and delicate flavor. If the ripening process is allowed to continue, however, the taste becomes more pronounced, resembling that of Camembert; the influence of the air on the rind makes it a very special little cheese. A correct amount of air in the ripening room is a decisive factor for quality. *Fromage "à la Pie"* is always eaten practically fresh. *Brie de Melun*, on the contrary, is well-ripened; unlike other Brie varieties, the mold formation in this cheese takes place spontaneously, and no *Penicillium candidum* is added. After ripening, the cheese has a homogeneous structure, a reddish or blue-white layer of mold, and a nutty flavor, which is not less powerful than the aroma. Varieties of Brie de Melun are *Brie de Montereau* or *Ville Saint-Jacques*. *Cendré de Brie* is coated with ash, and has a gray-black rind. *Fromage de Dreux*, a cousin of Brie, used to be wrapped in chestnut leaves.

Apart from Brie, the surroundings of Paris offer quite a number of cheese varieties, many of them little known outside their place of origin. *Olivet* is a farmhouse cheese from Orleans, wrapped in leaves and preserved in the ashes of vine stalks. The factory version is a rather sharp, white mold cheese, sometimes packed in hay *(au Foin)* or in ashes *(Cendré)*. There is also an *Olivet Bleu*. *Vendôme* and *Villebarou* are both interesting cheeses, difficult to find but worth searching for. Much better known is the fresh cream cheese *Boursin*, widely exported in cardboard boxes. Its light taste is often strengthened by the addition of garlic and herbs, or with a coating of crushed peppercorns. *Selles-sur-Cher* is a very savory *chèvre*, covered with salt and charcoal. *Fontainebleau* rivals Petit Suisse; it is a very light, creamy

Name	Milk	Type	Rind	Form	Weight	% Fat content
- de Meaux				flat disc	0.4-3 kg	40-50
- de Melun				flat disc	0.4-3 kg	40-50
- de Montereau				flat disc	0.4-3 kg	40-50
Bruccio				basket	500 g	45
Cachat				basket	100 g	45-50
Camembert				flat disc	200-300 g	45-55
Cantal				cylinder	35-45 kg	45-50
Carré de l'Est				rectangular	100-200 g	40-60
Carré de Saint-Cyr				rectangular	varying	45
Castillon				flat disc	0.5-1 kg	45
Cendré de Brie				flat disc	250 g	40-50
Chabichou				truncated cone	100 g	45
Chaource				flat disc	500 g	45-50
Chèvreton d'Ambert				loaf	400 g	40-45
Chevrotin				truncated cone	100 g	45
Dauphin				oval, bar	200-500 g	50
Demisel				rectangular	75-100 g	40
Emmental				cartwheel	60-130 kg	45
Fontainebleau				container	varying	60
Fromage "à la Pie"				basket	600-800 g	40-50
- de Dreux				flat disc	150-500 g	30-40
- d'Epoisses				low cylinder	250 g	45
- de la Mothe				flat disc	250 g	45
- de Ruffec				flat disc	250 g	45
- Nantais				rectangular	300 g	40
Géromé				flat disc	0.3-4.5 kg	40
Gournay				flat disc	100 g	45
Gruyère de Comté				cartwheel	20-55 kg	45
Laumes				loaf	0.6-1 kg	45
Livarot				flat disc	300-500 g	40-45
Manicamp				rectangular	200 g	40-45
Maroilles				rectangular	200-800 g	40-50
- Gris				rectangular	200-800 g	40-50
Mimolette				ball	2.5-4 kg	40
Monceau				rectangular	600 g	45
Munster				flat disc	0.3-1.5 kg	40
Neufchatel				varying	100 g	40-45
Niolo				rectangular/basket	500 g	45
Olivet				flat disc	300 g	45-50
Orrys				low cylinder	10 kg	45
Pelardon				flat disc	80-100 g	45
Petit Suisse				small cylinder	30 g	60-75
Picardon				flat disc	75-100 g	45
Poivre d'Ane				flat disc	75-200 g	45
Pont-l'Evêque				cube	300 g	50
Port-du-Salut				low cylinder	1.3-2 kg	45-50
Reblochon				flat disc	600 g	45
Rollot				flat disc	200-300 g	45
Roquefort				cylinder	2.7 kg	50-60
Sainte-Maure				tall cylinder	300 g	45
Saint-Marcellin				flat disc	75 g	40-60
Saint-Nectaire				flat disc	1.7 kg	45
Saint-Paulin				low cylinder	1.3-2 kg	45-50
Sartenais				ball	0.5-1 kg	45
Selles-sur-Cher				flat disc	150 g	45
Tomme au Marc de Raisin				flat disc	1.5-2 kg	20-40
- d'Aligot				container	varying	45
- de Savoie				low cylinder	2-3 kg	10-30
Venaco				rectangular	500 g	45
Vendôme				flat disc	250 g	50
Villebarou				flat disc	450 g	45

Key to symbols on page 6. 1 kg = 2.2 lbs.

BELOW: An attractive display of cheeses in the window of a *fromagerie*. Top row from left to right: Livarot, Epoisses, Fromage Nantais, heart-shaped Rollot and Bleu de Bresse; below, left: Brie Coulommiers, Fromage de Dreux, Dauphin, and a number of soft, white-mold cheeses.

and spongy cheese, excellent for a sweet dessert, and is sold as such in the famous Paris café *La Coupole*. Finally, *Chaource* is a wonderful, soft, white-mold cheese, milky to fruity in taste and possibly a touch sour, with a very fine but penetrating aroma.

Many foreign cheeses are produced in France, including *Cheddar, Gouda, Edam, Gorgonzola* as well as cheese spreads. There is a market for these cheeses, but they have a hard time competing with the genuine, natural cheeses that France has to offer.

Paris and French cuisine
Paris became the gastronomic center of the western world because of at least three factors: the imagination and skill for improvisation of ordinary people in the preparation of their food; the importance of elegant, refined cuisine at the royal court; and the radiating influence of French politics and diplomacy. None of these factors should be ignored – least of all the first one. The brilliance of the court life at Versailles, so close to the densely populated and hard-working capital contrasted with, and supplemented, the solid traditions of French country cooking.

The essence of French cuisine is not in complicated, sumptuous recipes, but in excellent ingredients and well-tried methods of preparation. It is not for nothing that the food in even the smallest Paris restaurants is unsurpassed. And so it is with cheese. Every Frenchman knows how cheese should be eaten; the experience of centuries has enhanced his knowledge of the specific quality and character of the many varieties. No meal in France is complete without cheese, eaten with crisp French bread and its ideal companion – wine.

Germany (Federal Republic)

A mighty, lowland plain dominates that stretch of Europe south of the Baltic Sea. From the Soviet Union, it sweeps through Poland, East Germany and the northern territories of West Germany, to reach the Netherlands and the border of Denmark. Along the North Sea, the polders and dykes join up in the west with the Dutch lowlands. For centuries during the Middle Ages this vast area west and north of Danzig was a great trading center. For one thing, there were many well-placed seaports: Lübeck on the Baltic, and Hamburg and Bremen on the Elbe and Weser rivers, which feed into the North Sea.

Together these cities formed the powerful trade federation known as the Hanseatic League. Since the league monopolized most of the produce of northern Europe, it follows that a considerable variety of cheese found its way to and from the transit ports. Furthermore, this was good dairy country. Ostfriesland, Schleswig-Holstein and Niedersachsen – where, unlike Bavaria with its big landowners, farmers owned their own property – are among the most important cattle-breeding regions. This is the natural homeland of the black-patched Frisian-Holsteiner cows. Further to the south the fertile lowlands deteriorate into the desolate Lüneburg Heath, which affords scant opportunity for dairy farmers.

West Germany, in fact, has greatly contrasting landscapes. In the central German highlands, from the Rhineland across to the Bayrischer Wald, rivers run between beautiful hills, which are clad with vineyards and surmounted by castles – the fairyland of the brothers Grimm. Cheese, a traditional fairy food, is made here, although most farms have fewer cattle than those in the north.

Further to the southeast, the central plateau climbs up to the heights of Swabia and Bavaria, where Lake Constance – the Boden See – straddles the Swiss-German border. In the Allgäu Alps east of the Boden See, an area outstanding for cattle breeding and dairy production, the well-known cheese town of Kempten is found. The Allgäu is a truly Alpine landscape of dark pine forests, where the springtime meadows are carpeted with mountain flowers, and the herds of brown cattle are located by the flat, metallic ringing of the cow bells. The Allgäu has now

ABOVE: Drachenstein, a small village surrounded by woods and meadows, in the Baden-Württemburg region, the home of a fresh cheese called Topfen.

LEFT: The brown Allgäu cattle of southern Germany on their way to the fresh, alpine meadows.

superseded the north as a cheese-producing region.

Monasteries, merchants and cheesemakers

Homemade, nonrenneted cheeses were made by the northern Germans over a thousand years ago, and they probably bore close resemblance to the present Sauermilch cheese.

When people learned the skill of making good rennet, a more stable product was established, and cheese-making spread from Schleswig-Holstein all over East and West Prussia. In the castles of the Teutonic knights, founded by the Baltic Germans, cheeses were made: *Herrenkäse* for the nobility and lower quality *Gesindekäse* for the commoners. The village of Lieben-werder, a well-known trade and export center, was even renamed in 1341 as Käsemarkt ("cheese market"); about the same time the cooperative Holsteiner-Meierei system was established, whereby farmers communally processed their milk.

Even so, cheese production far from met home requirements, and in the centuries that followed, cheese was imported from Holland via Hamburg, Bremen and Emden. Northern German merchants visited the weekly markets of Amsterdam and other Dutch cities, while Rotterdam and Dordrecht supplied German provinces via the Rhine. Dutch Edam cheese, colored red since the thirteenth century, was so appreciated by the Germans that the foreign makers of other cheese types began coloring their cheeses red, to be sold as Edam.

Many of Germany's most popular cheese types are copies of, or variations of, foreign originals. The Allgäu has a centuries-old tradition of making *Emmental*, but the quality varied considerably, in spite of the efforts of one Josef Stadler, who in 1821 sent for two experts from Switzerland to try to control the fat content, temperature and ripening. Yet methods remained primitive: the cheese kettle still hung over the open fire; temperature was judged with the elbow; rennet was imperfect; and pressing was done with stones. Drastic improvements came about with the introduction of the *gärkellers* in the 1870s, places established to facilitate the ripening of cheese. The Allgäu Emmental is now a quality product.

LEFT: The massive, thatched roof of a typical farmhouse in the Black Forest, designed to bear the heavy winter snows.

Although Germany produces a great variety of cheeses, with a wide range of flavors, shapes and sizes, plus a remarkable number of fresh- and sour-milk types, there seems to be a particular affection for those pungent, strong cheeses which in some examples have the power to fell trees. It is not really known why these cheeses are so admired – perhaps it is the traditional love of the heroic; possibly Siegfried was raised on a diet of black bread, beer and Handkäse, those archetypal, hand-molded farmhouse cheeses whose modern descendants so readily betray their whereabouts.

Not content with the indigenous types, the Germans looked around for inspiration and finally borrowed, later to naturalize, Limburger and Romadur – the famous "stinking cheese" of Belgium – to which they added the lively Munster cheese from Alsace. The Belgians, at any rate, seem fairly unconcerned that their Limburger has moved several hundred miles downwind.

Another suggestion is that Germany's assertive cheeses compliment the national taste for highly flavored, gamey meats, such as boar, pheasant, hare and venison – or that a strong cheese needs to be washed down by copious draughts of German beer.

Emmental was not the only cheese to make the Allgäu a famous dairy region. From 1830 Karl Hirnbein, advised by the Belgian Herve cheese specialist Grosjean, manufactured

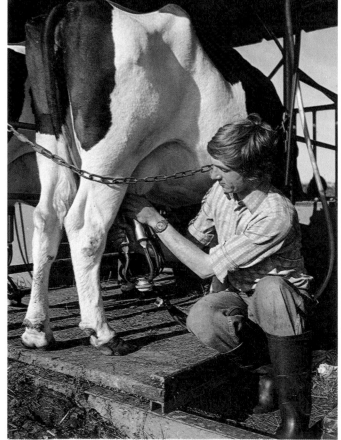

BELOW: Niedersachsen is one of Germany's most important cattle-raising and milk-producing areas; the Frisian-Holstein cattle are the most important breed. Here, the black-and-white cows are milked by machine.

soft Allgäu *Limburger* and *Romadur* cheese. Hirnbein's Limburger was such a success that it is now one of Germany's most important cheeses, in spite of a period of falling interest, which may have brought about a change in consistency – modern Limburger is more solid. There are loaf and block-shaped Limburgers of different weights. The required fat content and names of the cheeses are precisely specified: *Halbfettstufe* (20–30%), *Dreiviertelfettstufe* (30–40%), *Fettstufe* (40–45%), *Vollfettstufe* (45–50%) and *Rahmstufe* (above 50%). The Romadur cheese has an additional type, 60%, and finally there is a *Doppelrahmstufe* with a fat content up to 85%. The quantity of the dry matter is also regulated.

Limburger is difficult to make, because this piquant cheese with its reddish bacteria flora is extremely sensitive to both temperature and moisture degree in preparing and ripening. This original Belgian cheese has been almost wholly adopted by Germany, and is manufactured on a large scale. The dry salting by hand has now been replaced by the brine bath: 24 hours for the big Limburger cheeses, 7–12 hours for the small, and 2–4 hours for Romadur, according to fat content. During the first stages of ripening, the cheeses are placed close together; they are separated as soon as the flora appears. The cheeses are then given a mechanical wash with coryne bacteria, from four to eight and smooth, with a strong, spicy aroma. This cheese is like Romadur, becoming ripe after two or three weeks, and the longer it ripens the more pronounced is the goaty aroma. For the white type a similar quantity of goat's milk is used, between 60 and 70%, but after the brine bath the cheeses are dipped in a solution of whey and Camembert culture; it is ripe after eleven days, and then packed in foil. The cheese bears the white rind flora of Camembert, and has a lighter consistency than orange Gaiskäsle. It develops some holes, has a milder flavor, and a mushroom aroma which becomes more piquant and goaty as ripening progresses.

ABOVE: Both the farmer and his cow are of sturdy German stock – only the farming methods have changed.

ABOVE: A small Münster cheese, the German version of the original French cheese of the Vosges mountains.

times depending on the size of the cheese. To prevent the flora from being washed away, the wash is kept and used again.

After three or four weeks of ripening the cheeses should show a yellow-brown rindless surface, without cracks but with a somewhat sticky flora. They have a white to yellow-colored paste, which is crumbly, and a pliant, soft core. Consistency varies with the fat content – lower fat Limburgers are firmer, and in the fourth week of ripening the flavor changes from spicy to piquant; Romadur cheese is softer and milder, and is ripe after two weeks.

The *Frühstückkäse* ("breakfast cheese") is a small, round Limburger that ripens in its packing and can be eaten almost fresh, or only a little ripened. Also from the Allgäu is a variety of Limburger called *Weisslacker Bierkäse* – excellent with beer – with a white, waxy flora. Although a small cheese of only 60 g (2 oz), it has a prolonged brine bath of 2–3 days, and consequently is a slow ripener, taking some 5-6 months, but can be stored for over a year. The cheese is semihard with a very sharp, piquant flavor, reminiscent of bacon.

The *Allgäuer Gaiskäsle* is made in two types, the orange and the white. The former is prepared from a mixture of 60-80% raw goat's milk and 20-40% pasteurized cow's milk. It develops a thin, yellow to red-brown rind with a coryne flora; the paste is light yellow

ABOVE: Limburger is similar to the Belgian Herve cheese. It originates from around Liège, Belgium, but most is now made in Germany.

ABOVE: Karwendel is a soft cheese with a fat content of 50%. It is made in the Allgäu, an alpine region in southern Germany, and a great cheese area.

Other regions, other countries

Another German cheese of foreign ancestry, originating in the French Vosges, is *Münster*, with its soft to semihard paste and red rind flora. It sounds German enough anyway, for an umlaut has been added to the original name, Munster, to avoid any confusion. The cheese comes in weights of 125, 500, 600 or 1,000 g (5 oz to 2 lb 5 oz). It is fine, mild and close-textured, and has a white to yellow color, with a thin skin instead of a rind.

Weinkäse ("wine cheese") is named for its affinity with the fruity Rhine and Moselle wines. The cheese has a white to yellow color; a glossy, delicate paste; and develops a thin skin in the manner of the Münster. It is a flat, round little cheese weighing about 75 g (2.6 oz), with an orange surface flora and fat contents of 30, 40, 45 or 50%. *Butterkäse* has a yellow-brown or red rind, but sometimes develops no rind at all. It was once a soft cheese type, but it is now made slightly more firm – a good Butterkäse should be elastic and easy to cut. The flat round type weighs .5 to 1.5 kg (1.1 to 3.3 lbs), and the sausage-shaped variety weighs 2 kg (4.4 lbs). A similar cheese is *Schnittkäse*: the mild and somewhat sour-tasting paste should never be pappy, chalky or contain holes, faults that do occur with this type of cheese.

The well-known *Tilsit* cheese was first made by Dutchmen living in Tilsit, East Prussia (now Sovetsk, USSR). Today it is also made in West Germany, as is the less strong variant *Ansgar*. From the border region of the Marsch, behind the sea dikes of Schleswig-Holstein comes a cheese

that shares several characteristics with the Tilsit. This is the *Wilster Marschkäse*, a loaf-shaped, semihard cheese and one that is easy to cut, with irregular little holes and a light, somewhat sourish flavor; it is also a very quick ripener. The French cheese Port-du-Salut, first introduced by Trappist monks, is one of the most popular of all cheese types. Several countries make a version, and in Germany it is known simply as *Trappistenkäse,* made according to the French recipe either as a 1.5 kg (3.3 lbs) round, or 2.7 kg (5.9 lbs) loaf-shaped cheese, with a 45% fat content.

If you cannot identify a cheese by its appearance, you may confirm your suspicions merely by tasting it. No two comparable cheese types are exactly similar, even though they may share similar names. *Edelschimmelkäse* and *Edelpilzkäse* are names that can refer equally to blue-veined cheeses or to cheeses with a Camembert-like white rind flora, but their flavors are sharply distinctive. The latter cheese is made with pasteurized milk (mostly cow's milk, but sometimes mixed with ewe's milk) to which is added a starter and a culture of

ABOVE: View of a modern cheese factory in Waging. Curd from the cheese vats on the upper floor flows via the chute, which can turn a full circle, down to the filling apparatus on the lower floor. Here the molds are filled with cheese.

LEFT: Farmhouse Handkäse, a cheese molded by hand, here flavored with caraway seeds.

LEFT: Another type of Handkäse, the Mainzer Roller, with its typical round shape.

LEFT: The small Weinkäse ("wine cheese") goes well with a glass or two of Rhine or Moselle wine, hence the name.

Penicillium roqueforti – the cheese might have been called Roquefortkäse, but the name Roquefort was protected. The mold veins are evenly spread, and the texture of this fine cheese is smooth, with a slight tendency to crumble. The color is light yellow, the taste piquant to sharp, and the fat content usually higher than the required minimum of 45%. Also belonging to this group of cheeses is *St. Mauritius*, a small cylindrical-shaped cheese, mildly aromatic with a rind on which a combination of white and red mold can develop. In its unripe stage it is white to cream-yellow with a porous texture, becoming smoother as it ripens and reddening towards the rind.

Three very popular German cheeses are: the *Caramkäse*, shaped either as a sausage, or in blocks of 1 to 2 kg (2.2 to 4.4 lbs), with a smooth rind enclosing a supple, close-textured paste, more aromatic in the smoked version; the bar-shaped *Tapi* cheese, with its butter-yellow color, elastic consistency and fresh, sour taste; and the mild, though slightly more piquant *Parmesello*, a hard, low-fat cartwheel, used for grating.

Fresh, unripened cheeses are of prime importance in the German cheese range. Fresh cheese – in German, *Frischkäse* – is subdivided into the following main types: *Speisequark, Rahmfrischkäse, Doppelrahmfrischkäse* and *Schichtkäse*, according to the cream or fat content. Regional names for Frischkäse tend to vary, however, so that in the Allgäu it's *Zieger*, but in Niederhein it's called *Klatschkäs*, while in Württemberg and Matte in central Germany, it's either *Topfen* or *Luckeleskäs*. Frischkäse must be made from pasteurized milk, or in special cases from a high-quality, soluble milk powder.

The preparation of Frischkäse requires more starter than other cheeses, also less rennet, a low curdling temperature and a longer curdling time. Sometimes herbs or spices are worked in. All varieties have an even, soft consistency, no rind and a fresh, light, sour taste. As most are very soft they are packed in plastic cups or tubs. Their color varies from milk-white to cream-yellow, depending on the fat content: less than 10 % (*Mager*), 10-20 % (*Viertelfett*), 20-30 % (*Halbfett*), 30-40 % (*Dreiviertelfett*), 40-45 % (*Fett*), 45-50 % (*Vollfett*), 50-60 % (*Rahm*) and 60-85 % (*Doppelrahm*).

Cream cheese sandwich

Low-fat curd cheese is known as Quark, the fat having been removed by skimming. When a certain quantity of the skimmed fat is replaced and mixed with the lean curd, the cheese takes the name *Speisequark*. Cheese factories skim their milk with a centrifuge, which can handle large quantities, and produces a better-quality product. The soured warm or cold milk is thickened, and then enriched by adding the calculated amount of cream; low fat Speisequark is very popular with dieters. Popular too is Quark mixed with fruit pulp, a thinner, moister product because of the fruit, which constitutes 19-22 % of the bulk. *Labquark* or *Labfrischkäse* is prepared by using mainly rennet (*Lab*) for curdling; sometimes the curd is lightly pressed. It is white and somewhat crumbly, with a neutral flavor. As we shall see, Labquark is sometimes used in making Sauermilchkäse.

Rahmfrischkäse is made by adding cream to Speisequark until the desired fat content is reached. The mixture is

ABOVE: A landscape characteristic of Holland; a polder mill in the dairy country of Schleswig-Holstein.

ABOVE: The "Shepherd's Dance" maintains the rural, rustic traditions, and is held every year in the medieval town of Rothenburg.

not completely homogeneous since the curd is pressed before the cream is added (thus the fat is not blended with the whey), and the cheese has a creamier taste. The disadvantage, however, is that fat is more exposed to air due to the incomplete casein enclosure, and the flavor is therefore inconsistent. Rahmfrischkäse is sold in foil-wrapped cubes of 50 or 62.5 g (1.8 or 2.2 oz), in wooden boxes of six.

Schichtkäse is made in layers. It was formerly made by putting a layer of lean Frischkäse into the cheese mold and adding, half an hour later, a layer of fat Rahmfrischkäse, and after a while a top layer of Frischkäse. Today all layers have an identical fat content. After 24 hours in the mold, the Schichtkäse possesses a firm, smooth texture with very few holes and a fresh, sour taste. It comes in packs of 250 and 500 g (9 oz and 1 lb 2 oz). *Fromgap* is a flat, round, fresh product weighing 160–190 g (5-6 oz). It is a white to cream-yellow cheese, sometimes spiced, and is spreadable and freshly aromatic.

Sauermilchkäse

Sauermilchkäse deserves a special place. As *Handkäse* (hand-made cheese), it has been prepared for centuries on farms dotted all over the German countryside. There are still many *Sauermilchkäsereien* in central Germany, Niedersachsen and Hessen. The raw material is *Sauermilchquark*, which unlike Speisequark uses only a starter and no rennet. In the past, the skimmed milk was allowed to sour spontaneously, but today the milk is pasteurized and a culture of lactic acid bacteria is added. Sometimes the mass is lightly pressed and then vacuum packed or deep frozen – in the past it was stamped firmly into barrels for storage and transport.

Home-made Sauermilchquark used to be called *Zieger* (it still is in the Allgäu), which included a ripened version, but the name now applies to albumen cheese. Heating whey causes the albumen protein contained therein to coagulate, producing a type of curd that can be mixed with milk. The protein in Sauermilchquark, as in most cheeses, is casein, while the protein of Zieger is entirely albumen unless, of course, milk is added.

Sauermilchkäse, prepared from ordinary Sauermilchquark, and occasionally in combination with

Labquark, was first made in the late eighteenth century by a Swiss family living in the Harz mountains. A century later production was taken up by factories around Hildesheim and Mainz, and improved by the invention of grinding and molding machines. Two types of Sauermilchkäse were developed, both with a surface flora; the varieties of these cheeses depended on color or shape, or both. In Mainz they made *Gelbschmierekäse* or *Rotschmierekäse*, and their variations were *Harzer, Mainzer, Handkäse, Korbkäse, Spitzkäse* and *Strangenkäse*. They came flat and round, or in a bar or cube. The surface of these cheeses varies from yellow-gold to reddish-brown. The surface is moist; the paste smooth and close-textured; the taste piquant to sharp; and some varieties contain spices.

The names Hand-, Korb, Spitz and Strangen also prefix the second type of Sauermilchkäse, the *Schimmelkäse*, made in the Harz and other mountain areas. These are treated with *Penicillium camemberti* or *Penicillium candidum* according to region. The cheese itself is light yellow in color, the mold either blue-gray or white, depending on the culture used. The paste is smooth and firm, and has a mild, aromatic taste. Rich in protein and low in fat, it is a good diet cheese.

Buttermilk, skimmed-milk and beestings cheeses
Buttermilchquark belongs to the

ABOVE: A farming custom shared with the Swiss: cattle are garlanded with flowers when they move from the valleys to the upland pastures in the spring.

LEFT: A chef makes the sandwiches – with cheese as an indispensable ingredient – for an appetizing *Brotzeit*.

Frischkäse group. Usually made from a mixture of (sour) buttermilk and skimmed milk, it curdles at 38°C (101°F) without rennet. Although production is small, it provides a means of using up the superfluous buttermilk.

The farmers of Paderborn and Nieheim in the Westfalen area make a cheese according to an old recipe, leaving the skimmed milk to thicken spontaneously. They then warm it, drain off the whey and lightly press the curd. The cheese is left to ripen in wooden vats, after which salt and kummel are added by kneading. The cheeses are hand-shaped and stored in boxes lined with hop leaves, which transmit their special flavor. This *Nieheimer Hopfenkäse* is so dry that it must be grated. The cheese is also made in factories, the Sauermilchquark being obtained from suppliers. This factory cheese is ground, preripened, mixed with salt and kummel, molded mechanically and packed – alas, not always with hop leaves – in boxes of 1.5-2 kg (3.3-4.4 lbs). It dries much quicker and is less hard than the farmhouse cheese.

Biestkäse, or *Kolostrumkäse*, hardly rates as a cheese. Beestings is the name given to the first milk obtained from a cow after calving. It has a quite different composition from ordinary milk, being more viscous, saltier and darker in color, and it solidifies when heated to 60°C (140°F); moreover, the albumen and globin content is con-

LEFT: A display of German fresh cheeses of the Quark type.

with salt, pepper, chopped chives and chopped onion; or with hot, boiled potatoes in their skins, an appetizing delicacy. Fresh cheese is also very good with fruit, jelly or syrup. Quark comes into its own in main courses like Quark Haluschka (creamy macaroni, Quark and baked bacon), or in the form of Quarkschnitten (slices of Quark baked in fritter batter), Quarkkartoffeln, Quarkknödel and Quarkpfannkuchen. Rightly famous is the German Quark pastry, from the simple Quarkapfelkuchen (apple pie and Quark) via the refined Quark-auflauf (Quark soufflé) to the delicious Quarksahnetorte (Quark and cream tart).

The amount of Quark eaten by the Germans is enormous. The nation's annual per capita cheese consumption averages more than 11 kg (24.2 lbs), 5 kg (11 lbs) of which is Quark, and the latest figures show an increase. Soon it may be Quark *über alles*!

The German daily schedule allows the people plenty of opportunity to enjoy their vast range of cheeses. In common with the breakfasts of the Low Countries, *Frühstück* might include a selection of cheeses and cold meats, and this meal is followed several hours later by *Zweites Frühstück*, the second breakfast which can be either a hearty repast or merely a couple of cheese sandwiches.

Cheese could well complete the lunchtime *Mittagessen*, and will almost certainly make its appearance at the end of the day when *Abendbrot* is served. It is even possible for the dedicated cheese lover to squeeze in a slice or two during *Kaffee*, the afternoon break when people go to the *Konditorei* for coffee and cakes.

siderably higher. In farm kitchens a kind of porridge is made by warming the beestings and stirring until it thickens. In the Allgäu it is often salted and placed in the oven in a wide plate until the heat causes the milk fat to rise to the surface.

All Frischkäse varieties attract microorganisms and are sensitive to heat, light, dust and other influences. For this reason, severe quality regulations exist in Germany, and cool storage and fast, refrigerated transport is essential.

Cheese in German cookery

Cheese occupies a very important place in German homes. In the big cities, food shops offer a wide variety. The delicatessen store of Dallmayer in Munich, for example, with its marble pillars and fountains, has a display of 130 different types of sausage – and 180 varieties of cheese! Cheese is not only eaten on brown bread or on pumpernickel, but often accompanies ham in veal cutlets (schnitzel): super-schnitzels are filled with ham and cheese and covered with bacon or ragout. All German fresh cheese varieties are extremely popular mixed

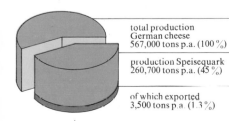

total production German cheese 567,000 tons p.a. (100%)

production Speisequark 260,700 tons p.a. (45%)

of which exported 3,500 tons p.a. (1.3%)

Name	Milk	Type	Rind	Form	Weight	% Fat content
Allgäuer Gaiskäsle	⌂ 🅰 ●	❖ ❖	flat disc, cube	62.5-125 g	50
Butterkäse	⌂ ■	❖			
Caramkäse	⌂ ■	□	flat disc, bar	½-2 kg	45-60
Frischkäse	⌂ ○		bar, loaf	½-2 kg	45
(includes Speisequark			container	62.5-500 g	1-85
Rahmfrischkäse Doppelrahmfrischkäse Schichtkäse)					
Limburger	⌂ ■	❖	cube, loaf	180-1000 g	20-50
Münster	⌂ ●	❖	flat disc	125-1000 g	45-50
Nieheimer Hopfenkäse	⌂ ■	—	ball	115 g	40
Romadur	⌂ ●	❖	loaf	80-180 g	20-60
St. Mauritius	⌂ ●	❖	bar	125 g	30
Sauermilchkäse	⌂ ■	❖	varying	100-250 g	1½-10
(includes Gelbschmierekäse Rotschmierekäse Harzer Mainzer Handkäse Korbkäse Spitzkäse Stangenkäse)					
Tilsiter	⌂ ■	❖	cartwheel	1.5-20 kg	30-50
Trappistenkäse	⌂ ■	❖	low cylinder, loaf	1.5-2.7 kg	45
Weinkäse	⌂ ●	❖	flat disc	75 g	30-50
Weisslacker Bierkäse	⌂ ■	❖	cube	60 g	40
Wilster Marschkäse	⌂ ■	❖	loaf	6 kg	45-50

Key to symbols on page 6. 1 kg = 2.2 lbs.

Switzerland

There is an almost unique, fresh, invigorating atmosphere in the Swiss landscape, an appealing, rural, well-ordered neatness, too, that makes so much of the country memorable to the visitor. For a large proportion of the population, however, Switzerland is a modern, forward-looking, industrial nation. Nevertheless, it is also a country of romantic and picturesque views. In some areas there are castles, monasteries and medieval towns. Rivers flow gently through beautiful valleys, but in the mountains they tumble wildly through deep ravines and form countless waterfalls.

The landscape is overpowered by the Alps. The contorted, double-folded and pleated rocks have fractured, exposing their old crystalline cores. Above the forests and grasslands tower the mostly white-shrouded, massive peaks, sometimes sharply etched against the vivid blue sky, other times hidden in clouds or wreathed in mist. It is usually with astonishment that the visitor finds palm trees, camelias and orange groves growing in a mild climate on the protected southern slopes.

But then Switzerland has over 40,000 square kilometers (14,400 square miles) of varying contrasts. It isn't all Edelweiss, cuckoo clocks, cheese, clinical counting houses and flourishing winter sport centers for tourists. There exist many intimate, secluded mountain villages, where strangers are never seen. Whereas the large cities developed into focal points of industry, commerce and international diplomacy, the inhabitants of those isolated valleys remained faithful to their age-old manners and colorful regional dress. On the mountain slopes people work for their bread and cheese with a persistence and ingenuity which helped to make their country one of the richest in the world.

The Swiss Confederation consists of twenty-two independent cantons, and has a republican and federal constitution. Each canton is ruled by its inhabitants according to their needs and circumstances, and most people speak at least two languages. The traditional Swiss neutrality does not mean that the country keeps itself apart from world events. Proof to the contrary is that a modified version of its flag has become the symbol of the Red Cross, a symbol of altruism and

ABOVE: For centuries these alpine pastures have supported the fine dairy herds responsible for some of the world's great cheeses.

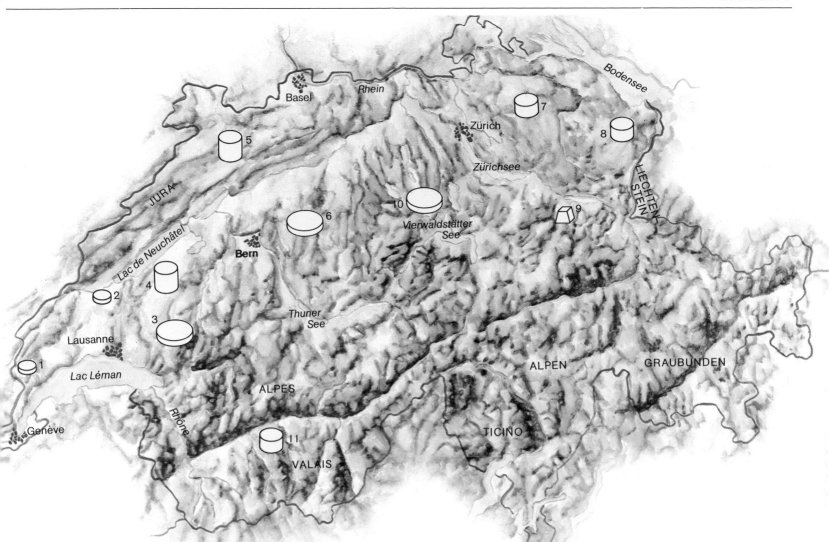

Appenzell 8
Emmental 6
Glarner Schabzieger 9
Gruyère 3
Raclette cheeses 11
Royalp 7

Sbrinz 10
Tête de Moine 5
Tomme Vaudoise 2
Vacherin
  Fribourgeois 4
Vacherin Mont d'Or 1

BELOW: Herding cattle at the end of summer from the mountain pastures to the valleys – and vice-versa in the spring – is an occasion that demands traditional costume for the herdsmen and garlands for the cattle. A scene near Appenzell, south of Lake Constance.

RIGHT: That cheese is an important part of Swiss life and culture is evident from this postage stamp, showing milk being poured into the cheese vats.

humanitarian ideals.

From a military point of view, Switzerland has gigantic, natural lines of defense which have always dissuaded conquerors, but since early history a lively trade route developed through the difficult mountain passes. Even the Romans knew where to find the entrance gates, and they were the first to discover the Alps as a holiday resort. Additionally, they were in search of Helvetian cheese, which at that time was already renowned for its fine quality – the Romans were cheese connoisseurs par excellence.

Switzerland gradually improved its reputation and eventually perfected some of the world's great cheeses – as we shall see. To most Swiss farmers, dairy culture is more important than agriculture. They raise first-grade cattle, and maintain their traditions of craftsmanship and expertise; each

individual district has its own cheese specialities. The success of Swiss cheese has produced a host of foreign imitations; many such copies, however, bear little resemblance to the true product. No wonder that the Swiss are careful to guard their reputation: genuine Swiss cheeses carry the name "Switzerland" in addition to the cheese type. Thus the name "Emmental Switzerland" is the guarantee of origin to look for.

BELOW: Two famous cheeses – Gruyère and Emmental. The Gruyère above has hardly any holes, and is smaller than the "big wheel" Emmental, with its many large holes. The red stamp "Switzerland" is a guarantee of authenticity.

This famous Swiss cheese owes its name to the Emmental valley in the canton of Bern. Cheese has been made here for hundreds of years by the Sennen, cowherds who stayed the entire summer in the high alpine meadows, using their remote mountain huts as dairies. These men were excellent cattle breeders, who milked and tended their cattle; the cheeses they made had good keeping properties. Loading their cheeses on donkeys, they traveled to the markets in the valleys, and even to Basel and Strasbourg to sell these cheeses to the public. They purchased the best meadows and doubtless owned the finest cattle. In those days their cheeses did not have the enormous dimensions of today's Emmental, "the king of cheese." A cheese then weighed a modest 4 to 12 kg (8.8 to 26.4 lbs). Only in the sixteenth century did the Sennen discover how to make larger cheeses which could be kept even longer.

With the expansion of the cities, and the improvement of roads and other means of transport, the demand grew for a cheese that could travel well. The St. Gotthard Pass, constructed in the thirteenth century, had opened up Italy as a market. But it was mainly during the Thirty Years' War in Germany, during the first half of the seventeenth century, that Swiss cheese production grew rapidly. Emmental cheeses were transported in Rhine barges to Rotterdam in Holland, and other ports, where they were sold for ships' stores.

The resources of the Sennen were unable to cope with the increased demand for their cheese, and increasing their herds meant finding bigger pastures. Accordingly, they began to produce cheese on the *Gemeinalpen*, communal meadowland which was more or less in public ownership. Communities that owned these meadows, as well as private land-owners, hired cheesemakers to tend the cows and sell the cheese which they had made with their own equipment.

New ideas and experiments in dairy farming during the eighteenth century uprooted the conviction that good cheese could only be made high on the alpine meadows. The first small cheese dairies were soon established in the valleys, using milk from cows that were sometimes stabled throughout

LEFT: No other country can make a Gruyère or Emmental with the skill of the Swiss; traditional craftsmanship can't be copied. The picture shows Emmental curd being drained of whey in a cheese cloth.

ABOVE: The curd is placed in the press. After pressing, drying and maturing, a fine cheese of about 100 kg (220 lbs), with a diameter of about 1 meter (3.3 feet) is produced.

the year. These were fed on a balanced diet of hay, clover and concentrated food.

The number of village dairies rose dramatically when it became apparent that no dealer could distinguish the difference between alpine and valley cheese. Practically every village has now got its own small cheese dairy, where the master cheesemaker, assisted by two or three workers, makes three or four Emmental cheeses a day. Genuine Swiss Emmental is produced far beyond the original boundaries of the Bern canton, and a weekly output of about two dozen cheeses per dairy is the national average. Three cheeses a day might not seem much of an output until you consider the fact that an Emmental is by no means a small cheese. An Emmental weighing 80 kg (176 lbs) will require 1,000 liters (1,100 quarts) of milk, the yield of some eighty cows. As the average farm has only ten to fifteen head of cattle, milk must be brought in twice daily from several farms.

Careful steps to a great cheese
Emmental cheese is one of the few cheeses to be made from raw milk only, and as the risk of defects in the cheese is great, considerable skill is required in its manufacturing. The traditional preparation methods have been officially proclaimed, and the observance of the regulations is closely supervised. Not only could mistakes

RIGHT: A Senn from Rosenlauital in the Bernese Oberland cleans the milking utensils in front of her farmhouse. Note the collection of cowbells above the door.

A. Genuine Swiss Emmental is produced in relatively small village dairies. The atmosphere is quite different from the large, automated, stainless steel production lines seen else-where. Fresh raw milk is brought in each morning from the surrounding farms.

B. The milk is heated to approximately 33°C (91°F), starter and rennet are added, and the milk curdles in 30 minutes. The cheesemaker cuts the curd, the watery whey separates and finally the curd particles are the size of grains.

C. The curd is after-heated or "cooked": it is brought to 53°C (127°F) in 30 minutes' time and stirred for 45 minutes. This makes the curd drier and more solid. When it is judged ready by the cheesemaker, he lifts the curd from the whey.

D. In order to do this, he passes a cheese cloth, fixed to a flex-ible frame, under the curd mass in the cheese vat. He re-moves the frame, and with a helper he ties the cloth into a knot. All the curd is in the cloth, most of the whey remains in the vat.

E. As the mass is hoisted out, more whey leaks away.

F. The mass is lowered into the wooden mold, still in its cloth, and pressed.

G. During the day, the young cheese is turned at regular intervals. Pressure is gradually increased. In the evening it is quite dry and drained of whey.

H. The great wheels are sprinkled with dry salt, and then floated in a brine bath for one to two days.

J. After the salt bath, the cheeses rest in a cool cellar.

K. In the warm and humid ripening rooms the Emmental de-velops its unique properties. This is where it gets its holes, due to gas formation in the cheese paste, and here the aroma and flavor develop.

occur with the feeding of the cows, the condition of the stable, the milking and quality of the milk, but also in the preparation of rennet or the cheesemaking itself. Moreover, the ripening process in the warm curing room must proceed in a regular fashion, for it is here, and here only, that previous mistakes are revealed, and the whole cheese might have to be thrown away.

A well-made Emmental reaches perfection in the curing room. Under the influence of the correct bacteria cultures, the cheese acquires its sweet-dry flavor, its hazelnut aroma and its shining, cherry-sized holes, caused by the carbonic acid gas which cannot escape from the paste. The rind of Emmental is dry and hard, and colored from golden-yellow to brown. Once or twice a week the cheeses are turned and rubbed with a moist cloth. Turning is now done mainly by machine, but in the old days the cheesemaker had to turn the heavy-weight cheeses by hand.

An officially-approved Emmental bears the legend "Switzerland" plus an indication of the fat content. Exported cheese must have the stamp "Switzerland" printed in red, and radiating out from the center like the spokes of a wheel. After a ripening period of four to five months the taste is still mild, and it takes seven to ten months of maturing before the flavor becomes more pronounced, when a "tear" (a drop of brine) might be spotted in the eyes. Emmental is a perfect cheese for sandwiches, hardened as it is by after-heating during its preparation, and it is also as such excellent for cutting and grating. In hot dishes it is inclined to draw threads, but in rice dishes or in savory pastry it is unsurpassed.

ABOVE: Along the Alpine chain, huge glaciers and moraines spill into the valleys, and from the water-shed countless rivers are formed carrying pure mountain water to the lowland pastures; such natural gifts are important factors in the making of fine Swiss cheese.

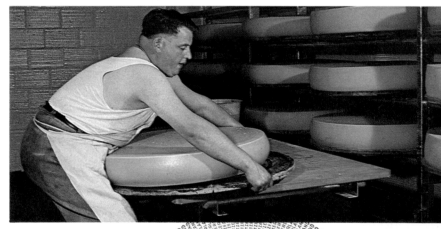

LEFT: The heavy Emmental cheeses must be turned from time to time in the storage cellars, a task requiring strength and long practice – and a diet that includes cheese.

RIGHT: Guarantees of origin protect the product, and the customer, from the many imitations that fail to match the unique character of Swiss cheese.

ABOVE: The export stamp, in red, is printed on the rind of the cheese with this franking machine.

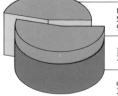

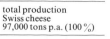

total production Swiss cheese 97,000 tons p.a. (100%)

production Emmental 51,100 tons p.a. (55%)

of which exported 37,600 tons p.a. (73%)

Gruyère, or *Greyerzer*, cheese is the smaller, but equally famous relative of Emmental; it shares with Emmental the red "Switzerland" stamp on the rind, and, in addition, bears an alpenhorn symbol. Gruyère cheese originated in the region of Gruyère, in the canton of Fribourg, where the Swiss black-and-white cattle are found. In 1115, the first Count of Gruyère founded the Abbey of Rougemont and levied a church tax which included payment in cheese from the region. Five centuries later the same type of cheese could be found in the market in Turin, Italy, where it was transported by road, and in the French city of Lyon, which could be reached from Switzerland via the Rhone. Today Gruyère is made in the entire western, French-speaking part of Switzerland.

The weight of a Gruyère cheese varies from 30 to 40 kg (66 to 88 lbs), half that of the average Emmental; it is also ripened differently – in cooler and more humid rooms, causing practically no gas formation to occur. This is apparent from the miniscule cracks when the cheese is cut; only a few small holes occur, none larger than a pea. During the curing period the rind is kept moist, and a red-brown rind deposit forms, giving the cheese its distinguished flavor. To bring the cheese to full maturity requires a curing period of at least ten to twelve months. Five-month-old Gruyère is also marketed, but it is much milder and still elastic in consistency.

The classic fondue
The paste of a well-ripened Gruyère cheese is moister than that of Emmental. When heated it hardly draws any threads, and is therefore excellent for use in hot dishes. When

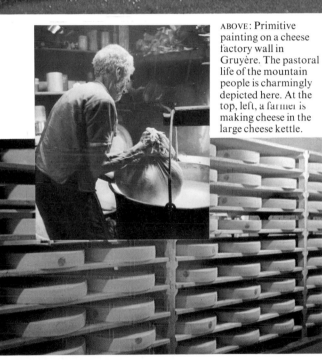

ABOVE: Primitive painting on a cheese factory wall in Gruyère. The pastoral life of the mountain people is charmingly depicted here. At the top, left, a farmer is making cheese in the large cheese kettle.

TOP LEFT: Cheese-making in a *Sennhütte* high on the Hinter-fallenalp in the Toggenburg in northeastern Switzerland. The Senn has knotted a cloth around the curd and is lifting it out of the whey, which remains behind in the kettle.

LEFT: A bank of Gruyère cheeses in the maturing room.

BELOW LEFT: The old town of Gruyère that gave its name to the cheese. It used to be the capital of the Gruyère region in the canton of Fribourg. A great deal of chocolate, as well as cheese, is made in this area.

grated and cooked as a topping it gives a beautiful, even, and not too dry crust. The matured variety, which melts easily, is especially suitable for cheese fondue. Fondue, like the Dutch Kaasdoop, was originally a dish of expedience and utility, employing scraps of cheese and stale bread. It eventually acquired sophistication, with wine, kirsch and garlic being added to the melted cheese mixture. It came from the mountains via the cities, and has been adopted by the rest of the world. The Swiss make it with a combination of Gruyère and Emmental, in a ratio which depends on individual taste – Gruyère is more highly flavored, Emmental blander. A true fondue should only be made with Swiss or French Emmental and Gruyère. Cheeses of a lesser quality, or those not easily adaptable to heating, are likely to produce a stringy, sharp-tasting gluc. In fact, many people who have never tasted the real thing have been misled by poor imitations. (See the recipe section of this book.) Fondue may be served with dry white wine, but most Swiss prefer tea, or a sip of kirsch now and then.

The relative hardness of Emmental or Gruyère depends largely on the after-heating of the curd, a process that usually leads to a cheese's being called a "cooked cheese," which is a rather misleading term. *Sbrinz* is Switzerland's third variety of hard cheese, where the finely cut curd is heated to an even higher temperature than Emmental or Gruyère. It is made in the center of Switzerland, where a sturdy race of brown cows graze the high mountain pastures. The cylindrical cheeses weigh from 25 to 40 kg (55 to 88 lbs), and during the fifteenth century were being exported via the St. Gotthard Pass to the south – a considerable proportion of the production still goes to Italy.

The curing period of Sbrinz cheeses is impressively long. After their brine bath they go to an *Abschwitzraum* ("sweating room"), where the temperature is 20°C (68°F). Here they sweat fat and water, and the rind is regularly wiped. After a minimum of four months, the cheeses are placed upright in racks, so that air can circulate around them: they must then mature for eighteen months to two years.

The long curing period makes Sbrinz a very aromatic and full-flavored cheese and, owing to the decomposition of the casein, one that is easy to digest. Another Sbrinz variety is sold as *Spalen*, or *Spalenschnittkäse*, named after the vats in which they used to be packed. It also goes under the name *Innerschweizer*.

A good judge of cheese
The Swiss enjoy the hard, sharp-tasting Sbrinz in many ways. Not cut, but broken off and crumbled on freshly-buttered bread, it is considered a delicacy. It lends itself well to grating, draws no threads when heated, and is excellent for use in soups, sauces and cooked dishes such as cheese soufflé, where one-third of Sbrinz may be substituted for Emmental or Gruyère. Despite the hardness of the cheese, Sbrinz, when cut into thin slices with a cheese or cucumber slicer, melts on the tongue. It is thus sold in delicatessen shops in Saanenland under the name of *Hobelkäse*.

The rigorous inspection accorded to Emmental and Gruyère is also granted to Sbrinz. Farmers, cheesemakers and dealers have formed their own organization, the Schweizerische

ABOVE: Sbrinz cheese, ancestor of Gruyère and Emmental, is a hard, well-matured cheese that is cut into fine slices with a sharp slicer. Thus prepared, it is sold in delicatessens as Hobelkäse. Sbrinz cheeses are here being prepared in Saanenland.

ABOVE: Even the smallest rural villages contribute to Switzerland's dairy industry. The terrain of the country is better suited to cattle than to crops.

Käseunion, which controls the entire production of Emmental, Gruyère and Sbrinz and supervises the marketing both at home and abroad. Experts assess the cheeses for their consistency, color, aroma, taste and appearance, and points are awarded. A high award provides an extra premium to farmers as well as cheesemakers.

Cheese folklore
Food plays an important part in the symbolism of folklore, and cheese in particular. In Valais and the Bernese Oberland, the dead used to be buried with bread and cheese to nourish them in the long journey to wherever they were bound. In some districts, the Sennen still distribute cheese among the poor. An ancient custom that is still observed is the procession to and from the high alpine meadows in the spring and autumn seasons. One of the Sennen heads the procession, dressed in his most colorful costume, accompanying the *Meisterkuh* or *Herrkuh*, the "master cow," who carries a milking stool between its garlanded horns. In Valais and Graubünden everybody eagerly awaits the annual cow fight, a very innocent and simple version compared to the Spanish spectacular; here the cows merely try to push each other over, and the winner is given the title *la reine*, "the queen," or *vacca pugnèra*, "fighting cow."

LEFT: This brightly
painted cask, an
example of Swiss folk
art, bears a picture of
the traditional festive

homecoming of the
herdsmen and cows
from the high Alpine
meadows before the
approach of winter.

In addition to its hard cheeses, Switzerland has many semihard varieties with a higher moisture content; they ripen earlier and do not keep as long. Appenzell cheese derives its name from the East Swiss canton of Appenzell where it was originally made, but today it is also manufactured in the cantons of St. Gallen, Thurgau and Zürich. In the Middle Ages, the cheese was so popular, especially in neighboring countries, that there was an ever-increasing shortage on the home market. This was why, from 1571 onwards, the cheese merchants were only allowed to export butter and cheese that exceeded the cantons' requirements.

Soon after preparation, the cheeses are delivered to the cheese merchants, who attend to their ripening, a process that varies from three to six months. In the beginning they are turned daily, then twice weekly, and washed in a mixture of water, white wine, salt, pepper and herbs. The correct composition of this mixture used to be kept secret, but today the cheesemakers exchange recipes and information.

Washing is an important factor in the development of the particular

LEFT: Cheese scraped from the melted surface of a cheese set before an open fire and piled on a plate, is a national Swiss favorite called *raclette*.

BELOW: *Käseteilet* in the Justistal, in the Bernese Oberland. The cheeses made and stored in the mountain huts during the summer are solemnly divided among the cattle owners.

flavor and aroma of Appenzell cheese. A good sized piece of well-ripened Appenzell lends a cheese fondue a full-flavored, very fine aftertaste.

An Appenzell speciality is *Rasskäse* ("sharp cheese"), which is washed the same way, but which has a much lower fat content; it is pale in color with a pungent flavor.

The specialities of Valais

Where the river Rhône flows through the canton of Valais on its way to Lake Geneva you will find the semihard cheeses such as *Gomser*, *Bagnes* and *Orsières*, usually referred to by the collective name of *Raclette* cheeses. *Racler* is a French word meaning "to scrape," and in the region of origin Raclette cheese is used in the preparation of a very popular melted-cheese dish. The cut surface of the cheese is melted before an open fire, or an electric element, and scraped onto a plate, where it is joined by potatoes baked in their jackets, onions and gherkins. The dish takes the name of the cheese, and to be suitable for *raclette*, the cheese must melt evenly and easily, must have a fruity but not too dominating flavor, and must be creamy but not too chewy when served.

As with fondue, raclette should be served with either tea or kirsch, and never with wine, although for the non-Swiss this is, of course, a matter of personal taste.

The remarkably spicy yet not overpowering taste of Raclette cheese is due to the special quality of the milk from the alpine meadows of Valais. The cheesemakers in this region still use raw milk, mostly from Eringer cattle, a breed which varies from red to dark brown in color, or sometimes a splendid black. Because the canton is unable to meet the total demand for such milk, Swiss cheesemakers in other localities have started to produce Raclette cheese using a standardized, usually pasteurized, milk of a specific fat content.

A Raclette cheese, with its reddish rind and weight of 5 to 7 kg (11 to 15.4 lbs), is considered ripe after four to six months. Cheeses of seven months' maturity are preferred by some connoisseurs because of the more mature taste and the greater ease of melting.

BELOW: Derelict *Sennhütten* built in 1607. The buildings were used as primitive alpine dairies.

Less renowned than the great Swiss cheeses, but nationally as popular, are those known as *Bergkäse* ("mountain cheese"), which often have individual names, such as *Justistal, Brienzer Mutschli* or *Nidwaldner Bratkäse*. Despite the arrival of small dairies in the valleys, cheesemaking is still an alpine speciality in the high *Sennhütten*, and the cheeses are usually transported to a nearby village, and left in a *Salzer* or *Gäumer* – places where they may ripen. Nearly every small alpine meadow has its own special cheese. They are usually of a hard type with few holes and washed rinds, and are eaten in the region of production. Of exclusive local importance are the small, cylindrical goat's milk cheeses with rind molds, such as *Formaggini* or *Agrini* from Ticino, the canton whose southernmost point touches Como, Italy. These are made in some areas from milk given by goats who graze the sparsely vegetated, rough mountain slopes.

Poor Folk's Cheese

Green cheese, called *Glarner Schabzieger* or *Sapsago*, is a semihard, fatless cheese made from cow's skimmed milk, and not from goat's milk as is sometimes suggested. Lactic acid is added to the milk, which is then heated to nearly boiling point to coagulate both the casein and albumen, and then ripened under pressure at 20°C (68°F). This causes milk and butter acid fermentation; the lactic acid is a preserving agent. The cheese's green color is due to the addition of a herbal mixture, which includes a clover variety grown exclusively for this cheese. Schabzieger has been made in the canton of Glarus for over a thousand years, first by monks, who used the cheese as food for the monastery community, and also as a medicine for stomach ailments, although the monks' cheese did not contain herbs.

Today the herbs are added after the cheese has ripened for a few weeks, at which point it is ground finely and mixed with the herbs before being pressed into the shape of small cones (*Stöckli*) and sold, or dried. The dried variety, which can be kept almost indefinitely, is finally rubbed to a fine powder and packed in small cartons, each equipped with a sprinkler lid. As the taste of the cheese is so spicy and

BELOW: A consignment of milk arrives at a cheese factory. The milk is weighed immediately on arrival, before being processed. Other particulars regarding the milk, origin, type and quality are carefully noted.

strong, only a little is needed to flavor a slice of bread, which is why it has been called the "poor folk's cheese." Mixed with butter or cream, Schabzieger is eaten on toast, or added to salads, soups and various other dishes. Owing to its low fat and high protein content, it can be highly useful in a restricted fat diet.

A slice of monk's head

Tête de Moine or *Bellelay* cheese used to be made by monks at the Abbey of Bellelay, near Moutier in the Bernese Jura, but was later produced by the local farmers and delivered to the abbey as a church tax. It is made with rich milk from the summer meadows, ripened from three to five months, and marketed from September to March as a winter speciality. The cheese has an exceptionally delicate flavor and taste; it is smooth and creamy, cylindrical in

LEFT: *In memoriam.* Here in Mals in the principality of Liechtenstein, and in certain other places, it is the custom to nail these wooden symbols to the stable when the *Herrkuh,* the leader of the herd, dies. This series of plaques represents quite a few generations.

RIGHT: Symbolism again, in the form of ancient cheese stamps. They were designed as personal insignia by the Sennen and cheese merchants to identify origin or ownership of cheeses.

shape, and weighs 1 or 2 kg (2.2 or 4.4 lbs).

The name "monk's head" originates from its appearance when it reaches the table. It is preferably served whole, and cut by slicing across the top; this top piece is usually replaced as a lid and gives the cheese a patch, rather like a monk's tonsure. The Tête de Moine may also be cut crosswise, in two halves. Experts, after having cut away the edge a few centimeters from the top, will preferably pare the cheese with a knife, and eat the piece on bread sprinkled with pepper and cumin. A fresh white wine should be served with it – the same wine that is used for wetting the cloth in which the remaining cheese is stored.

The Vacherin cheeses

The west of Switzerland produces two types of Vacherin cheese of which the first, *Vacherin Fribourgeois*, has two varieties: *Vacherin à la Main* and *Vacherin à Fondue*. Vacherin Fribourgeois can be traced back in official accounts of banquets held in Fribourg during the fifteenth century. The rind of these cheeses is a brownish yellow, and the Vacherin à la Main has a strong flavor, maturing after three to four months – earlier it is somewhat sourish. Vacherin à Fondue tends to be runny, and is therefore wrapped in a cloth and packed in chip boxes. It is especially good when used to make fondue. For example, Fondue Moitié-Moitié is made of half Gruyère

BELOW: Young cheeses, made in the alpine huts of the Sennen, are kept in these wooden storage houses for further ripening. Cheeses made and stored in the mountains have a fresh aroma of alpine herbs.

and half Vacherin. The ability of Vacherin to dissolve completely in water, before it reaches boiling point, is a solution to those fondue specialists who prefer not to use wine in the preparation of the dish; fondue thus prepared is very appetizing.

Cheese of the forests

The second type of Vacherin, the *Vacherin Mont d'Or*, is protected and inspected by the Centrale du Vacherin Mont d'Or, named after the mountain in southwestern Jura, near the French border. The French cheesemakers produce small, soft cheeses of goat's milk (*chevrotins*) which inspired the farmers in the Swiss region to make something similar, but with the creamy milk from their sturdy, red-white Simmentaler cows. Towards the winter their milk yield was insufficient to produce large cheeses. Furthermore, it had an extremely high fat content, which caused the cheeses to remain unusually soft when emerging from the mold; they had to be prevented from collapsing by encasing each cheese in a container of pine bark. Consequently, Vacherin Mont d'Or has a particular, resinous aroma unique to the cheese, donated by the forests of its birthplace. It is only made during the last four and a half months of the year. The marketing period ends with the beginning of warmer weather, for the cheese's delicate constitution could not stand the summer heat.

When this new product was sold for

the first time in Lausanne in 1880, it became so popular that cheese dairies were soon obliged to assist with production; today sixty such dairies make the cheese. The drained curds are collected by *affineurs*, who ripen them on pine shelves in the special cellars of the Vallée de Joux. The shelves absorb large amounts of moisture from the cheeses, and they are constantly changed and dried; the workshop of the *affineur* can be recognized by the hundreds of boards, placed outside under cover.

After the tenth day of ripening, the rind has developed its reddish-brown coloring, but the cheeses continue to be cured for up to four weeks, after which they are packed in pine boxes. Maturation depends on expert ripening and curing processes, plus accurate judgment: a too fresh cheese has an undeveloped flavor; a too mature cheese loses its quality and reveals short and sharp-edged wrinkles on the surface. A correctly matured Vacherin Mont d'Or has a reddish glaze, and the taste is mild and creamy. It may also have some very small holes, and the rind a surface with several long, flowing folds. The cheese is served in its box. The people of the Jura prefer the Vacherin served with potatoes and cumin seed, accompanied by a dry, white wine (a red wine would overpower its special flavor).

The Swiss Tomme

There is another speciality of the Swiss Jura – *Tomme Vaudoise*, called after the canton where we also find the soft Vacherin. Tomme is more than of just local importance, unlike · certain varieties of the French Tomme. The flat and round cheeses, weighing approximately 100 g (3½ oz) each, are ripe after seven to ten days. Their sealed, soft, almost liquid consistency is enveloped by a rind which has a faint white deposit, in between which long rows of red spots occur during longer maturing. The taste is very mild, the aroma modest. If the cheese is less than whole-fat, it is stated on the packing. Tommes are also made elsewhere in Switzerland, formerly by dairy merchants, who sold these *Rahmkäsli* to their customers. They are now made in cheese dairies, using pasteurized milk.

Swiss Tilsit

Towards the end of the last century, a

ABOVE: Cheese fondue is not only an enjoyable dish – it's a national pastime, where the Swiss gather round a communal bowl of melted cheese, mixed with either milk or wine, depending on the recipe. Tea is a frequent accompaniment to fondue – or a glass of kirsch.

BELOW: An ancient type of Swiss cheese, colored green with herbs, is this Schabzieger, sold either in the cone shape, or grated in cartons. The picture shows two old-style labels.

young cheesemaker from the East Swiss cantons made a journey to East Prussia and returned with the recipe for *Tilsit*. The first experimental production caused quite a stir – this semihard cheese was quite different from the much harder varieties with which the Swiss were familiar. Once successfully copied, it needed one hundred cheese dairies to meet the demand. Swiss Tilsit developed rapidly from an imitation to a real Swiss cheese, which became entitled to bear the national quality mark and a new name, *Royalp*; it cannot even be entirely compared with Tilsit made in other countries. Most Royalp cheese is prepared from raw milk instead of the more usual pasteurized milk. Moreover, the Swiss leave the curds floating in the whey, and afterwards the cheese is lightly pressed.

The red rind of Royalp is similar to that of other Tilsits. The fat content may differ: usually it is 45% but can be lower, which makes the mild flavor a little stronger. Cream Tilsit is particularly fine and delicate. When made from pasteurized milk, it has a less interesting taste, but is preferred by those who dislike such a distinctive flavor and aroma to their cheese. In any case, all Tilsits are mild in flavor if their maturing period does not exceed two or three months, but to be in peak form the cheese should mature for at least four to five months, and not be eaten older than seven months. It is excellent for use in certain salads, and makes a delicious combination with fruit and nuts.

A few foreigners

Besides the original Swiss cheeses, Switzerland also produces a number of foreign varieties such as *Brie, Camembert, Romadur, Limburger, Munster* and *Reblochon*, each of these being soft cheeses; there are also fresh varieties such as *Petit Suisse, Double Crème Carré* (a little firmer than Petit Suisse), *Cottage Cheese* and *Curds.* Owing perhaps to the influence of tourism, they appear more and more in shops and stores. The average Swiss consumes 10.7 kg (23.5 lbs) of cheese per year – and he does it in style. Petit Suisse, for example, is served on a platter with an assortment of garden herbs, and a different flavor can be chosen to dress each mouthful.

Distribution of mountain cheeses

In places where cheese is still being made on the alpine meadows, such as in the Justis valley, the distribution of cheeses amongst the owners of cows, in proportion to the milk yield, is cause for celebration. The event is called *Käseteilet*. One of the most beautiful places in Switzerland is chosen for the occasion, at the entrance to the Justis valley, some five hundred meters (16,500 feet) above the Thunersee. In a meadow with an exquisite view overlooking the forests and mountain ridges, stand three fine old warehouses, and it is here that the cheeses made during the long summer by the Sennen are stored.

The festivities start as soon as the sun has dispelled the morning chill of the high mountains. For once, the peaceful silence is broken by the approach of cars and motorcycles; the rapidly increasing crowd of cattle farmers and other dwellers have arrived to take part in the *Kaseteilet*. The warehouses are officially opened, the cheeses taken from the dark rooms, passed from hand to hand, and end up in piles of five on wooden benches, a total weight of about 70 kg (154 lbs) to a pile. This is the average yield of one cow per summer. The *Meistersenn* or *Bergvogt* then places plaques bearing the initials of the cattle owner on each of the piles. Everyone then knows what he is entitled to, and no disputes are expected to arise, except for the good-natured, competitive exchanges during the ensuing eating, drinking and merriment – such as who has the finest cows, the lushest meadow and, of course, the best cheese!

The end of the beginning

As the fall approaches, and before the arrival of snow and ice and tourists in pursuit of winter sports, the mountain herdsmen bring their cows down from the high alpine meadows, for the cattle must be sheltered during the long, cold months until the return of spring.

This event is more than just a manifestation of colorful folklore; it is an essential part of the agricultural year. In the Bernese Oberland, the men light bonfires in the upland pastures, set fire to logs and roll them, crackling and blazing, down the mountain slopes to announce the herd's descent. Perhaps this is a similar ritual to the cheese-

ABOVE: *Alpabfahrt* in the Bernese Oberland. The cows are crowned with a bouquet of flowers and herbs as they descend the mountain slopes on their way to winter stables in the valley.

They have spent the summer in the alpine meadows, often above the tree line. *Transhumance* is the name given to this herding of cattle from the mountains to the valleys.

Name	Milk	Type	Rind	Form	Weight	% Fat content
Appenzell	⌂	◖	☐	low cylinder	6-8 kg	50
Emmental	⌂	■	☐	cartwheel	80-100 kg	45-48
Glarner Schabzieger	⌂	◖	☐	truncated cone	45-100 g	1
Gruyère	⌂	■	☐	cartwheel	30-40 kg	45-48
Raclette cheeses	⌂	◖	☐	low cylinder	5-8 kg	52
Royalp	⌂	■	✤	varying	4-5 kg	15-55
Sbrinz	⌂	■	☐	cartwheel	25-40 kg	45-48
Tête de Moine	⌂	◖	✤	cylinder	1-2 kg	52
Tomme Vaudoise	⌂	●	✤	flat disc	100 g	25-45
Vacherin Fribourgeois	⌂	◖	✤	cylinder	7-12 kg	45-50
- Mont d'Or	⌂	●	✤	flat disc	0.3-3 kg	45-55

Key to symbols on page 6. 1 kg = 2.2 lbs.

rolling ceremonies practiced in Britain, notably in Gloucestershire, where large cheeses are rolled down Cooper's Hill.

As it winds down from the mountains, the procession announces itself by the distant tinkle of cowbells – the leader of the herd has the largest and most sonorous bell – and eventually you see the men and animals approaching in the distance. The journey takes many hours before it is completed; it is hard work for the herdsmen, for the cows keep breaking formation to forge on ahead, attracted by a kind of bovine nostalgia for the warmth and comfort of their stables, perhaps dimly recollected from the previous winter. As they return, the entire village rushes out to meet the procession, and to celebrate their safe return before the arrival of the dark months ahead.

These celebrations are a very ancient and well-established part of alpine farming life, and one that might seem rather at odds with the highly mechanized and progressive dairy industry for which Switzerland is famous. Such traditions, however, serve to remind the people in the cities that cheese is a national, and essentially *natural*, product, made from fresh grass that becomes wholesome milk – cheese is cut off from its origins when processed by the factory.

Italy

Few countries are easier to subdivide at a glance into various large, consolidated land masses than Italy, the boot that ever threatens to prod Sicily in the direction of Spain. In the north the plain of the river Po is girdled by the mighty Alps; southward runs the backbone of the peninsula – the Apennines, stretching from the northwest all the way to the southernmost point; across the Strait of Messina we find Sicily, and above is Sardinia and the smaller Italian islands.

The rivers running down from the Alps supply the lovely Italian lakes, which in their turn flow out into numerous tributaries of the Po, the fountain of life for the Lombardy Plain. This extensive basin, situated between the Alps and the northern Apennines, forms the largest plain of lowland Italy, much larger than the sunny Campagna di Roma and the even sunnier and more southern Campagna Felice near Naples. In Lombardy the summers are hot, but the winters chilly and misty. On both sides of the Po and its widely branched delta on the Adriatic Sea, early farming communities found a land that promised rich cultivation, where the kind of crops that were later established – rye and corn, sugar beet and rice – can often be harvested twice yearly.

The plain and the mountain slopes are no less important for cattle raising and dairy farming: the excellent cattle types yield milk for the preparation of cheeses that are famous throughout the world. This same area is also Italy's most industrialized region: many thousands are employed in the large factories of Turin, Milan and Verona, which has helped to make the northern Italians more affluent and progressive than their countrymen in the south.

South of Lombardy the soil conditions and the climate begin to show a marked change. Below Naples the volcanic ridge of the Apennines slopes sharply into the sea on either side. The flanks of the mountains in Roman times were covered with silver-gray olive orchards and dark cypress woods, that were later stripped bare to provide timber for Italy's mighty merchant and war fleets. Then erosion took a hand, and the soil dried out and the ground silted up after heavy rainfall. For centuries efforts have been

RIGHT: An attractive display of cheeses, hams and salami, some of the basic ingredients of a great national cuisine.

ABOVE: The Tuscan landscape was featured in the paintings of the Italian Renaissance, and has changed but little over the centuries. This town is San Gimignano, to the southwest of Florence.

Asiago 13
Bel Paese 5
Caprino 15
Fiore Sardo 20
Fontina 1
Gorgonzola 6
Grana Padano 9
Mascarpone 8
Mozzarella 14
Pannarone 12
Parmigiano
    Reggiano 11
Pecorino Romano 16
Pecorino
    Siciliano 18
Pressato 10
Provolone 17
Ricotta 19
Robiola 2
Robiolino 3
Stracchino
    Crescenza 4
Taleggio 7

made to make these barren regions fertile again by irrigation and drainage, often with significant results, but this is by no means true for all of the peninsula.

The vegetation displays great local variations, according to the soil and climate, which is in turn affected by the mountains and the sea. Along the coast the summers are hot and increasingly more arid as one moves south. On the islands too one finds diverse conditions: there is a softer, Mediterranean climate on the smaller islands and along the shores of the larger ones.

All over the mainland of Italy agriculture is the primary means of existence. Farming in most areas is characterized by wine production, olive cultivation and the growing of semitropical fruits. Because of the lack of sweet pastureland, there are few cows. Sheep and goats are the most important producers of milk; furthermore, they are cheaper to maintain and are more resistant to harsh conditions. An animal that has long thrived in central Italy is the buffalo, which is kept not only for its good quality milk, but as a draught animal, being more powerful than the ox and more able to withstand hot and dry seasons.

The traditions of Italian cheese and its importance in everyday life go back to before the Christian era. Virgil, the pastoral poet, tells us that, "Milk gathered in the early morning light is curdled at night; but that of twilight the herdsman puts in wooden vats and brings to the city, or is made into cheese for the winter, having been slightly salted." In antiquity, sheep's and goat's milk were both preferred for making cheese. Not only the large farms, such as those excavated near Pompeii, but also the city households had a separate cheese kitchen, or *caseale*, as well as rooms in which the cheeses could mature. Usually, cheese-making took place in the spring or early summer. Cheeses were made in considerable variety: there were salted and unsalted ones, hard and soft cheeses in the form of loaves, millstones, flattened cones or bricks, some unspiced, some spiced or with other additions.

Milk and honey

Various Roman authors wrote fairly comprehensive studies of cattle breeding and dairy farming. In his book *De Agricultura,* the oldest extant work in Latin, Cato gives instructions for the summer and winter feeding and stabling of herds. He also gives a number of recipes, including one for a cheese pastry which seems to be a Roman invention. At least two sorts of pastry, Libum and Placenta, could be purchased ready-made – they were served in the home, but also featured in religious devotions. Honey was used as a sweetener, as sugar was unknown. Cato did not indicate exactly which cheese was used, but he did say that it was to be rubbed until fine, so perhaps it was a kind of Ricotta. He sounds surprisingly modern when he stresses again and again the need for strict hygiene in cooking.

In *Rerum Rusticarum*, the writer Varro enumerates the various qualities of sheep, giving detailed instructions about care in sickness and in health, and also discusses many other aspects of farming. Virgil also had decided opinions about livestock: "Goats require attention and no less care than sheep, and are quite as profitable; goats deliver more young, sheep are excellent milk producers." An animal's reaction to the correct sensory stimulus when being milked was not unknown to him either: "The

BELOW: Gioconda – "a delicious table cheese" – and an obvious choice for the label: Leonardo's famous painting of the Mona Lisa, La Gioconda.

BELOW: Milking a goat, from a Roman relief dating from the third century A.D.

more the pail foams while milking, the more richly the milk will flow from the udders."

The cheesemakers of Rome

In the middle of the first century A.D., the agricultural writer Columella gave a very complete and unusually detailed account of everything concerned with farming in *De Re Rustica*. He cites the preparation of cheese as particularly important in isolated regions, where there may be a surplus of milk which cannot be easily disposed of. He suggests using a vegetable starter – such as thistle flower, safflower seed or the juice of green fig bark – for the curdling process, instead of rennet from animals. He also refers to the pressing, salting, rinsing and ripening of cheese, and states that cheese undergoing these processes is especially suitable for export: "It does not then acquire any holes, nor does it become too salty or too dry; the first mistake shows up when the cheese has been insufficiently pressed, the second if it has been salted too much and the third if it has been dried in the sun." In Columella's day, the predecessor of the modern Caciocavallo cheese was already very popular. The curdled milk which had thickened in a warm container was suffused with boiling water, kneaded and formed by hand, or pressed into beechwood containers A brine bath might then follow, which would harden the cheese, prior to its being smoked above a fire of straw or apple wood; in the big cities this was done in special smokeries. The cheese was made in the form of braids, bottles, or the heads of horses and deer. It seems that it was a particular favorite of the Emperor Augustus who, being a patron of the arts, knew quality when he saw it.

Tricks of the trade

The Augustan age of cheesemaking has been well-documented, and detailed recipes remain, such as this one for cream cheese: "Take a new bowl, with a hole and a plug just beneath the rim; fill it with fresh

LEFT: Pecorino, the famous Italian cheese made from sheep's milk. Pecorino has been made since before Roman times, and Pliny is among those authors who mention it. Legend says that Romulus, the founder of Rome, made this cheese from both sheep and goat's milk.

sheep's milk and add a bouquet of garden herbs, such as marjoram, mint, onion and coriander, suspended upside down so that the stalks and roots are clear of the milk. After five days remove the plug and allow the whey to run off. Close the hole as soon as the milk begins to flow out. After three more days, separate the whey in the same fashion, take out the herbs and discard them. Sprinkle dried thyme and marjoram into the curd, and chives if you wish, then mix thoroughly, and after two more days separate the whey again. Now add finely rubbed salt, and stir. Close the bowl tightly with a lid, and open it only when you are going to eat the cheese."

There were many tricks of the trade, as Columella describes, and they must have evolved over centuries of empirical cheesemaking. Putting fresh pine seeds in the pail beneath the goat helps to curdle the milk. Adding pulverized seeds or herbs to the milk or the curd makes for many varieties in flavor. Fresh cheese can be eaten after a few days by putting it directly from the basket or mold into a brine bath and then allowing it to dry a little in the sun. Dry sheep's cheese can be given an after-treatment in the springtime by soaking large pieces in good grape must in a vat sealed with pitch; the vat is sealed for twenty days, and herbs are added before eating. "But," says Columella, "even without herbs, it isn't bad at all." Cows are described as being more sensitive to heat, cold, soil conditions or altitude than are goats and sheep. He also differentiates four Italian and six foreign breeds according to size, vigor and temperament. Such types include the large, white Umbrian cattle (to this day the most numerous in Italy) and the productive and hard-working Alpine breed, probably the ancestors of the famous, brown Swiss cattle.

Cheshire – the Roman's favorite

During the era of the Roman emperors, the cheese regions were extremely productive, especially with new kinds of cheese. At the *velabrium*, the dairy market in Rome, cheeses were imported from conquered lands under Roman occupation. There were cheeses from the alpine meadows of Helvetia; Gallic cheeses from the Massif Central, Nimes and Toulouse; Greek ones from the Peloponnesos;

ABOVE: A shepherd near the Temple of Juno, Agrigento, Sicily. Traditions are deeply rooted in the peasant communities of southern Italy.

RIGHT: Medieval monasteries were cultural centers where, amongst other things, domestic knowledge was carefully preserved. Quite a few monastery cookery books remain, and include recipes for making cheese.

cheese from the Middle East; and even cheese from Britain. Legend maintains that the Romans were so fond of Cheshire cheese that they built a wall around the city of Chester to ensure the continued progress of its production!

Conversely, vast quantities of Italian cheese left Italy, including the hard cheeses which could survive the long journeys and were popular with the Roman legions. Eventually, the collapse of the Roman Empire put an end to the cheese culture of antiquity. Nothing more is known about cheese production in Italy until the tenth century. It is certain, however, that some aspects of Rome's cultural knowledge were preserved in Christian monasteries, including the techniques of wine production, farming and cheesemaking. When the time came the monks spread their knowledge abroad, hand in hand with the preaching of religion.

Parmesan, the hard, grainy, drum-shaped cheese, is the queen of the Italian cheeses. Because of the very long and slow maturation, and the low moisture content, the cheese is particularly hard and the crust extremely tough and thick. For these reasons it can survive long transportation and extremes of climate, becoming, with age, richer in taste and aroma, rather than deteriorating. Parmesan is certainly the most famous of that group of cheeses known as _grana_, because of their grainy texture, or more precisely _Formaggio di Grana_.

The grana is a very ancient cheese type that originated in the Po valley. Homer, in the eighth century B.C., knew of a tasty, long-keeping kind of cheese which was transported over vast distances, a very hard product that had to be ground with an iron grater. The Spanish poet Martialis, living in Rome in the first century A.D., mentions a hard, moon-shaped cheese, first made by the early Etruscans of northern Italy. These records suggest that grana cheese was well established long before the Roman Empire came into power. After the fall of Rome, however, the plains of the Po were allowed to deteriorate into an infertile, swamp-like area. Only gradually was it brought into cultivation again, by various monastic orders, who also revitalized the cheese industry.

A mountain of cheese

With perseverance, and over a period of five hundred years, the old traditions found new roots. Parmesan evolved from the old Etruscan recipe, and was made in the tenth or eleventh century. Its birthplace was the town of Bibbiano near Piacenza, an area which in those days belonged to the province of Parma, from which the cheese took its name. Records show that the city of Parma supported a lively trade in _Parmigiano Reggiano_ cheese as early as 1364, and the production region south of the Po soon extended as far as Bologna. In Florence, on the other side of the Apennines, Parmigiano Reggiano was already in considerable demand, as is apparent from Boccaccio's description of a land of plenty in his _Decameron_: "There was a mountain made entirely of grated Parmesan cheese, and on top of it people were making nothing but macaroni and

LEFT: The label from a small package of Parmesan cheese.

ABOVE: A stack of fine, drum-shaped Parmesan cheeses, the color of gold and almost as expensive. The cheeses are stamped with their official denomination.

BELOW: Notice the very dark rind of this Parmesan cheese, made from earth mixed to a paste with oil. The picture is an old promotion hand-out from a cheese manufacturer.

noodles, which they boiled in capon broth and threw downhill...."

Meanwhile, north of the Po, the cheesemakers produced _Grana Padano_ in more or less the same way, following the example and the success of Parmesan. The centuries-old issue over the birthright of both types ended in 1955 with the legal protection of their names, and the precise determination of the regions of production, following a decree by the Italian government.

Parmigiano Reggiano

Parmesan cheese is produced between the middle of April and the middle of November in modern creameries, which continue to maintain some elements of traditional craftsmanship. The cream, for example, is allowed to rise naturally in 100-liter (110-quart) vats, without the use of a centrifuge. The following morning, this skimmed evening milk together with fresh morning milk is poured into double-walled tanks to settle. After the milk has soured and curdled, the curd is carefully cut so that no fat escapes into the whey. It is then stirred vigorously with a large rod until it

LEFT: Landscape near
Monte Cassino
between Rome and
Naples, in the heart of
the Italian peninsula.

becomes very fine; meanwhile, the steam between the double walls of the vats brings the temperature up to 54°-58°C (129°-137°F). The mass then cools for a quarter of an hour, as the cheesemaker continually monitors the consistency of the curd particles and the acidity of the whey. The curd is gathered in a cloth, which hangs in the whey for a short while, before being put under the press in a wooden hoop and lid, where it is turned every hour. The salting time takes up to three weeks, depending on the weight; the curing time, two or three years. The cheeses are turned and brushed every other day to begin with, later twice a week and finally once a week. After a year they may be provided with a protective coating made of dark, fine earth mixed with oil. The crust of a mature Parmesan is practically bullet-proof, and the cheesemaker is obliged to test its quality by hitting the cheese with a small hammer – the characteristic ring of truth is pleasing to the trained ear.

Guarantee of excellence
Under its impressive crust, a mature Parmigiano Reggiano hides a straw-yellow, very hard, dry paste without any holes; it is very crumbly and melts on the tongue. The taste is deliciously spicy, but not piquant and certainly not sharp, and despite the low fat content it is rich and full. Parmesan is best known as a grating cheese, and very few dishes of pasta or rice are complete without a liberal sprinkling of grana cheese.

Parmesan is categorized according to maturity as *vecchio* (old); *stravecchio* (very or extra old); *tipico* (four to five years old); and *giovane* (young, table cheese).

The Consorzio del Formaggio Parmigiano Reggiano guarantees the origin and quality of the cheese, inspecting and labeling export cheese with extra care. Both the milk supplier and the cheesemaker are subjected to the strict control of the Consorzio, as are the cattle and pastures.

Grana Padano
While Parmesan is made in a limited area, and over a limited season, Grana Padano is a cheese for all seasons and is made throughout the Lombardy Plain. In the manufacture of Grana Padano, pasteurized milk has now almost entirely replaced raw milk. It is processed in much larger vats than Parmesan, and the evening and morning milk are processed separately, while the milk for Parmesan is always mixed. There are other minor differences in the two recipes, although they follow the same basic pattern. Grana Padano matures more quickly and becomes flaky. The longer the cheese matures, the more clearly can the tiny, hard grains be felt on the tongue; *grana*, of course, refers to the granular structure, while *padano* means "of the Po." The color is usually lighter than that of its great rival, being almost white in some cases. As a table cheese Grana Padano is much less common than in its grated form. It is preferred in cooking and in soups since it doesn't tend to form threads.

There are other varieties of grana, including one from the neighborhood of Lodi, the low-fat, sharper and sometimes slightly bitter *Grana Lodigiano*, which has small eyes and weighs up to 50 kg (110 lbs). Another type is the *Grana Lombardo* from the province of Milan. The production and inspection of grana cheeses is controlled by the Consorzio per la Tutela del Grana Padano.

LEFT: Everywhere in Italy you can find small, well-stocked groceries with a fine display of cheeses from many parts of the world. Centrally placed in the group are the hard, grating cheeses such as Parmesan and Pecorino, so important in the Italian kitchen.

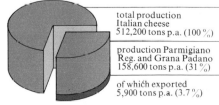

total production
Italian cheese
512,200 tons p.a. (100%)

production Parmigiano
Reg. and Grana Padano
158,600 tons p.a. (31%)

of which exported
5,900 tons p.a. (3.7%)

Centuries ago, the cattle that grazed on the lush summer pastures of the Italian Alps were herded south at the approach of winter. One of the several resting places along the route was the small town that gave its name to a great and famous bluish-green-veined cheese – *Gorgonzola*. The milk from these cows was made into cheese, a rather poor quality milk to be sure, for the cattle were tired from their long journey, and it was for this reason that the cheese was originally called *Stracchino Gorgonzola* (from *stracco* meaning "tired"). There are several legends that describe the genesis of this blue cheese; all are fanciful and probably apocryphal, and suggest that the blue mold came about as the result of a happy accident.

Gorgonzola is known to have been made for at least a thousand years, and was initially matured in the caves of the valley of Valassina, which were no doubt ideal for the formation of *Penicillium* mold. Later, maturing rooms were constructed all over the region. Until the nineteenth century Gorgonzola remained a typical regional product of small cheese-makers. The curd of the evening milk, which had been curdled immediately and had ripened overnight, was transferred the next morning into a mold of wooden rings lined with a cheese cloth, and covered afterwards with the warm, new curd of fresh morning milk. These two curds were considered essential in the manufacture of Gorgonzola. After being pierced to allow the invasion of air, the cheese was left to develop its mold for several months; the entire maturing procedure took over a year to complete.

A cheese of unusual mildness
In today's modern cheese factories, Gorgonzola is made according to a less time-consuming process – it would seem that the world is impatient for each consignment of Gorgonzola cheese. The quality, however, is by no means impaired by the urgency. This is how the cheese is made: *Penicillium gorgonzola* is added to fresh, pasteurized milk, together with an acidifying agent. The curd particles are cut and stirred until they are the size of hazel nuts, and are then packed in portions into cloths, placed in aluminum molds and are turned regularly and salted in a humid but warm room. After two weeks of maturing, this time in a cold,

ABOVE: A wedge of genuine Italian Gorgonzola. It is no longer merely a region cheese: as one of the world's most famous cheese types, Gorgonzola is much in demand wherever cheese is appreciated.

LEFT: Dolcelatte, meaning "sweet milk," is the trade name of a well-known factory-made Gorgonzola.

BELOW: One of the many attractive little towns of northern Italy, Como on the Lago di Como.

LEFT: Paglierini is a delicious, soft cheese with a subtle aroma. Its name derives from the straw mats (*paglia*) on which it is sold. The cheese is a regional speciality of Piedmont.

moist environment, one side of the cheese is pricked for mold development. Ten days later the other side is given identical treatment. The total maturation period is a mere three months. The taste and aroma are possibly less pronounced when compared to those cheeses made by the old method, and the body of the cheese is somewhat softer. It is elastic in consistency and possesses small holes. In color it is white to straw yellow, with blue-green veins and a wrinkled, reddish crust. Gorgonzola is packed either whole or in segments, usually in aluminum foil. It is unusually mild for a blue cheese, and thus is excellent as a dessert cheese, especially when accompanied by a glass of, say, Valpolicella or Barolo.

Gorgonzola can be used in cooking to make a number of attractive dishes. Try it in place of Roquefort in salad dressings. The Milanese like to stuff ripe pears with Gorgonzola; in the north they mix it with the fresh cream cheese Mascarpone.

The *Gorgonzola Bianca*, or *Pannarone*, is only lightly salted and does not form a mold, except on the crust where it is washed away. After maturing for about a month it acquires a piquant, slightly bitter taste. White Gorgonzola is made only in some parts of Lombardy, mainly around Lodi, and has attained considerable popularity in Venice.

Many years ago, the traditional cheese of northeastern Italy, *Asiago*, was made on the southern slopes of the Dolomites. Through the improved breeding of their cattle, the farmers increased the milk yield, and cheese production shifted from the primitive dairies to cooperative factories in the foothills. The factories were founded by cattle owners and cheesemakers together, and by 1910 there were 176 in existence. The home of Asiago cheese is the province of Vicenza, west of Venice. Asiago is a hard cheese, which comes in two varieties: the semifat *Asiago d'Allievo*, made from skimmed evening milk and fresh morning milk, a cheese which is rather piquant and popular as a grating cheese; and the full-fat mountain cheese *Asiago grasso di monte*, with its much smoother texture. The latter is sufficiently ripe after about six weeks.

A descendant of the Asiago, called *Pressato*, is found locally in Lombardy and Basso Veneto. The fat content is inclined to be somewhat variable, depending on the basic ingredient – either skimmed or whole fresh morning milk, or raw and skimmed evening milk mixed with fresh morning milk. It may be enjoyed after a mere one or two months, but can be allowed to mature for longer periods. Pressato is a flat, round cheese with a brown-painted crust. Its texture is elastic, its color white to straw yellow, and its flavor mild to piquant. The body of the cheese contains many pea-size holes.

The delicious gift of Piedmont

From the Valle d'Aosta, north of Turin in the province of Piedmont, comes the wonderful *Fontina* cheese, which many connoisseurs would unhesitatingly place among the first

ABOVE: Cheeses galore displayed in a specialist food store in Venice.

ABOVE: Records show that Taleggio has been made since the eleventh century, and possibly well before. It is a semihard, mountain cheese, also made in the valleys, with a lovely, mellow taste.

LEFT: Indisputably one of the world's great cheeses, in perfect combination with a flask of wine – Fontina from the Valle d'Aosta, Piedmont.

half dozen great cheeses of the world. Originally a sheep's milk cheese, Fontina has become the most important source of income for the cattle owners of the area. Nowadays the summer milk of cows is processed directly in the cooperative mountain chalets, the milk being contained in small copper kettles heated over a wood fire. The maturing period lasts for three months, and takes place in cooperative curing rooms in the valleys. In winter and early spring, when the cattle are stabled, Fontina is made in the village factories; a few of the larger concerns, however, operate throughout the year. They boast big, double-walled, steam-heated vats that can accommodate hundreds of gallons of milk – a far cry from the traditional copper kettles still being used in the mountain chalets.

The semihard Fontina varies in weight from between 10 and 20 kgs (22 to 44 lbs). It has a flat, round form and a thin, smooth, brownish rind. The paste has only a few holes and is white to yellow in color. The flavor is faintly nutty, faintly sweet, and the texture creamy smooth.

Fontina takes its name from Mount Fontin near Aosta. It lends itself to the elegant dish *fonduta*, a Piedmontese speciality related to Swiss fondue. Fonduta is made with fresh, white truffles, Fontina cheese, eggs and milk, Fontina made entirely from the raw milk from the Valle d'Aosta bears the stamp of the Consorzi della Fontina Tipica. *Fontal* is the name accorded to Fontina-type cheeses made from pasteurized milk, regardless of whether they come from Aosta or other regions.

The fresh and delicate Stracchini

The trouble with *Taleggio* cheese, like certain others of the Stracchino group, is that it matures and loses its fresh flavor rather too quickly to travel any distance. With modern, refrigerated transport, Taleggio can be found outside the valley near Milan, after which it was named. The cheese was probably made there as early as the eleventh century, but is now made elsewhere in the Alps and on the Lombardy Plain. It has always been made during the cool months from a raw mixture of preripened evening milk and fresh morning milk. On the plains, in the large creameries, it is produced throughout the year from large quantities of pasteurized milk. The curd is not pressed but is turned regularly in the vat. Rubbing with brine during the curing period allows the formation of the flaky, reddish, soft rind. The consistency of the cheese is compact and sometimes rather brittle; the color is white to pale yellow; and the taste mild yet fruity, as the cheese melts on the tongue. The traditional method of preparation undoubtedly results in a fuller and more characteristic aroma.

Lombardy and Piedmont together produce *Stracchino Crescenza*, and the best quality cheese is said to come from Milan and neighboring Pavia, to the south. It is a delicious dessert cheese which matures so quickly that an unexpected rise in temperature can spoil the entire production. For this reason, Stracchino Crescenza used to be made only in winter, but today it is made throughout the year in factories with air-conditioned rooms. The texture can be soft and melting (*pasta cremosa*) or more solid (*pasta sostenuta*).

Theme and variations

Although not strictly a Stracchino cheese, *Robiola* is a Stracchino type – soft, delicate and quick to mature. A square-shaped cheese of between 250 and 500 g (.5 to 1.1 lbs), it was previously made from a mixture of cow's, sheep's and goat's milk, usually partly skimmed. Nowadays it is made entirely from cow's milk. The curd is hardly cut at all, and the cheeses ripen in straw or linen-lined wooden boxes. The temperature in the curing room is kept low, and the cheesemakers rub the cheeses regularly with a brine cloth as soon as mold begins to form. The *tipo dolce* with its delicate, mild taste matures in 8 to 10 days; the fully mature, full-bodied *tipo piccante* develops its light truffle aroma in 30 to 40 days.

Originally, Robiola came from the Alpine foothills of Lombardy, but is now made over a much larger area of northern Italy. A smaller version, called *Robiolino*, has a lovely, smooth and creamy exterior. The curd is extensively worked until very soft and smooth. With the aid of molds, the cheeses are shaped into bars or rolls. The fresh type tastes a little sourish; the more mature type is fuller and creamier.

From the same area comes a number

LEFT: Sentinel haystacks near a small and primitive farmstead at Soltera.

LEFT: Bel Paese, a modern factory cheese that has attained international status. Its mildness forms a good contrast to the stronger flavored cheeses on the table.

BELOW: The label of a mixed cheese, and a regional speciality. It tells us that the cheese is made from the pure milk of goats *(capra)* and sheep *(pecora)*.

BELOW: Sheep grazing in an almond orchard near Catania, Sicily. Many Italian cheeses are Pecorinos, made from the milk of ewes, and large flocks of healthy sheep are among the country's main assets.

of descendants of the Robiola, bearing the collective title of *Italico*, as well as all kinds of fancy names. These are soft cheeses with or without surface flora, and among them is the famous cheese *Bel Paese*, which means "beautiful country." Invented in 1929, Bel Paese is a flat, round cheese from Lombardy, weighing .5 to 1 kg (1.1 to 2.2 lbs). It matures for only a short time, and with its soft, mild taste is a worthy member of this selection of dessert cheeses.

Finally, Mascarpone deserves a mention, although it hardly rates the title of "cheese" as it is made from fresh cream and doesn't ripen at all. It was originally made only during the autumn and winter in Lombardy, but is now made throughout Italy. Mascarpone is strictly a desert cheese, although one recipe from around Trieste advises that it be mixed with Gorgonzola, mustard and anchovies. The product is made from whole cow's milk and is sold in muslin bags. It is globe-shaped like certain versions of Mozzarella, and the creamy yellow paste is very soft, having the consistency of thick cream. Mascarpone is usually served with fruit and sugar, and may be flavored with liqueurs such as Strega or Chartreuse. Some types are sold with a candied fruit inside the cheese.

Following the route of the sun, southwards down the Apennine peninsula, the traveler will notice how the cattle pastures gradually give way to the more arid, burnt-umber territories of sheep, goats and buffalo. Interesting cheeses are made everywhere. The sheep of the Sopravissina breed yield great quantities of lovely, fat milk during their lactation period, which all goes to make fine *Pecorino* cheese. Pecorino is the name given to all Italian cheeses made from ewe's milk, and there are, of course, many varieties. Pecorino was made in the time of Pliny, and in the first century A.D., Columella recorded a recipe for *Pecorino Romano*, the oldest and best of the type. It is made in both central and southern Italy, while on the island of Sardinia, which supports 2.5 million sheep, *Pecorino Sardo* is a major industry.

Until the end of the last century, Pecorino was a true shepherd's cheese. Salt makers then began to take over the salting and curing of the fresh curds, and started simple dairies themselves. These progressed to become large, modern cheese factories which made Pecorino (together with the cheese Provolone) the most important export cheese after grana, especially to the United States with its considerable Italian population. Pecorino matures in about eight months, and the weight varies. The smooth crust of the cylindrical cheese was previously treated with oil mixed with earth, but

ABOVE: Both a milk-producing and a draught animal, the water buffalo is found in southern Europe and Asia, where it survives the hot climate more easily than do cattle. True Mozzarella is made from buffalo milk.

today this is done with a red-brown synthetic material. The texture of the straw-yellow cheese is hard and compact. It is made of fresh ewe's milk, first heated, then curdled by lamb's rennet; in Sicily they add peppercorns to the curd, to make the piquant *Pecorino Pepato*. Although Pecorino may be used as a table cheese, it is used principally for grating and in cooking.

As the rapidly rising Pecorino industry demanded more and more of the Sardinian sheep's milk, it seemed as if the shepherd's cheese *Fiore Sardo* would become extinct. But with new methods of preparation, factories began to improve the quality, and the cheese survived. Fiore, made from raw milk, can either be eaten fresh after salting, or after several months of maturation in a cool, dry environment, which allows it to develop a full, piquant flavor.

Whey and albumen cheeses

Although it is generally referred to as a cheese, strictly speaking, *Ricotta* isn't a cheese at all, since it is not made from the pressed curds of milk but from the whey, the by-product. It is prepared either from sheep's milk whey, *Ricotta pecora*, or from cow's milk whey, *Ricotta vaccina*. More specifically, the Ricottas are named after the region of origin: thus we have *Ricotta Romana*, *Ricotta Sarda* and *Ricotta Siciliano*, all made from the whey of sheep; and *Ricotta Piedmontese* made from cow's

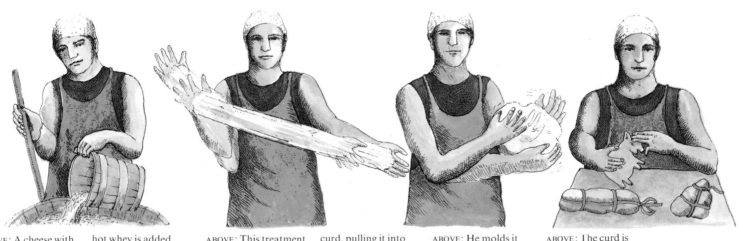

ABOVE: A cheese with an unusual method of preparation is the kneaded or plastic-curd cheese. The cheesemaker adds hot whey to the curd. After a pause the whey is run off, and fresh, hot whey is added. Immersed in the whey, the curd rests for 20-30 minutes at a temperature of about 45° C (113° F).

ABOVE: This treatment makes the curd tough but elastic. Cut into pieces, and then into smaller strips, it is again immersed in hot water and whey. The cheesemaker now starts to knead the curd, pulling it into long threads. This accounts for the generic Italian name for the cheese: *Formaggio di pasta filata* – "... paste that threads." The curd is intensively worked until ready for the next stage.

ABOVE: He molds it into ball shapes, and these are also immersed in the hot whey mixture.

ABOVE: The curd is now so elastic and malleable that it can be modeled into a variety of shapes, whatever may suit the cheesemaker's fancy: melons, sausages, piglets, lambs, people.

whey, which usually has a softer texture.

Whey contains no casein protein (this has been left in the curd), but does contain the protein albumen, as well as part of the milk fat, minerals and vitamins. The albumen sets at a high temperature, incorporating the other constituents. Ricotta was once a product of expedience through poverty, but these days milk is added.

There are three varieties of Ricotta: the unmatured, unsalted *tipo dolce*; the salted, dried and somewhat firmer *tipo moliterno*, and – solely around Bari on Italy's heel – the *tipo forte*, which matures in long, wooden containers. All types are round in shape; weight 1 to 1.5 kg (2.2 to 3.3 lbs); and are fresh, white, and softly crumbling in texture, with a pleasant mildness and a touch of sweetness in the taste. On Malta, *Rkotta* is made in practically the same way, except that it is not a whey product, but a curious combination of three parts cow's milk to one part filtered sea water; it is sold by weight from eathenware bowls.

The sculpted cheeses
Some types of curd, when treated in a certain way, become very pliant and malleable. Such cheeses are known as kneaded cheeses, or plastic-curd cheeses, and their Italian name is *Formaggio di pasta filata*, which denotes that the curd can be drawn out in stringy lengths. The milk is usually raw cow's milk, and to obtain the desired whiteness, winter milk is preferred, summer milk being considered too yellow. The curd is first heated in warm whey to about 45°C (113°F), when it will stretch into tough, elastic fibers. It is then cut into long, thin slices and immersed in hot water and whey, at which point the cheesemaker kneads it vigorously by hand, in much the same fashion as a baker might knead his dough. At a certain point his experience will tell him that the curd is ready to be shaped. He molds it into balls of a specified weight, which are again placed into hot water and modeled into a variety of shapes. Next the cheeses are transferred to cold water in order to make them firm, and then to a brine bath where they remain for several days, before being taken out and dried. Unless the cheese is to be matured for any length of time, it is then dipped in

LEFT: The most typical shape of these plastic curd cheeses (Provolone, Caciocavallo, Ragusano, etc.,) is the pear shape. They are suspended on strings, perhaps because some types were once smoked.

paraffin wax. The intensive treatment of the hot curd produces a very compact paste with a smooth finish.

One of the most famous varieties of *pasta filata* is *Provolone*. In times gone by, people preferred it well matured and smoked, a tradition since Roman times. Today, the milder Provolone with its firm, close, occasionally crumbly texture, and its delicate, light taste is more popular. Provolone, a name which originally meant "large oval," or "large sphere," is molded in a wide variety of fanciful shapes, then tied round with a cord by which it is suspended, and which leaves its impression in the crust. Other types of kneaded cheese are the Sardinian *Casigiolo* and the loaf-shaped *Ragusana* from Sicily, which at six months is a delicious table cheese, but when older is best for grating. There is also *Caciocavallo*, an ancient variety whose name means "horse cheese," or "cheese on horseback," and which might refer to the fact that the Romans – who made this cheese – fashioned it in the shape of a horse head. There is another explanation: Caciocavallo cheeses were often hung in pairs over a pole, as one might straddle a horse, and were also made of mare's milk.

Cheese where the buffalo roam
Mozzarella cheese has achieved world fame due to its being a main ingredient in the ubiquitous pizza. True Mozzarella is made from buffalo milk, but since there are too few buffalo to meet the demand, cow's milk is used, sometimes mixed with buffalo milk for the sake of authenticity. True Mozzarella should be very moist, delicate of flavor, and slightly giving as you bite into it. The cheese is eaten fresh, often with sliced tomatoes and a few anchovies. The shape varies from the usual oval ball to a wide range of forms, including those known as "buffalo eyes" (*occhi di bufala*) and "buffalo eggs" (*uova di bufala*). A very special kind of Mozzarella called *Manteca* contains a piece of whey butter in its center.

Finally, *Caprino* is a cheese made from goat's milk, and has existed since recorded history. The aroma of the white paste, and the distinctive, fresh but sourish taste clearly denote the origin of the milk. Caprino is a soft cheese, sold fresh from the wooden containers in which it is packed.

Name	Milk	Type	Rind	Form	Weight	% Fat content
Asiago	⌂	■	□	low cylinder	9-13 kg	36-52
Bel Paese	⌂	●	❖	flat disc	0.5-2 kg	50
Caprino	⌂◿⌂	○	—	container	varying	40-45
Fiore Sardo	◿	▲	□	low cylinder	1.5-4 kg	45
Fontina	⌂	▲	□	low cylinder	10-20 kg	45
Gorgonzola	⌂	▲	✂	low cylinder	6-12 kg	48
Grana Padano	⌂	■	□	low cylinder	24-40 kg	32
Mascarpone	⌂	○	—	container	100-125 g	70
Mozzarella	⌂*	●	□	ball	0.5-1 kg	44
Pannarone	⌂	●	□	low cylinder	6-9 kg	52
Parmigiano Reggiano	⌂	■	□	low cylinder	22-36 kg	32
Pecorino Romano	◿	■	□	low cylinder	6-22 kg	36
- Siciliano	◿	■	□	low cylinder	4-12 kg	40
Pressato	⌂	●	□	low cylinder	9-14 kg	30
Provolone	⌂	■	□	varying	1-6 kg	44
Ricotta	⌂◿	○	—	flat disc	1-1.5 kg	20-30
Robiola	⌂	●	❖	loaf	250-500 g	48-50
Robiolino	⌂	●	❖	bar	50-100 g	30-45
Stracchino Crescenza	⌂	●	—	loaf	0.05-4 kg	50
Taleggio	⌂	●	❖	loaf	1.7-2.2 kg	48

＊ Buffalo

Key to symbols on page 6. 1 kg = 2.2 lbs.

LEFT: Pizza as pizza should be – large as a cartwheel, and made from fresh Italian vegetables, Mozzarella cheese and perhaps a few slices of of garlic-scented salami.

LEFT: Reblochon is a French Alpine cheese, made under almost identical conditions in Italy. It was perhaps originally a monk's cheese, and has been made for hundreds of years.

BELOW: Traveling in Tuscany, you can buy your lunch from a roadside food stall: salami, bread, wine and, of course, cheese.

Without cheese, Italian cooking would be missing one, perhaps even two dimensions. Nowhere in the world does cheese play a more important role in the kitchen than in Italy. This is true for everyday cooking as much as for refined cuisine. The most diverse dishes are prepared with cheese, or embellished with it – soups, pasta (what is pasta without cheese?), meats, sauces, desserts and pastry. In an attempt to praise Italian cooking, it is often favorably compared to French cooking, yet they are as different and individual as chalk and cheese. Italian cooking is boldly and everlastingly *Italian* – it is not French, and stands supremely in its own right. The historical influence of French cooking is of no consequence when it comes to evaluating the quality of Italian cuisine, with its deep foundations and traditions harkening all the way back to Roman civilization. What has really stood the test of time is the matchless, satisfying combination of pasta, wine and cheese.

The cheesecake of history

Roman gastronomy has had both a famous and infamous reputation, partly due to the fanciful writings of contemporary historians, and partly to our belief that despotic rulers are inevitably prey to every vice including gluttony. Roman emperors, then, feasted on incredible amounts of food, and were notorious for regurgitating halfway through their meal (perhaps we should say "orgy"), in order to make room for the next course. Less well documented is the daily diet of the average citizen. Cato's *De Agricultura*, which we have already mentioned, informs us that the average Roman enjoyed bread, *puls* (a kind of porridge), meat, wine and

cheese. He also includes a recipe for a cake called Libum, which might well have been his favorite cheesecake: "Wash hands and the utensils carefully. Grind down two pounds of cheese [this would probably have been either Ricotta or salted, fresh cheese] in a mortar; add one pound of meal or, for a softer cake, half a pound of fine flour, and mix thoroughly. Form the mass into a loaf, place it on leaves, and bake slowly on a hot fire under a heatproof earthenware dish." The recipe does work, and it makes a very good and nourishing cake.

Pass the cheese, *per favore*

Each region of Italy has its own culinary traditions, its own staple preferences and its own methods of preparation, which have always depended on the climate and what the soil can be coaxed to provide. On Sardinia, for example, the barbecue has been commonplace since well before Roman times, and the habit of passing home-made sheep's cheese from person to person, as a group sits around the open fire, still remains.

Italy produces her own special type of rice for risotto; corn is grown for polenta, or corn meal; and durum wheat for the pasta. Pasta has more variety than the whole range of sounds capable of being produced by a symphony orchestra and its names are sweet music to the Italian ear: spaghetti, fusilli, macaroni, tagliatelli, lasagne, tortellini, ravioli, rigatoni. The home of pasta is Naples – but the Neapolitans are too generous to keep it to themselves. The north of Italy demands the flat, ribbon-shaped *pasta all'uova*, made from eggs and flour, which is so good with butter and parmesan cheese, or the *salsa Bolognese*; but there are also pastas in the form of butterflies, little hats (Cappelletti), little wheels (Ruote), shells (Conchiglie); some to toss into soup, some to boil or fry or fill – and almost always they are sprinkled with a generous handful of grated cheese, or cooked with cheese, or covered by a cheese sauce. Italy enriched the world with its fonduta and gnocchi, its cheese pastry, its pizzas and above all its cheeses for the table, to be eaten on their own, or with fruit, and washed down with Italian wine. It is for this reason, as much as any other, that both Petrarch and Dante called Italy the *"Bel Paese"*!

Cheese in your home

There is no doubt that the majority of cheeses have a beauty and attractiveness entirely their own. After all, some cheeses have taken hundreds of years to perfect, it is right that they should be uniquely appealing. A fine wedge of farmhouse Brie on a straw mat; a yielding Camembert in its chipwood box; a fresh goat's milk cheese wrapped in bright green or autumn-tinted leaves; a noble piece of blue-veined cheese next to a bunch of grapes; a mellow, honey-colored slice of old Gouda on a simple, wooden cheeseboard – all of these promise delight and are the ambassadors of good taste.

Cheese is both cosmopolitan and democratic, for it is eaten almost throughout the entire world. Cheese is most frequently enjoyed just as it comes, in generous portions accompanied by crusty, fresh bread or crackers, and washed down with beer or wine. It is equally important in the kitchen, as an ingredient to simple, wholesome dishes and in highly refined cuisine. Cheese has a traditional place on the table, is taken in sandwiches to work, and is indispensable in the good restaurant. The increasing, worldwide popularity of cheese is due not only to its remarkable variety, but also because modern transportation and storage techniques have made the selection available to most areas, and thus more easily available to the average consumer than ever before. This new emphasis on cheese follows the current trend in the interest in food generally, encouraged by food manufacturers, by advertising, and by shops everywhere.

Cheese has its own, individual nature. It should be carefully treated both by those who make it and by those of us who eat it, if we are to gain the maximum enjoyment from each particular aroma and flavor.

Room temperature

In the first place, cheese must be eaten at the right temperature. Soft, semihard and hard varieties are best enjoyed at about 20°C (68°F), and fresh cheeses a little cooler. If a cheese is stored in a cold cellar or in the refrigerator, it should be allowed to reach room temperature to unfold its taste and aroma to the full; this may be a matter of one hour, but sometimes much longer, depending on the difference in temperature between the storage place and the room, and also,

ABOVE: Cheese and wine – two of life's pleasures to be enjoyed in a relaxed, and preferably sunny, atmosphere.

of course, on the type of cheese. A hard cheese requires more time than a soft one. In the final analysis, however, it is largely a matter of personal preference. Only experience will tell you exactly how long is needed for each cheese to reach the temperature where it treats your nose and tongue to the perfection that it promises.

Storage

Where should you keep your cheeses between purchase and consumption? The spot you choose must not be at too low a temperature, as the cutting surface of the cheese and also the rind are inclined to dehydrate, impairing taste and smell.

Granted, in these days of modern houses with central heating it is no easy task to find a cool, not cold place. If you have a cool cellar you are lucky, because nothing is better. Preferably, the cheeses should be placed on clean, unpainted and unvarnished wooden boards. The cut surface of a cheese can be smeared with butter before being covered with aluminum foil or shrink foil, or wrapped in a damp cloth. But do this only with semihard or hard cheeses. Soft cheeses are never put in

ABOVE: An evening at home with a few friends, some well-chosen cheeses and a good glass of wine.

BELOW: A communal dish that has been made for centuries in the Swiss Alps – the famous fondue. There are various recipes employing different cheeses; two classic recipes can be found

on p. 109: Fondue Neufchâteloise and Fondue Fribourg.

a damp cloth; they can best be kept in their own wrapping, if this is not of cardboard only. If it is in cardboard, remove the cheese and wrap it in aluminum foil or transparent film.

Refrigerators can, of course, be used; yet the temperature there – 3°-4°C (37°-40°F) – is really too low for cheese. Protect the cheese by placing it in a plastic bag, which should be tightly closed; then wrap the entire piece in aluminum foil or transparent film, or place it inside a plastic box. The crisper, or vegetable bin, at the bottom of the unit and the space inside the door are the least cold. Never wrap small pieces of cheese together: their flavors would mingle and they would lose their individuality.

Cheeses should never be placed in the freezer, where the temperature is −20°C (−4°F), as most cheeses will be destroyed or at least their quality hopelessly impaired. For example, cheese spreads lose their creamy structure and become unpleasantly crumbly. Yet, there are some varieties better capable of withstanding the freezer climate, such as Quark types. These should be thawed slowly, and afterwards must not be refrozen.

How long can cheeses keep?
The semihard and hard cheese varieties can be kept for weeks; they may be bought in fairly large quantities, which is sometimes cheaper than buying small pieces. Store them carefully and cut each time a piece large enough to be eaten within a few days. A full-size cheese certainly looks attractive on a cheese board, but to bring it repeatedly to room temperature does not improve the cheese, even though doing so once will not harm it.

Much more sensitive are the soft cheeses, due to their higher moisture content and the fact that their surface ripening or mold development continues. There are three groups. Soft cheeses with a tendency to become runny – such as Brie, Camembert and Liederkranz – have a very short life. When you buy them, they should be newly or almost ripe. Eat them at once or the next day: if you need to keep them longer, wrap them in aluminum foil at room temperature. Remember that once a cheese turns liquid, it will not solidify in the refrigerator but only dry out. Cheeses with a firmer paste, such as Pont-l'Evêque and Reblochon, can be kept in the refrigerator for some days. These cheeses continue to ripen, however, and once they are past their peak, the quality quickly deteriorates. Speedy consumption is thus recommended. Fresh cheeses and thick cream cheeses (Cottage Cheese, Speisequark, Crème Chantilly and Petit Suisse, for example) are less sensitive and can be kept in the refrigerator for some weeks, even if they have been opened or cut into.

Finally, there are foil-ripened and vacuum-packed cheeses. They may be stored for long periods as long as their wrapping is not opened.

Do not discard
Soft cheeses cannot be stored too long at room temperature without becoming runny and overripe. In comparable circumstances harder cheeses start to "sweat" their fat. However, wrongly treated cheese need not be totally discarded. The fat drops can be wiped off with a dry cloth. Should the cheese become too dry, it can still be ground or grated and then sprinkled on sandwiches or used in casseroles, soups, or other hot dishes. Next time look for a better storage place! Molds may also

ABOVE: A fine assortment of British cheeses, with special crackers known as "Bath Olivers."

BELOW: An attractive buffet of cheeses and other snacks, for a party held in an old farmhouse.

be wiped off without causing any health risk. If the mold has penetrated into the cheese then a layer can be cut away. Even dried blue-veined cheese need not be thrown away: a lovely cheese cream can be made of it by adding it to butter or cream.

Selecting and serving cheese
The intriguing variety of the world's cheeses – fresh, soft, semihard, hard, mild, strong and sharp-tasting, with either bland, spicy, pithy or fruity aromas – guarantees that there is surely something for everybody. And how exciting it is to find new cheeses, experimenting and trying to gather from the packaging what the contents promise. On the other hand, the wide choice can be very difficult too.

What is needed is some method of deciding how and when to use which cheeses. Perhaps some guidance can be given here.

With bread, the semihard to hard cheeses are preferable and everybody knows best what he or she likes. A mild or perhaps a more pronounced type? Members of a family can have diverging tastes in cheese as well as other things. Satisfy everybody by putting both a mild young cheese and an older or more pithy cheese on the table.

On the cheese plate following the main meal there should be at least three types of cheeses, widely differing in character. The food and drinks being served are among the things that influence the cheese selection. This is discussed at greater length in the section on cheese and wine (see p. 96).

For cooking, flavor is not the only point to be concerned about; the texture and melting qualities are also important. Sometimes you need a good melting variety which does not pull into threads (e.g., for Raclette or hot cheese canapés). The thready varieties have their place too (e.g. in fondue). And sometimes – as for cheese schnitzels – you need a cheese that becomes soft but does not melt completely. For soups and sauces you can choose among the piquant and hard types which are so suitable for grating. Consult the recipe section beginning on p. 100 for further information.

Another important thing to take into account is the best time to enjoy each particular cheese: breakfast, for example, is hardly the time to have a

ABOVE: French cheeses, selected and carefully arranged on a cheese board. This variety covers a wide range of flavors and aromas.

piece of Roquefort with a glass of Burgundy. Nor should a cheese dessert be served after a Japanese sukiyaki or Chinese meal. But few Italian spaghetti dishes are complete without cheese. Your own good taste, backed up by some knowledge and experience, is your best guide in the world of cheese.

Nutritive value

Cheese has an important place in the diet. Not only is it good to eat, and a pleasant additive to the enjoyment of life, it is a complete food in itself. Cheese contains almost all the nutrients the human body needs, and in a concentrated form. It contains the proteins casein, albumen and globulin, of which casein is the most important. Casein is found in milk and milk products only. These cheese proteins are particularly valuable since they are built up from amino acids from which humans can synthesize their own body protein.

Moreover, most cheeses are rich in milk fat. During preparation and ripening, the fat has been partly broken down, like the proteins, making it easily digestible.

Average composition of cheese per 100 g (3½ oz)

Name	% Fat Content	Fat in grams	Proteins in grams	Carbohydrates in grams	% Moisture	Calories
Blue	45	30.5	21.5	2.0	40	368
Camembert	45	22.1	20.9	1.0	53	286
Cheddar	48	32.2	25.0	2.1	38	398
Cottage Cheese	4.2	4.2	13.6	2.9	78	106
Danbo (10% fat)	10	5.5	34.5	1.0	56	191
- (30% fat)	30	15.4	28.6	1.0	52	257
Emmental	45	31.0	29.0	1.0	36	399
Gouda	48	29.0	25.0	1.0	42	365
Parmesan	40	26.0	36.0	2.9	33	390
Speisequark						
- (5% fat)			13.5	3.4	81	72
- (45% fat)	45	11.3	8.7	3.4	75	150

Cheese contains several vitamins: the water-soluble vitamin B as well as the fat-soluble vitamins A and D. It also has an impressive list of minerals. Indispensable for the human body are calcium and phosphorus, both of which can be obtained, for the greater part, from milk and cheese.

Cheese lacks those fattening carbohydrates – such as milk sugar – which have largely been converted into milk acid during the production process.

Along with the protein, fat and carbohydrate values, we have indicated the caloric value of some cheese varieties in the list on this page. The calories have been calculated according to the "energy value" of the various cheeses. The caloric value per weight unit fluctuates with the fat and moisture content of the cheese. The lower the caloric value, the higher the moisture content of the cheese; the higher the caloric value, the fatter the cheese. The moisture content can only be indicated approximately as it decreases as the cheese gets older.

Cheese and wine

We may wonder why it is that wine has long been considered the true and perfect partner to cheese. One reason is that cheese on the palate seems to require a foil, and by choosing wine we provide a contrast which is at the same time complementary; we can prove this to ourselves by judicious comparison, and by tasting.

The harmony of cheese and wine cannot be easily achieved with other beverages. The taste of cheese is not generally improved by coffee, neither is it enhanced by tea, although the Swiss prefer to serve tea instead of wine with their favorite fondue. Beer is a better choice as a partner to cheese, and is often preferred in countries that do not produce wine: beer and Cheddar cheese is an established tradition in England, while in Norway the pungent Gammelost is well tempered by the local brews

ABOVE: A simple, well-prepared meal is enjoyed in the romantic atmosphere of an Italian wine cellar.

LEFT: Stilton cheese with a glass of port, a classic combination shown here with a piece of Cheddar.

Since they are so closely allied in origin, it might seem logical to partner cheese with a glass of milk, but the assertive flavor and clinging texture of many cheeses are neither resolved nor enhanced by milk, for milk is too similar. We might be forced to conclude that alcohol is at the heart of the matter, were it not for the fact that whiskey and gin are decidedly unsympathetic to cheese. So we are left with wine, with its fruity, earthy, aromatic, benign and often heady qualities – these are the ideal companions to the special qualities of cheese.

Yet even here we must exercise a certain amount of selection and judgment, for there are almost as many varieties of cheese as there are wine. Although some eccentric tastes might suggest combining a peppery cheese with a sweet wine, we might begin with

Some successful cheese trays

The key to success is: Combine different types with interesting flavors. Include at least one soft cheese with white mold or red rind growth, one semihard or hard type, one blue-veined cheese and possibly a goat cheese or a fresh type. Processed cheese has no place on the cheese board. It is always nice to include a little-known speciality that you may have found. The following combinations include simple and inexpensive, as well as more extravagant suggestions.

Boursin	*Bel Paese*	*Boursin*
Camembert	*Emmental*	*Emmental*
Gouda	*Camembert*	*Havarti*
Danablu	*Pont-l'Evêque*	*Reblochon*
		Camembert
		Neufchâtel
		Banon
		Maroilles
Brie	*Reblochon*	*Munster*
Cheddar	*Jarlsberg*	*Bleu de Bresse*
Banon	*Vacherin Mont d'Or*	*Stilton*
Gorgonzola	*Taleggio*	
	Bleu de Bresse	
Camembert	*Tomme au Raisin*	*Banon*
Gruyère	*Gouda*	*Vacherin Mont d'Or*
Munster	*Appenzell*	*Edam*
Bleu des Causses	*Carré de l'Est*	*Chaource*
Sainte-Maure	*Livarot*	*Cantal*
	Munster	*Emmental*
	Bleu d'Auvergne	*Pont-l'Evêque*
	Roquefort	*Bleu de Bresse*
Brie		
Saint-Paulin		
Chabichou		
Munster		
Roquefort		

a simple rule: The wine that accompanies most types of cheese should not be sweet. There are one or two exceptions, however. Connoisseurs usually insist that Stilton cheese be served with port wine which, though heady and strong, is decidedly sweet. The reason for the survival of this partnership is because port was the gentleman's after-dinner drink of eighteenth-century England, and since cheese was served at the end of the meal, it naturally found port as its partner: port was the aristocratic wine, Stilton the aristocratic cheese. Others may point out that the ideal partner to Stilton cheese is a fruity Burgundy.

The rules that govern our selection of wines to accompany cheese should be regarded more as suggestions than strict guidelines, but they have evolved from experience gathered from centuries of careful judgment. It is generally acknowledged that a wine and a cheese of the same general character prove to be the most successful partners. A fresh, slightly

---

Some successful wine and cheese combinations

Banon (France)
Fruity red wine or dry rosé, such as Côtes de Provence.

Bel Paese (Italy)
Supple, but not too light red wine, like Barbera or Chianti.

Bleu d'Auvergne (France)
Robust, full-bodied red wine such as Châteauneuf-du-Pape or other Rhône wines.

Brie (France)
Fruity red wine of character; or possibly a good white wine, such as a fine white Burgundy.

Camembert (France)
A lively red wine, neither too light nor too heavy; St. Emilion would be a good choice.

Cantal (France)
Ripe, rather luxurious, red wine, perhaps a fine Burgundy or a full-bodied Rhône wine.

Carré de l'Est (France)
A rather full-bodied red, or a light, spicy white wine, such as Alsace.

Chabichou (France)
A bone-dry white wine, such as Sancerre or Pouilly Fumé.

Cheddar (Great Britain)
A reliable claret, a good Burgundy or Rhône wine, or perhaps a strong dry white wine.

Cheshire (Great Britain)
A reliable claret, a good Burgundy or Rhône wine, or perhaps a strong dry white wine.

Danablu (Denmark)
Powerful reds like Rhône or Rioja.

Edam (Netherlands)
A not too overpowering red wine, such as a fine Bordeaux.

Emmental (Switzerland)
Fresh whites (the Swiss Fendant is very suitable), or light reds (perhaps a young Beaujolais).

Gorgonzola (Italy)
Robust, full reds; among Italian wines, a quality Barolo is a good choice.

Gouda (Netherlands)
A not too overpowering red wine, such as a fine Bordeaux.

Gruyère (France, Switzerland)
Fresh whites (the Swiss Fendant is very suitable), or light reds (perhaps a young Beaujolais).

Maroilles (France)
A powerful red wine, like Rhône or Rioja.

Mozzarella (Italy)
Fresh whites, preferably Italian Soave or Verdicchio.

Munster (France, Germany)
The spicy white Gewürztraminer is the local companion in Alsace; a pithy red wine is also very good.

Parmigiano (Italy)
Full-bodied reds, like Sangiovese or the sparkling Lambrusco.

Pont-l'Evêque (France)
Rather full red wines such as one of the better Beaujolais types (Moulin á Vent, etc.).

Port-Salut (France)
Light, agreeable red wine or a not too heavy white.

Provolone (Italy)
A supple and fruity red wine, preferably not too young.

Reblochon (France)
White and red Savoie wines; also rather full reds from the Rhône area.

Roquefort (France)
Cahors, Roussillon; a glowing red wine like Châteauneuf-du-Pape.

Saint-Nectaire (France)
Powerful reds from Rhône, Provence, Languedoc.

Saint-Paulin (France)
Light, agreeable red wine or a not too heavy white.

Stilton (Great Britain)
Vintage port or a full, ripe red wine of high quality.

Tilsiter (Germany)
A fresh white wine or a not too powerful red.

Weinkäse (Germany)
Rhine or Moselle wine.

sourish cheese is well suited to a dry, light, white wine: Chabichou, the goat's milk cheese from Poitou, France, is a good companion to a crisp white wine such as Sancerre, or a Muscadet from the Loire. Strong, aromatic cheeses demand a strong, robust wine: Provolone, for example, a pretty powerful cheese, needs a wine that can look it straight in the eye, a wine like Barolo.

Many combinations of wine and cheese are thus closely related by region of origin. A really earthy and tangy cheese, a blue such as Roquefort, demands a hearty red wine, and we do not have far to look: the vineyards of Châteauneuf-du-Pape, a mere seventy miles to the east of Roquefort village, produce the perfect partner – equally earthy and tangy.

On the cheese farms of Alsace, the strongly aromatic Munster cheese is balanced by serving it with the spicy, white local Gewürztraminer; in the *trattorias* of Piedmont, blue-veined Gorgonzola is best suited to a warmblooded Barolo or Barbaresco. In the same way, Reblochon goes well with the light white wines of the Savoie, such as Rousette; Emmental with the delicate Fendant wines from the Swiss canton of Valais; and Parmesan with a red San Giovese or a Lambrusco from Emilia.

Combining cheese and wine of the same region is a good first principle, but it is by no means invariable. Bearing in mind what we have said about sweet wines, it would be a pity to serve a fine *Beerenauslese* hock with a piece of Limburger; when in doubt, the rule of "like character" should be applied. This rule is also useful with cheeses produced by countries that do not make wine, countries like Holland, Belgium, England and the Scandinavian nations. English blue Cheshire has a salty tang that might go best with a St. Emilion from Bordeaux. Mature Dutch Gouda is splendid with wines of the Medoc, while many of the Scandinavian cheeses can be partnered with dry white wines, like Chablis.

The quality of the wine must also be considered when choosing the cheese. If you have stumbled across a treasure trove of Richebourg, that ambrosial wine from the Côte de Nuits in Burgundy, or if you have been saving a few bottles of Haut Brion for a special occasion, you are unlikely to serve them with cheeses like Limburger or

LEFT: When you serve a variety of international cheeses, you may want to accompany them with a selection of wines. Cheese and wine should be presented in ascending order of fullness of taste. Match the mild cheeses to the younger, simpler wines – white or red – and the sharp or well-matured and strongly flavored cheeses to the richer and more robust wines, mature Burgundy, the Italian Barolo, or even port wine.

BELOW: The faintly sweet, nutty Emmental is perfect when accompanied by brown, whole-meal bread and a glass of light red wine.

Romadur, cheeses that you can recognize even before you've seen them. Romadur, Belgium's famous "stinking cheese," needs a rough and ready Chianti to keep it in its place.

On the other hand, a cheese and wine party does *not* have to cost a fortune. A good piece of advice is to aim for simplicity, particularly when on unfamiliar ground. A large selection of cheeses and wines is pleasing only to the expert; to the uninitiated it merely leads to confusion.

Serving cheese and wine
Someone once said that the first duty of a wine is that it should be red. To this we might add that its second duty is to accompany food. There are some fruity and very distinctive white wines that can be enjoyed by themselves – those from the Mosel or Rhine for example. But most reds are best drunk

BELOW: A selection of French cheeses, perfectly matched with a full-flavored Burgundy.

with food, for it is food that somehow gives an added dimension to their flavor. As a food cheese is particularly gifted in this task.

One of the most acceptable moments to serve cheese and wine is at the end of a good meal. In most European countries, this is usually before the dessert, when a few different types of cheese are placed on the table to be enjoyed with the remaining red wine. In France, cheese is an inseparable part of the dinner.

In keeping with the simple approach, the cheese board on the dinner table should offer a limited selection of types. For one thing, appetites are somewhat flagging by the time cheese is presented. There should be a sufficient portion of each type (about $3\frac{1}{2}$ oz per person). A list of possible combinations can be found on p. 97.

The popularity of the wine and cheese party as a social occasion has increased with the availability of the staple ingredients. You could, if you felt sufficiently confident, offer just *one* cheese, such as a whole Cheddar, Stilton or a Gruyère, with a variety of wines to choose from.

The combination of wine and cheese should be supported by additional elements: bread, an assortment of salad things, a few condiments. While the French will always choose bread first and foremost, other nationalities might prefer crackers or crispbreads. Scandinavia and Germany have a great selection of rye and black breads and crispbreads, well suited to the kinds of cheese they produce. Some sophisticated Italians claim that it is vulgar to eat *grana* as a table cheese, but you might well discover the joy of a piece of fresh Parmesan accompanied not by bread but by crisp celery, a few radishes and, of course, a glass or two of fruity Lambrusco.

Make an experiment and decide whether Camembert cheese goes best with a crusty French *baguette* or a slice of pumpernickel, and whether Danish Tybo with caraway seeds should be accompanied by sour rye-bread or a slice of challah (the braided loaf found in Jewish cookery). English farmhouse Cheddar seems designed to be a life-long partner to farmhouse bread, yet it goes equally well with "water biscuits" (an early corruption of the word *wafer* biscuit) or the elegant, crisp crackers known as Bath Olivers.

BELOW: The Ristorante de Filippo in Valle d'Aosta, Italy, where they know about good food, good wine and good cheese – especially the local and famous Fontina cheese.

With your cheeses and wines there should be an imaginative selection of breads and crackers, including fresh and crusty French bread, brown bread and granary bread, rye and knäck-bröd, toast and an assortment of wafers and crackers. Some people disapprove of butter with bread and cheese, nevertheless it should be included for those – and there are many – who prefer it. There should also be cheese knives, plates and napkins, salt, and fruits such as grapes, apples and pears, for these go extremely well with cheese.

The quantity of wine needed must be calculated in relation to the possible thirst and drinking habits of the party. If you are serving light white and rosé wines during summer, thirsts may be considerable, and for this reason it is a good idea to include beer, iced water and fruit juices in your selection of drinks. But your first consideration is to the wine, and you should count on about three-quarters of a bottle per person, or three bottles shared between four people.

In wine-drinking countries, and with those familiar with wine, it is customary to serve wines in order of importance: light or modest ones first, leading up to a grand climax. A host serving claret from Bordeaux might begin with a few bottles of *Cru Bourgeois* wine, fairly inexpensive, through to something such as Château Talbot, or a more classy Pauillac wine, and terminate (if he can afford it) with something really grand like Château d'Yquem. It is difficult to present wines in some semblance of order at a wine and cheese party, unless you are prepared to guide your guests through the selection. You can put all your wines on the table at once – or perhaps start with some light wines and bring on the big guns later.

When all is said and done, it is the individual taste – your taste – that is the most important guide to choice. Take a piece of mature Pont-l'Evêque and try it with a glass of full-bodied Burgundy. If you don't agree that this is an ideal combination, try the cheese with a glass of claret, or a white Burgundy, or even a hock. You will soon find, in this pleasant and pioneering fashion, the cheese's true companion. It is the individual, and not the cheese nor the wine, that really decides the ideal match.

Recipes with cheese

The history of food and cooking is an integral part of the fascinating story of human culture and civilization. When we try to imagine what the daily life of other peoples in other times must have been like, we should discover what food they ate, how they cooked, which utensils they used and invented, and how they managed to provide themselves with the necessary ingredients for the daily meal. It is also true the other way around: when we get to know a foreign cuisine, we not only discover new dishes and new flavors, but we are also invited to taste and to experience something of the character and the way of life of the people who created the dishes.

It is particularly true in the twentieth century that cookery has become truly international. Refrigerated transport has made it possible to enjoy fresh Italian vegetables, British lamb, and soft French cheeses in virtually every corner of the world.

Cheese has its own place in the culinary world. Of course, it classifies first of all as a complete and nourishing food. It is also a lovely snack, to be enjoyed with a glass of wine in the company of good friends. It is part of any French dinner. And it can be used in the kitchen, as the chief ingredient of many a dish, or as a refined flavoring.

In the selection of recipes that follow, you can find many suggestions. Use your imagination to develop, change or vary them to your own tastes and preferences. Herbs and spices, for instance, may be adapted to your taste. The cheese types prescribed (we have often indicated them in general terms) can be interchanged. You can find substitutes easily enough in this book.

The recipes are loosely divided according to their nature, from breakfast dishes through lunch snacks to hot dinners. The recipes will serve four persons (of average appetite), unless otherwise stated.

Standard American measurements have been used throughout. Please consult the "Conversion Tables" on p. 112 for British and metric equivalents.

Breakfast

What a curious experience – eating a food that you positively know was prepared in exactly the same fashion two thousand years ago. The experience is yours when you try one of the Roman recipes which have been preserved in writing. Marcus Porcius Cato (234-149 BC) recorded the recipe for Savillum. This is likely to have been an everyday food in ancient Rome. It is a compact cake of corn grits with a mixture of cheese and honey. The Romans baked it in an earthenware pot in the glowing embers. It can be prepared in advance and served cold at breakfast. Cut a thick slice, spread some more honey on it – delicious!

ABOVE: An arrangement of British products on a traditional pub table: a York ham, a Stilton and some Cheddar, a pint of beer and a pie. Only the wine is non-British.

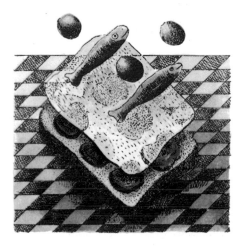

Savillum
Oil, 8 oz corn grits,
1 lb Ricotta, 8 oz
honey, 1 egg, poppy
seed

Grease a heatproof dish with oil. Mix the grits, cheese, honey (save a little of this) and beaten egg together. Place the mixture in the dish, cover, and bake in an oven preheated to 400°F for 50 minutes until done. Then cover the top with the rest of the honey, scatter poppy seeds over it and put the Savillum, still uncovered, back into the oven for a few minutes. It can also be fried on top of the stove in a frying pan and the honey may also be mixed through the dough all at once.

The Romans also had a recipe for Pulmentum, the predecessor of today's Polenta, the corn porridge that is such an important part of the menu in central and southern Italy. The Romans, by the way, did not have maize yet (this came from America many centuries later); they used millet or spelt as the chief ingredient of this dish. There were many variations on the theme, prepared with milk, fresh cheese, honey, etc.; and the parallel with today's breakfast cereals can not be denied. Another version of the Polenta is the Rumanian Mamaliga, so thick that it hardens when cooled. The Rumanians break it into bits and eat it with eggs, sour cream and cheese.

Polenta
2½ cups water, 1 tsp
salt, 4 oz corn grits,
butter, 4 oz Parmesan
cheese

Bring the salted water to a boil in a pan with a thick bottom. Sprinkle in the corn grits while stirring continuously, making sure that the water continues to boil. Cook over a low flame for about 30 minutes, stirring occasionally, until the Polenta is done.

The mush must be thick enough for a spoon to stand up in. It is eaten topped or mixed with butter and grated cheese. Once it has become cold it can also be fried in oil and eaten with tomatoes and grated cheese.

In most countries the cooked breakfast is unknown, and if it does exist (e.g., the famous British breakfast), eggs, bacon or even fish are preferred rather than cheese. In a gastronomical country like France, the *petit déjeuner* is nothing but a cup of coffee and an unbuttered roll. Sandwiches with cheese are a more nourishing start of the day, and they are the mainstay of the Dutch breakfast. The thriftiness of the Dutch is exemplified by the use of the cheese slicer which produces impossibly thin slices: the careless big chunk of cheese is taboo at breakfast.

Lunch
At lunchtime, there is more time and perhaps more appetite to take some trouble over the preparation of an appetizing snack. Nothing is more simple than hot cheese canapés in their many variations. The great thing is that you can prepare them a few hours in advance and keep them in the refrigerator; they need only a few minutes in the oven, preheated to 450°F, or under the grill, and they are ready. Welsh Rarebit is a bit more complicated to prepare, but well worth the trouble.

Quick Pizza
4 slices of white bread,
butter, 2 tomatoes,
salt, pepper, 4 oz
Cheddar or Gouda
cheese, anchovy
fillets, black olives

Toast the slices of bread and butter them. Peel the tomatoes, cut them in slices and place them on the slices of toast. Sprinkle salt and pepper and the grated cheese on top. Decorate each slice with a latticework of anchovy fillets cut lengthwise, and halved black olives in between. Place the slices underneath a hot grill until the cheese has melted.

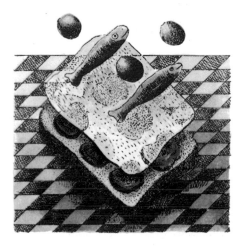

Welsh Rarebit
4 slices of bread, 3 Tbs butter, 7 oz grated Cheddar, 8 oz beer (pale or stout), 2 egg yolks, 2 tsp mustard, cayenne pepper, paprika

Cut the crusts off the bread, toast the slices and keep them warm. Melt the butter on a low heat, stir well and add the grated cheese and the beer gradually. Continue stirring until the mixture is smooth. Mix in the loosened egg yolks, mustard and pepper, pour the sauce over the slices. They can then be put under the grill and sprinkled with paprika, but this is not essential.

Croustades Montagnardes
Bread, sliced cheese, chives

This is the simplest form of cheese canapé, the bottom of which is a slice of toasted bread and the top melted cheese. Real farmer's bread with a slice of not overmature cheese on it, sprinkled with fresh chives needs no additions at all.

BELOW: Croustades Montagnardes, a simple and very tasty snack at any hour of the day.

Gouda and Asparagus Canapés
4 slices white bread, 2 Tbs butter, 3½ oz ham, 1 can of asparagus spears (about 12), 4 slices semimature Gouda cheese, parsley, paprika

Toast the slices of bread and butter them. Place one slice of ham with 3 strained asparagus spears on it on top of each slice. Cover the slices with a slice of cheese and put them under the grill or in the oven until the cheese has melted. Garnish with chopped parsley or ground paprika.

Sauerkraut Toast
4 slices white bread, 2 Tbs butter, 3½ oz sauerkraut (preferably the sort made with wine vinegar), 4 thick slices of smoked bacon, 4 slices semimature cheese or processed cheese, paprika

Toast the slices of bread and butter them. Boil the sauerkraut for 10 minutes in a little water, drain and divide between the toast slices. Fry the slices of smoked bacon and lay them on the sauerkraut. Cover the slices with cheese and place under the grill or in the oven until the cheese has melted. Sprinkle them with paprika before serving.

LEFT: Gouda and asparagus canapés are a delicious combination of ham, cheese and asparagus spears.

The Italian Pizza has conquered the world. It can be served as a complete meal, is fun to make and fun to eat. It is a good example of typical Italian cooking: simple, resourceful but filling. It is composed from the inexpensive ingredients of the region: tomatoes, often planted between olive trees and ripening quickly in the hot southern sun; anchovies, caught in the Mediterranean since time immemorial; and Mozzarella, produced from the milk of buffalo and cows. This cheese is really indispensable when making a genuine Italian pizza; additionally, Parmesan cheese may be grated on top.

But the ingredients vary; every pizzeria offers a selection of pizzas, each with a different flavor and taste. The dough is kneaded with vigor and skill; it is rolled, tossed and formed with a rapid spinning motion into a wafer-thin, round of dough. It is topped with the selected ingredients and put into the oven on a long, wooden shovel.

These days you can buy ready-made pizzas which only need warming in the oven. There are also cartons with all the ingredients, enabling you to make quite a good pizza with a minimum of fuss. But nothing is better than an entirely home-made pizza, starting from a rising yeast dough and prepared with fresh ingredients. As far as the cheese is concerned, apart from Mozzarella there are many other suitable kinds; the cheese should melt well and not draw into threads. Try Gorgonzola or another blue-veined cheese (with tomato, bacon and herbs), or Cheddar (with snips of onion, garlic and parsley), or Emmental (with diced ham, beaten egg and capers), or Parmesan (grated over mushrooms, paprika and black olives). But let us not forget the original recipe: Pizza Napolitana.

Pizza Napolitana
For the dough:
2¼ cups flour, 1 tsp salt, 1 oz yeast, 1 tsp sugar, approximately ⅔ cup water, 2 Tbs olive oil

For the topping:
2 onions, 2 Tbs olive oil, 2 cloves of garlic, 8 oz fresh tomato puree, 12-13 oz Mozzarella cheese mixed with 1½-2 oz Parmesan, thyme, basil, oregano, salt, pepper, sugar

Sift flour and salt in a bowl. Stir the yeast and sugar with some tepid water until the yeast becomes liquid. Make a hollow in the flour, pour in the yeast, cover it with a thin layer of flour and place the bowl covered with a clean cloth in a warm place, away from drafts.

As soon as the yeast forms bubbles, gradually add the remaining tepid water and olive oil. Start stirring from the hollow. Work liquid and flour in the bowl with a fork until the dough forms into a ball. Place the dough on a board dusted with flour and knead till it looks shiny and elastic and comes away from the hand easily. Put the dough back in the bowl, replace the cloth and leave the dough rising in a warm place for about 1 hour. Divide the quantity into four portions and knead each portion again on the flour dusted board. If the dough is still slightly sticky, use a little more flour. Shape each ball into a thin round shape, bend the edges up a little and place them onto a baking tray dusted with flour.

For the topping: fry the finely chopped onions on a low heat in the olive oil until they are soft; add the chopped garlic, tomato puree and herbs and let it simmer for a few minutes. Season with salt, pepper and sugar to taste and divide the filling equally over the 4 bases. Grate the cheese, put it on top of the pizzas and add a few drops of olive oil. Place the baking tray on the bottom shelf of the oven, preheated to 450-500° F and bake the pizzas for approximately 10 minutes until they are golden brown.

While British dishes may look less festive than the exuberant Italian foods, Cheese Pie is still a very good and statisfying dish. It is savory and nourishing, and goes well with a good glass of beer.

Cheese Pie
For the pastry:
4 Tbs butter, ⅔ cup flour, 1½ tsp salt, 2-3 Tbs water

For the filling:
3½ oz bacon, 9 oz Cheddar, ¼ cup milk, 2 eggs, parsley, paprika

Using two knives, cut the butter into the flour to which the salt has been added. When the butter has been cut fine, gradually add water and make a ball of the paste, still using the knives. Roll the pastry lightly on a board dusted with flour. Turn the pastry, dust flour on the top and repeat the rolling several times. Leave the pastry folded for about 1 hour in a cool place and then roll it out thinly. Line a thinly buttered pie dish with the pastry. Place the fried bacon in it, followed by the sliced cheese and pour the eggs, beaten loose with milk, on

BELOW: Pie crust filled
with thick slices of
aubergine – but you
can choose any filling
you like.

top. Place the pie on the bottom shelf
of an oven preheated to 450°F and
bake for about 20 minutes until
golden brown. Sprinkle with paprika
or chopped parsley.

Aubergine Pie

This is a tasty variation of the Cheese
Pie. Cut an aubergine in finger-thick
slices. Lay these on the filling of the
cheese pie and scatter grated cheese
over them. In this way, by choosing
other fillings, one can embroider
endlessly on the theme of cheese pie.

There are almost as many omelette
recipes as there are ingredients. The
basic ideas is simplicity itself: beat
eggs with milk, mix in some savory or
sweet extras, and let set over a fire. As
so often, it is the many possible variations that make the dish so interesting,
and among the recipes there are quite
a few where cheese plays an important
part. For the basic Cheese Omelette
and the tasty Soufflé Omelette, any
sort of cheese that melts well and
draws no threads can be used. An
omelette with a fresh salad is a complete meal and, many would say, one
of the best!

BELOW: There are
almost as many
recipes for omelettes
as there are ingre-
dients. The version
shown here is the
light, soufflé omelette.

Cheese Omelette
4 eggs, 4 Tbs milk,
2½-3 oz well-matured
grated cheese, salt,
pepper, 1 Tbs butter.

Beat the eggs and milk together and
mix 1½-2 oz of the grated cheese and
some salt and pepper through it.
B own the butter in a frying pan, pour
in the batter and allow it to set over a
low flame. From time to time draw the
congealed portions from the sides of
the pan to the center allowing the rest
to run out over the bottom of the pan
and set. This also makes the omelette
somewhat less compact. As soon as the
top is no longer liquid scatter it with
the rest of the cheese and fold the
omelette in half.

Instead of mixing the cheese
through the batter, one can also lay
slices of semimature cheese on top of
the omelette.

An omelette can also be made successfully with fresh cheese. Cover the
omelette with fresh cheese as soon as
it is no longer liquid, scatter chopped
herbs on it, and roll the omelette up.

Soufflé Omelette
4 eggs, 4 Tbs milk,
2½-3 oz Parmesan
cheese, salt, pepper,
2 Tbs butter

Separate the eggs. Beat up the egg
yolks with the milk and some pepper
until foamy. Whip the egg whites with
a little salt until very stiff and fold the
egg yolks carefully into the egg whites.
Allow the omelette to set without
stirring. Scatter the cheese over one
half and fold the other half over it.

Appetizers

At the end of a busy day, sit back and relax with a glass of your favorite drink and some snacks. Cheese is somehow a perfect companion to any drink, and can be enjoyed in many forms. Of course, you can just cut a solid piece of semihard cheese into small squares, decorated if you wish with little bits of onion, ginger, olive, pineapple, gherkin, etc. Just eat them from your hand – delicious! Cheese scones and cheese biscuits need a bit more preparation, as does the satisfying Cheese Pastry, which can be kept in the refrigerator and served cold. The cheese cream described under Chester Biscuits can be used in many other snacks: fill celery stalks with it, or shape it into little balls and dust these with grated cheese; serve with a cocktail pick and chopped garden herbs.

Chester Biscuits

For the biscuits:
1¼ cups flour, ¼ cup butter, 2 oz grated Cheshire cheese, ¼ cup finely chopped almonds, 3 egg yolks, salt, pepper

For the cream:
⅓ cup butter, 1 oz grated Cheshire cheese, 1 oz grated Parmesan cheese, salt, pepper, paprika

FOR THE BISCUITS: Knead all the ingredients together until a ball forms that sticks together. Set apart in a cool place. Later, roll the dough into a thin sheet, cut out rounds, lay them on a buttered baking tray and bake them in the middle of an oven preheated to 375°F for 15 minutes until golden brown.

FOR THE CREAM: Mix the ingredients thoroughly and put the cream on half the cooled biscuits, then lay another biscuit on top and press it down firmly.

Dinner

Cheese works wonders in many dishes. Theoretically, you could devise a complete menu where every course would be a cheese dish, and the whole still a reasonably varied and tasty meal. But don't put this into practice – imagination and variation are two of the most important aspects of the art of cooking. Still, cheese is the finishing touch to many dishes and gives them a refined taste that might otherwise be difficult to achieve.

A salad of fresh fruits and vegetables with cheese and a few other surprise elements is an original entrée: fresh, light and appetizing. These salads can be prepared well in advance and be served straight from the refrigerator. They look especially nice in a high glass bowl, sprinkled with some paprika or finely chopped parsley, and perhaps decorated with a slice of lemon.

Cheese Pastry

½ sweet red and ½ green pepper, 1 onion, 3½ oz butter, 3 eggs, 1 cup self-raising flour, 7 oz grated cheese, pepper, salt, paprika

BELOW: Cheese pastry, a savory loaf, baked in the oven but served cold. It is excellent as a satisfying snack, and can be given additional flavor and nutritional value by the addition of bacon to the recipe.

Wash the peppers, remove the seeds and core, and cut into small pieces. Chop the onion until fine. Beat the butter and eggs until frothy, add the flour and then mix in the red and green pepper, onion, grated cheese and pepper, salt and paprika to taste. Place the dough in a buttered cake tin and place the pie in the center of the oven, preheated to 375°F for about 50 minutes until golden brown. Allow it to cool, cut into slices and serve.

White Celery Salad

2 stalks white celery, 1½-2 oz blue cheese, 1½-2 oz semimature Brick or Gouda cheese, 1½-2 oz cashew nuts, 3½ oz peeled shrimp, 1 lemon, 1 Tbs oil, salt and pepper, 1 sour apple

Clean the celery and cut into thin rings. Crumble the blue cheese and dice the Brick or Gouda. Chop the nuts until fine. Shred most of the shrimp, reserving a few for decoration, and mix everything together.

Blend 1 Tbs lemon juice with the oil, add salt and pepper to taste, and dress the salad with this. Add the small pieces of apple only at the last moment to avoid discoloration. Decorate with the remaining shrimp.

Greek Salad
1 small green cucumber, 8-9 oz tomatoes, 3½ oz Feta or other sheep cheese, 2 Tbs tarragon vinegar, 2 Tbs olive oil, freshly ground pepper, paprika, thyme, basil

Wash the cucumber and dice it unpeeled. Mix in the peeled tomatoes and broken up cheese. Make a salad dressing of the tarragon vinegar, olive oil and herbs and mix it lightly with the rest of the ingredients.

Feta is fairly salty, so the salad probably does not need any additional salt.

Pear Cocktail
6-8 oz cheese (Fontal or some other crumbly cheese), 2 pears, 1 pint sour cream, the juice of 1 lemon, sugar, sweet red pepper

Cut the cheese and pears into fine strips. Blend the sour cream with the lemon juice and a little sugar and fold in the cheese and pear strips. Garnish the cocktail with strips of sweet red pepper.

Soup is an invitation to use your imagination and show your daring. When diced, cheese forms the body of the soup; when cut into fine slivers, it is a spicy flavoring; grated cheese sprinkled on top enhances the flavor and aroma of almost any soup. As a rule, soups should not be allowed to boil for any length of time after the cheese has been added; it may draw threads and become bitter in taste. It is better to add it at the last moment, or at the table. Remember that cheese contains salt, so do not salt your soup too heavily when you are going to add cheese.

The soups are followed by a few hot entrées, which you should probably prepare only for people with an exceptionally hearty appetite! For modest eaters, these dishes are a complete meal.

Leek and Cheese Soup
2 large or 4 small leeks, 1 onion, 1 clove garlic, 2 Tbs butter, 4 cups bouillon, thyme, basil, 2 oz short macaroni, salt, 3½ oz Gruyère cheese, 3 Tbs white wine

Cut the washed leeks into rings, chop the onion and the clove of garlic until fine and sauté them in butter until brown. Add the bouillon, thyme and basil and boil the soup gently for 15 minutes.

Boil the macaroni separately in plenty of salted water for 15 minutes until done and rinse in a colander with cold water. Stir it into the soup. Melt the cheese in the heated wine and continue to stir until a smoothly bound sauce has been achieved. Pour the soup into individual portions and pour the melted cheese over it.

Soupe à l'oignon
1-1¼ lb onions, 1 Tbs oil, 2 Tbs butter, 4 tsp flour, 4 cups strong beef bouillon, salt, pepper

For the croutons:
4 slices bread, 1½-2 oz grated Gruyère or Parmesan cheese

Slice the onion and sauté in oil and butter until the slices are glazed and golden brown. Turn them over occasionally. Sprinkle the flour over the onion and fry for a few more minutes. Then pour the bouillon over little by little. Allow the soup to simmer for 20 minutes, remove the excess fat and finish off with salt and pepper to taste.

The croutons are either placed in the bowls and the soup poured over them, or sit on the soup in the bowls and are liberally covered with grated cheese.

Dutch Cheese Soup
3 eggs, 2 Tbs cream, 2½ oz extra-mature Gouda, 1½-2 oz ham (finely chopped), chives, 3 cups bouillon, some Dutch gin, bread croutons

Beat the eggs with the cream and mix in the grated cheese, the finely chopped ham and finely cut chives. Bring the bouillon to the boil and pour into the egg mixture while beating continuously. Serve in bowls, accompanied by a glass of gin which may be added to the soup. The croutons are served separately.

RIGHT: Tartelettes au Roquefort, prepared with the famous sheep's milk cheese, and decorated with walnuts.

Tartelettes au Roquefort
3½ oz Roquefort, 1 oz walnuts, cognac, 1 egg yolk, about 1 Tbs cream, tartelettes (tart shells), parsley

Rub the Roquefort through a sieve. Reserve 2 walnuts and chop up the rest into small pieces. Blend the Roquefort with the chopped nuts, a dash of cognac, the egg yolk and enough cream so that a creamy cheese mixture is formed. Fill the tartelettes with this and bake them for 30 minutes in an oven preheated to 375° F until they are golden. Garnish with pieces of walnut and parsley. They can also be served unbaked (with an aperitif as a cold starter). The tartelettes must then be much smaller and the egg yolk may be omitted.

The tartelettes can be bought ready-made.

Provolone alla patte
7 oz Provolone, 16-18 oz tomatoes, salt, pepper, 1 clove of garlic or garlic powder, oregano, chopped parsley

Lay ¾-inch-thick slices of Provolone on aluminum foil on a baking tray. Peel the tomatoes, remove the core and cut the pulp into very small pieces. Blend with salt and herbs to taste. Put some of this mixture on the slices of cheese and place under the grill or in the top of an oven preheated to 375-400° F until the cheese begins to melt a little. Cut into small pieces, this is a delicious snack to have with an aperitif.

The *pièce de résistance* of most dinners is a good piece of meat, and many meats are very happily combined with cheese: steak grilled with a slice of cheese, veal with a creamy spread of butter and Roquefort mixed, cutlets filled with ham and cheese, ragout sprinkled with grated cheese, tongue of veal with a rich Sauce Mornay, etc. There are endless possibilities. We give the recipes of a few of the more famous dishes, followed by a cheese soufflé, some vegetables prepared with cheese, and a few interesting ways to prepare the faithful potato, so often neglected in cooking.

Kalbsrücken Kempinski
Salt, 4 veal steaks, 4 Tbs butter, 1½-2 oz mushrooms, 2 onions, 4 tsp flour, 1 cup bouillon, ½ cup cream, pepper, celery salt, basil, 1½-2 oz extra mature cheese, sweet red pepper or tomato

Salt the steaks, fry them in 1/3 of the butter on both sides until golden brown and place them in a flat heat-proof dish. Wash the mushrooms and cut them in slices. Chop the onions until fine and sauté them with the mushrooms for 5 minutes in half of the remaining butter. Salt and pepper to taste and divide the mixture over the steaks. Melt the rest of the butter in the same pan, add the dry flour and the bouillon little by little, stirring continuously until a smoothly bound sauce is formed. Add the cream and herbs. Pour the sauce over the mushroom-onion mixture, sprinkle the grated cheese over it, and place the dish in the middle of an oven preheated to 370° F for 30 minutes. Garnish with strips of red pepper or tomato.

Carré de Porc au Fromage (6 servings)
Salt, pepper, 2-2¼ lbs carré of pork (with ribs), 6 Tbs butter, 10-11 oz mature cheese

Fry the salted and peppered meat in butter for about 40 minutes until golden brown and done. Cut the meat between the ribs almost to the end. Place a thick slice of cheese in each groove and allow it to stick out about ¼-½ in above the meat. Then place the meat in the center of an oven preheated to 400-425° F until the cheese has melted (after about 15 minutes). Before serving place a paper cuff around each rib.

Cheese Soufflé

4 tsp butter, 4 tsp flour, 1¼ cups milk, salt, pepper, paprika, Worcestershire sauce, tabasco, thyme, 3 eggs (separated), 1½-2 oz extra-mature cheese, 1½-2 oz ham, 2 Tbs madeira, butter

Melt the butter, add the flour and very slowly add the milk, stirring gently until a smooth sauce is obtained. Mix in the herbs and spices. Stir the warm sauce through the beaten egg yolks, put everything back in the pan and mix in the grated cheese and diced ham. Finally stir in the madeira and finish off to taste.

Beat the egg whites until very stiff and fold them quickly and carefully into the sauce. Transfer the mixture to a buttered ovenproof dish (capacity 1 quart). Fill the dish no more than two-thirds and place in the bottom of an oven preheated to 375°F for about 30 minutes until done and golden brown. Place the lid next to the dish in the oven. When ready, cover it with the hot lid and serve immediately.

Fonds d'Artichauts au Gratin

3½ oz bacon, 7 oz mushrooms, 2 tsp butter, 4 artichoke bottoms, 1 cup Mornay sauce, salt, pepper, rosemary, 1½-2 oz Gruyère, paprika

Fry the bacon until crisp and golden brown. Pour off the excess fat. Wash the mushrooms and sauté them in butter for a few minutes only. Cut the bacon and the mushrooms into small pieces and stir them into the Mornay sauce. Add salt, pepper and rosemary to taste. Place the artichoke bottoms in an ovenproof dish, pour the sauce over them, sprinkle on the grated cheese and put the dish in the middle of an oven preheated to 350-375°F for about 20 minutes. Scatter paprika over it before serving.

Polpettine di Spinaci alla Ricotta

16-18 oz spinach, 8-9 oz Ricotta, 4 Tbs flour, salt, pepper, 3 egg yolks, 3½ oz grated Parmesan cheese, ¼ cup butter

Boil the washed spinach for 5 minutes, allow to drain thoroughly and chop until fine. Mix in the Ricotta, flour, salt, pepper, egg yolks and half the grated cheese and form into small balls. Slide them one by one carefully into a pan of almost boiling water and simmer for 3-4 minutes. Remove them from the pan with a slotted spoon, place them on a heated dish, dab with melted butter and sprinkle on the rest of the cheese thickly.

BELOW: Stuffed potatoes, baked in their jackets, and covered with a generous layer of cheese.

Stuffed Potatoes

6 large potatoes, ½ cup milk, 2½ oz Cheddar, Cheshire or Stilton, salt, pepper, season salt, 1½-2 oz grated cheese, ¼ cup butter, parsley

Brush the potatoes until clean, wrap them in aluminum foil and bake them in the center of an oven preheated to 375°F for about 1 hour until done. Cut off one end of each potato and hollow them out carefully. Mash the contents and blend with milk, diced cheese, salt and herbs. Fill the potatoes with the mixture, scatter grated cheese over them, dab with butter and put them next to each other in an oven-proof dish in the oven for another 20 minutes approximately until a golden-brown crust has formed. Garnish with a sprig of parsley before serving.

Emmentaler Rösti

2 onions, 3 Tbs butter, 1½-1¾ lb potatoes, salt, pepper, 1½-2 oz Emmental

Sauté the finely chopped onions in half the butter until golden brown. Peel the potatoes, grate them coarsely and scatter salt and pepper over them. Add the grated potato to the onion in the frying pan, press them down with the center of a spoon and fry them over a medium flame for about 20 minutes. Turn the cake as soon as the underside is golden brown and the top is glazed. To do this allow it to glide onto a board, put the rest of the butter in the frying pan and fry the other side of the Rösti until golden brown. Place the slices of cheese on top and put under the grill until the cheese melts and is golden brown.

We have kept until last what is no doubt the most famous cheese meal of all: the fondue. Invented by the Swiss Sennen, living high up in the Alpine meadows and in the solitude of the mountains, this dish was originally eaten in a primitive fashion from one communal pan. Modern Fondue has inherited these ancient traditions, for in Switzerland it is not a daily meal, but a festive one, to be enjoyed with old friends. The hostess prepares the fondue at the table and she takes care that everybody happily gathers round to enjoy this age-old cheese dish.

There must be an ample quantity of cut French loaves on the table, so that every one can dip pieces of bread in the fondue using long fondue forks. The fork is slowly twisted to cut the cheese thread and is slowly lifted to the mouth. Don't be in a hurry, you will enjoy the glorious flavor better . . . and you will not burn your tongue.

Herdsmen and farmers practice the fundamental skills of humanity. They represent all that is lacking in cultured man, especially the city dweller. Perhaps this hankering after lost things is the reason why many people like the sense of friendship and joy of life that is present in fondue.

Fondue Neuchâteloise
1 clove of garlic, 1 cup dry white wine, 10-11 oz Emmental, 10-11 oz Gruyère, 1 tsp corn flour, kirsch, nutmeg, pepper

Rub the fondue pan with a clove of garlic. Pour in the white wine and stir in the grated cheese. Continue stirring until the cheese has melted and the sauce is smooth. As soon as the mixture starts to boil, thicken with the cornflour mixed with a bit of wine. Add kirsch, nutmeg and pepper to taste. Leave the fondue to simmer gently on the fondue stand. Serve white wine or tea. As a break, a glass of kirsch can be served, which in French is neatly called *coup de milieu*.

Fondue Fribourg
2 cups milk or water, 28 oz Vacherin à fondue, black pepper

Place the milk or water in the fondue pan (rubbing with garlic is not necessary). Cut the cheese in pieces, place them in a pan and press them fine with a fork. Continue stirring. When the mixture is smooth, do not let it come to boil. If it becomes too thick, add a few spoonfuls of warm water. Season well with freshly ground pepper. The mixture can take quite a lot without becoming sharp. Serve with tea. In Fribourg the fondue is often spooned onto boiled potatoes.

Raclette
A typical dish of Valais, Raclette has the same function as fondue. The semisoft, full-cream Raclette cheese is halved, the rinds at the cutting surface are removed and the cutting surface is exposed to a brightly burning wood or charcoal fire – or to the heat of an electric Raclette device.

In the meantime the guests are kept busy. They peel the potatoes that have been cooked in their jackets, and put gherkins and silver onions on their plates. As soon as the cutting surface of the cheese liquefies, and the edges become golden, the host or hostess scrapes the half-melted cheese and the crisp edge onto one of the plates. The guests, therefore, do not all eat together, because Raclette must be eaten hot and each takes his or her turn. The pleasant fire, the smell of melting cheese, the contrast between hot Raclette and cool Fendant wine create a very special atmosphere.

Index of cheese names

This index lists the names of the cheeses mentioned in this book. Page numbers prefixed "D" refer to a data panel entry on that page. Page numbers prefixed "R" refer to recipes on that page. When a cheese is made in several countries, there is a separate entry or entries for the most important country or countries where it is made. Another entry refers to the remaining countries.

Acknowledgments

Grateful acknowledgment is made to the following persons and institutions for their assistance in preparing this book.

Picture sources

Picture research by Ann Horton.

ABC Press (*agency for* Magnum, Pressehusset and Scoop/ *photographers:* E. Erwitt, E. Lessing, G. Nielsen, J. Stacke, D. Stock, B. Uzzle)
Allgemeiner Deutscher Nachrichten- dienst
Art Directors Photolibrary (*photographer:* B. Fleming)
Barnaby Picture Library (*photographers:* Hedrich-Blessing, E. Manewal, E. Preston)
Bavaria Verlag (*photographers:* T. Fehr- Bechtel, Schmachtenberger, T. Sellhuber)
Kees v.d. Berg
British Information Services (British Crown Copyright)
British Tourist Association
R. ter Brerke
Camerateam
Danish Agricultural Productsere
English Country Cheese Council
Robert Estall
Mary Evans
Food from France
Foto-unit
Frans Halsmuseum, Haarlem
Frits Gerritsen
Photographie Giraudon et Lauros- Giraudon
Susan Griggs (*photographers:* M. Boys, S. Galloway, J. Garrett, N. Holland, A. Woolfitt)
Sonia Halliday
Robert Harding (*photographers:* R. Cundy, D. Harney)
Michael Holford

Sherry Kamp
Kon. Bibliotheek Albert I, Brussels
Koninklijke Nederlandse Zuivelbond
Landbrukets Sentralforbund (*photographer:* A. Svendsen)
Colin Maher
Mansell Collection
Mejeribrugets Hjemmemarkedskontor
ir. P. Meyers
Milk Marketing Board
John Moss
Norkse Meieriers Salgssentral
PAF International (*photographer:* Ch. Délu)
Paul Pet
Pictor (*photographer:* D. Braun)
Picturepoint (*photographer:* J. Baker)
Popperfoto (*photographers:* H. Chapman, M. Duris, J. C. Grelier, J. Mounicq)
Toine Post
Sem Presser
Reflejo
Peter Ruting
Schweizerische Käseunion
Simon Slop
Société Anonyme des Fermiers Réunis
Sopexa
Spectrum Colour Library (*photographers:* H. Douglas-Reid, M. J. Gilson, S. Meredith, E. S. Taylor)
J. W. Stoppelenburg
Svenska Mejeriernas Riksförening
Swiss National Tourist Office (*photographers:* Giegel, Müller)
John Topham Picture Library
Peter v.d. Velde
A. A. Verschoor
VVV, Gouda
ZEFA (*photographers:* W. Backhaus, Dr. K. Biedermann, W. Borrenbergen, W. Braun, E. G. Carle, W. Ernest, R. Everts, K. Göbel, H. Grathwohl, Dr. G. Haasch, W. Hasenberg, D. Hecker, B. Julian, G. Kalt, P. Keetman, Dr. H. Kramarz, K. Kurz,

Dr. R. Lorenz, H. Mante, G. Marché, M. Nissen, Paul, D. Pittius, Puck- Kornetzki, F. Saller, H. Schlapfer, G. Seider, A. Simonsson, Strachil, Teasy, D. H. Teuffen, H. Wiesner, Dr. H. Wirth).

Special thanks to
The Delicatessen Shop (John Cavacienti), London
Wells Stores (Patrick Rance), Streatley-on-Thames

Illustrators
Ritzo Bloem & Partners
Anke Engelse
Eddy Schoonheijt

Other sources, consultants and contributors
Pierre Androuet, Paris
ir. J. C. T. van der Berg, Wageningen
Fa. J. C. N. Boering (F. Sander), Dieman
Campina, Asten-Someren
Centrale du Vacherin Mont d'Or, Moudon
Centrale Paysanne Luxembourgeoise, Luxembourg
Comité Interprofessionel du Gruyère de Comté, Poligny
Confédération générale des Producteurs de Lait de Brebis et des Industriels de Roquefort, Millau
Coopérative laitière de Vicq, Vicq
Dutch Embassies in various countries
Hubrecht Duijker, Abcoude
English Country Cheese Council (H. R. Cornwell), London
Gerdabel, Amsterdam
Frans Grosfeld, Kortenhoef
Instituut voor Veeteeltkundig Onderzoek (S. Brandsma), Zeist
International Dairy Federation, Brussels
International Neighbor Group (C. Houtman), Eindhoven
Abraham Kef, Amsterdam

Landbouwhogeschool (Dr. H. Mulder, Dr. J. v.d. Poel), Wageningen
Mejeribrugets Hjemmemarkedskontor (L. Rasmussen), Århus
ir. P. Meyers, Veenendaal
Milk Marketing Board, Thames Ditton
Ministerie van Landbouw (Mr. Edam, ir. P. Tiersma, ir. D. Rozeboom), The Hague
Nationale Zuiveldienst, Brussels
Nederlands Instituut voor Zuivelonderzoek, Ede
Nederlands Zuivelbureau, Rijswijk
Norske Meieriers Salgssentral (R. Marcussen), Oslo
Ostmästaren, Riksost (Mr. Regouw), Stockholm
Produktschap voor Zuivel (P. Wehrmann), The Hague
Schweizerische Käseunion, Berne
Dave Smith, Grubbenvorst
Société Anonyme des Fermiers Réunis, Paris
Sopexa, Paris
ir. E. Steinbuch, Wageningen
Svenska Mejeriernas Riksförening (E. Westerberg), Stockholm
Syndicat d'Amélioration du Fromage Saint-Nectaire, Besse-en-Chandesse
Syndicat des Fabricants de Pont- l'Evêque et de Livarot, Caen
Syndicat des Fabricants du Véritable Camembert, Caen
ir. T. C. Tomson, Heiloo
Unigate, Wiltshire
Unions des Industriels Laitiers de Basse-Normandie, Rouen
Verband der deutschen Milchwirtschaft (Dr. Malich), Bonn
J. S. C. Verschoor, Rijswijk
Voorlichtingsbureau voor de Voeding (Drs. A. J. Bakker, A. A. van Vloten), The Hague
Zuivelkwaliteitscontrolebureau (A. Swarte), Amsterdam

Conversion tables

The recipes in this book are based on American measures. The solid American measures are ounces and pounds, equal to the Imperial measures. Butter, flour and a few other ingredients are given in American cups or tablespoons.

The liquid American measures are less than British Imperial Measures. In the recipes whenever "cup," "tablespoon" or "teaspoon" are quoted they are: American cup = 8 fluid ounces; American tablespoon = British dessert spoon; and American teaspoon = a small British teaspoon.

OVEN TEMPERATURES

Degrees Fahrenheit	Degrees Centigrade	Regulo Gas Mark	
240-280	115-135	$\frac{1}{4}-\frac{1}{2}$	Very slow
280-320	135-160	1	Slow
320-340	160-170	3	Warm
340-370	170-185	4	Moderate
370-400	185-205	5-6	Fairly hot
400-440	205-225	7	Hot

SOLID MEASURES

American/British		Metric
1 lb.	= 16 oz.	= 453 grams
2.2 lbs.		1000 grams = 1 kilogram
1 oz.		= 28 grams
$3\frac{1}{2}$ oz.		= 100 grams

LIQUID MEASURES

American (Standard Cup)

			Metric Equivalent
1 cup	= $\frac{1}{2}$ pint	= 8 fl. oz.	2.37 dl.
1 Tbs.	= $\frac{1}{2}$ fl. oz.		1.5 cl.
1 tsp.	= $\frac{1}{6}$ fl. oz.		0.5 cl.
1 pint	= 16 fl. oz.		4.73 dl.
1 quart	= 2 pints	= 32 fl. oz.	9.46 dl.
1.1 quart	= 1 liter	= 10 dl.	= 100 cl.

British (Standard Cup)

			Metric Equivalent
1 cup	= $\frac{1}{2}$ pint	= 10 fl. oz.	2.84 dl.
1 Tbs.	= 0.55 fl. oz.		1.7 cl.
1 tsp.	= $\frac{1}{5}$ fl. oz.		0.6 cl.
1 pint	= 20 fl. oz.		5.7 dl.
1 quart	= 2 pints	= 40 fl. oz.	1.1 liter
1 cup	= 16 Tbs.		
1 Tbs.	= 3 tsp.		